DILLINGER

A SHORT AND VIOLENT LIFE

BY
ROBERT CROMIE
AND
JOSEPH PINKSTON

DILLINGER

Originally published by
McGraw-Hill Book Company, Inc.

ISBN: 0-924772-06-9

Chicago Historical Bookworks Publishers
831 Main St. Evanston, IL 60202

Cover design by Dorothy Kavka
Evanston, Illinois

OTHER BOOKS BY ROBERT CROMIE

Chicago (with Arthur Haug)

The Great Chicago Fire

Par for the Course (Ed.)

Where Steel Winds Blow: Poets on War (Ed.)

Chicago in Color (with Archie Lieberman)

The Great Fire: Chicago 1871 (with Herman Kogan)

Little People (with Hy Roth)

A Short History of Chicago

INTRODUCTION

John Dillinger, who lived from 1903 to 1934, holds a unique place in the annals of American crime and folklore.

His outrageous escapades included an escape from a Wisconsin resort surrounded by FBI agents. Twice, he walked out of well-guarded prisons even though he was by far the best recognized prisoner in the country. He then led the police and the FBI on a wild chase that for months filled the front page of almost every daily newspaper in the country. During this time, he actually stopped off at his home in Indiana for a family gathering. He also attended, without being noticed by any of his pursuers, "A Century of Progress," Chicago's well-attended world's fair.

What Dillinger did was rob banks — lots of them. He was also notorious for brazenly holding up sheriffs' offices to acquire the guns needed so he could rob more banks.

Dillinger was both a criminal and a showman. He was an entertainer who loved giving the audience something to applaud.

Definitive answers do not exist to some questions about Dillinger. Was it a real gun or a whittled piece of wood with shoe polish on it that helped him escape from the Crown Point, Indiana, jail? Did Dillinger ever kill anyone? This book tries to examine these questions with an open mind and a solid investigation of the facts.

Polly Hamilton, Dillinger's "moll," reflected after being caught, "We had a lot of fun. It's surprising how much fun we had."

Dillinger today, however, is remembered not so much for his career and daring escapes as he is for his death. On July 22, 1934, he was gunned down by FBI agents in the alley next to the Biograph Theater on north Lincoln Avenue in Chicago. He was betrayed to the police by Anna Sage, known as the "woman in red." It was a violent end to a short life.

K.H.
Chicago, 1990

ONE

● "IT'S LIKE THE CORONER SAID, 'CRIME DON'T PAY!' DOES IT?"
—OVERHEARD AT THE MORGUE

It was July 22, 1934, and Chicago was suffocating under a heat wave. The mercury had climbed to 108 degrees at the municipal airport the day before, and no relief was predicted. Apartment dwellers thronged the beaches of Lake Michigan. Soda fountains, taverns, and air-cooled movie houses were doing a brisk business. Other Chicagoans, wearing their flimsiest garments, had left their stifling dwellings for the streets and whatever scant comfort the evening air afforded. But even sundown had brought no appreciable lifting of the heat that was oppressing the city for the third successive day.

Yet a number of men loitering near the Biograph Theater at 2433 North Lincoln Avenue not only wore full suits but kept the coats buttoned. This eccentric behavior was enough in itself to set them apart from shirt-sleeved passersby, but their ill-concealed air of expectancy made them still more conspicuous.

They lounged singly or in pairs, or sat quietly in parked cars within sight of the entrance to the theater. The marquee twinkled with an advertisement for *Manhattan Melodrama*, a motion picture about a gangster (Clark Gable) who came to a bad end. Some of the waiting men kept the rear exits of the Biograph under observation, and others were at the fire escapes. Those on the sidewalks behaved like idlers with nothing to do on a hot summer night. They gazed into store windows, smoked cigarettes, watched pretty girls as they went rustling by, or chatted amiably, as if waiting only for time to pass.

The cashier in the box office, uneasily aware that there had been a dozen holdups in the city that week, found the tableau unconvincing and spoke to the manager. He, in turn, telephoned the Sheffield Avenue police station to report a possible robbery attempt. Three plainclothesmen were sent to investigate. They were quietly but firmly informed that the strangers were on government business.

Melvin H. Purvis, thirty-year-old agent-in-charge of the Chicago office of the Federal Bureau of Investigation, had reached the Biograph with one of his men early in the evening. They sat in a parked car near the entrance, and every few moments Purvis went into a nearby tavern to telephone the hotel suite where other operatives were gathered. Samuel Cowley, thirty-four, special assistant to J. Edgar Hoover, chief of the Federal Bureau, remained at the downtown headquarters with an open wire to Hoover in Washington.

For this was a matter that commanded urgent attention all along the line: the probable end of the long and frustrating hunt for John Herbert Dillinger, the Indiana farm boy who had worked his way up in his chosen profession—bank robbery—until he now was Public Enemy Number 1.

About 8:30 Purvis and his fellow watcher saw a man and two women approaching the Biograph from the north. The man wore a striped shirt and gray trousers. His companions were Polly Hamilton Keele, a pretty twenty-five-year-old redhead in a light summer dress, and Anna Sage, a former brothel keeper of forty-five, wearing a bright orange skirt. Purvis walked casually toward the ticket window and waited as the man paid admission for the three.

Purvis watched until the three were inside, then quickly phoned Cowley and had someone instruct those waiting at the Marbro— Sergeant Walter Conroy of the East Chicago, Indiana, police force, and a government agent—to abandon their "stakeout" and come to the Biograph. Cowley telephoned Hoover, who gave orders to shoot only if Dillinger drew a gun. No machine guns, rifles, or shotguns were to be carried.

Within minutes after Purvis's call, sixteen federal agents were on watch, as well as five men from the East Chicago police force, all in positions that had been assigned to them earlier after a careful study of the various exits. The three plainclothesmen from the Sheffield Avenue station also remained at the scene, out of curiosity. It was a long wait in the hot summer night.

At 10:40, more than two hours after the full-scale vigil began, the main door of the Biograph was pushed open and the most-wanted man in the United States sauntered out, a woman on each arm. Dillinger turned left toward Halsted Street, where Mrs. Sage had an apartment, and his complete lack of concern showed that he had no hint that his amazing luck was about to end in a blaze of gunfire.

As the three passed the doorway of the Goetz Country Club, a tavern just south of the Biograph, Dillinger stared, incuriously, at Purvis, who was standing in the doorway. A moment later, when the trio was opposite the National Tea Company store, Purvis tried to light a cigar—the prearranged signal for his men to close in—but his hands were trembling so violently that he failed to do so.

The intended sign was caught, however, and two or three of the watchers walked unhurriedly in behind the threesome. None of the government men spoke, but the man who was being followed suddenly sensed that the scene was playing wrong. Mrs. Sage had dropped behind the other two just before the action began. Polly Hamilton, seeing men with guns, dug her elbow into Dillinger's ribs as a warning, and at the same moment he broke into a run, just at the mouth of the alley, his right hand tugging frantically at his trouser pocket.

All over the street guns flashed into view—Purvis tore the buttons off his coat getting his out in a hurry—and the customary night noises were drowned by a rapid series of shots, Chicago's theme song in the thirties. Four bullets struck Dillinger, one in the back of the neck, virtually at point-blank range. He was driven forward and down, landing on his face with his own gun still uncleared. Agent Charles Winstead is believed to have fired the fatal bullet.

As he fell, and almost before the echo of the shooting had drifted away, Dillinger's companions disappeared. A man who liked friends around him, John Dillinger was surrounded by cold-eyed strangers as he lay asprawl and dying in the dust of the alley. He was exactly one month past his thirty-first birthday. His straw hat and the glasses he needed only for disguise were broken beside him. With his white silk shirt neatly striped with green, he wore a gray tie touched with white to harmonize with the gray trousers, black socks, and white canvas shoes. He had a newly grown mustache, black-dyed plucked eyebrows, and fingertips that had been smoothed with acid. His rebuilt face showed the scars of plastic surgery.

The FBI men and police officers kept the crowds back but had nothing more to do. They waited for the final curtain rather like actors who had forgotten their lines and had no one in the wings to cue them. Sergeant Conroy rolled Dillinger onto his back and began searching him as Purvis knelt to inspect the gold ring Dillinger always wore and to remove the pistol, a .38 automatic with the safety still on, from the right-hand trouser pocket.

Then Purvis, who for almost five months had dedicated every waking hour—and probably some of his dreams—to the task of hunting down John Dillinger, sounded suddenly unsure of himself. He turned to a city policeman and asked, "What's the procedure now?"

Aid was summoned for two women who had been slightly wounded by ricocheting bullets. A police ambulance also arrived for Dillinger, who was taken to Alexian Brothers Hospital, a few blocks away. There he was pronounced dead at 10:55, and after a slight delay a deputy coroner authorized removal of the body to Cook County Morgue.

TWO

●● "HE WAS A GOOD ALL-AROUND BALLPLAYER. HE WAS A
GOOD BATTER, GOOD FIELDER, AND FAST—HE COULD STEAL
ANYTHING, SO THEY SAID."   —EMMETT HANCOCK

Audrey Dillinger sat on the front steps of the house at 2053 Cooper
Street in Oak Hill, a residential section of northeastern Indianapolis, late on the night of June 22, 1903, awaiting the arrival of a
baby brother or sister. Audrey had been awakened by noises in her
mother's room, and the midwife in attendance had told her to go
outdoors.

John Wilson Dillinger, Audrey's father, owned a grocery store at
2210 Bloyd Avenue in the same area. Business had been good and he
had bought four houses, in one of which he lived with his family.
The eldest of five children, he had come to Indiana from Alsace-
Lorraine with his father and mother. Years later he had married
pretty Mollie Lancaster of Cumberland, whose brother Dave was
a captain of police in Indianapolis and the strongest man on the
force. Audrey, the Dillingers' first child, had been born in 1889.

The second—for whose arrival fourteen-year-old Audrey had been waiting on the steps until nearly midnight—was a boy. He was named John, after his father.

He seemed like any other lively boy as he learned to walk and chatter, except that he was considered "cuter" than most of the other children in the neighborhood. Surviving photographs show him, a wide-eyed little youngster in the quaint garb of the day, sitting on a tricycle in front of the house on Cooper Street, or perched bravely on the high seat of his father's delivery wagon while the shirt-sleeved grocer holds the reins of a swaybacked horse.

Young Johnnie had the usual childhood ailments, said (no doubt) the usual clever things, got himself into the same mischief, and was petted or spanked as the occasion demanded. But he lost his mother earlier than most kids do.

Mollie Dillinger fell ill in 1906, underwent an operation, and died shortly before the year ended. Audrey had married Emmett Hancock a few months earlier, at the age of seventeen, and was living next door to her father. But on her mother's death she gave up her own house and, with her husband, moved back into the Dillinger home so that she could care for her baby brother—a habit she never relinquished.

Although the first of Mrs. Hancock's seven children was born in 1908, she continued to watch over Johnnie until 1912, when her father courted and wed Lizzie Fields of Mooresville. When the new wife moved in, the Hancocks went to a house on Roosevelt Avenue, not far away, where Johnnie became a frequent visitor and often played with Fred Hancock, five years his junior, and two other Hancock offspring, Mary and Norman. Mrs. Hancock taught piano, and Johnnie took lessons for a while but showed no particular interest.

Earlier, Johnnie had entered Public School 38, at Winter and Bloyd, in Oak Hill. He was not regarded as a brilliant pupil, but rarely gave trouble.

Earl Hendrixson, who was a classmate, says of him, "He wasn't a bad boy, I'll tell you that. He didn't do anything any other boy wouldn't have done: play hookey, steal cherries out of somebody's orchard. We were pretty fair at playing hookey, and when we did we'd just fool around, go here and there, up and down alleys and streets. We didn't do it too often, maybe every couple of weeks. We used to scuffle with each other, but it was all in good nature. Fist-fights and rassling both.

"Nobody'd get hurt. We wouldn't be mad at each other. It was just because we were the two strongest kids in the neighborhood. He'd try every day, if he could, to beat me, and once in a while it would come out in his favor. But he was just as well satisfied either way. When we were fighting we'd never go on if anyone said he'd had enough. He was good about that. I knowed kids a whole lot meaner than him. He'd never do anything behind your back—draw a knife or anything like that.

"He used to play ball pretty good, too. We had a kind of little neighborhood team. He liked to pitch, and would play the infield. In the summer we'd go up on the railroad tracks, or go swimming in Fall Creek, near 43d and Keystone. It was about three miles. There was an old covered bridge there then, and we'd walk or run. I could run like a deer, and he wasn't slow. I could run all day and never draw a long breath, hardly. He couldn't stay with me on that, but he was better than most.

"He got about average marks in school, and I never knowed any of the teachers to have any trouble with him. He hung around the grocery store, and the old Central Veneer Sawdust Mill. After fourth grade we went to P.S. 55, at Seventeenth and Sheldon—the George Washington."

Hendrixson's recollections are verified by Ralph Nelson, now a vice-president of the Citizen's Bank and Trust Company in Bloomington, Indiana, who was the same age as John Dillinger. Nelson attended both schools with John and lived a few doors from the Dillingers until 1917.

John, Nelson says, was never in any real trouble during those years, and seemed like any other boy in the neighborhood, except that he was "tougher" than most. Nelson says he never won a fight from Dillinger, not even, he ruefully admits, when some of his buddies arranged to distract John during one scrap so that Ralph could belt him while his attention was elsewhere.

All the boys used to hitch rides to school on a Marmon truck which delivered bread to the Dillinger grocery, Nelson says, and cops and robbers was one of their favorite games. Young Dillinger—in those days—didn't care which category he was in.

John's teachers shared his classmates' views, at least according to what they told reporter Fred Pasley in 1934.

Miss Elizabeth O'Mara, a grammar-school teacher, said, "John was no different from any other boy. True, it was often necessary to punish him, but I always got full cooperation from his father in this. I can say positively that at the time I knew John Dillinger he showed no inclination to steal. Other boys, you know, had stolen change from my desk. But John, although he had ample opportunity to do so, never touched a cent. He was intensely interested in anything mechanical, caring little for academic subjects. It was this indifference to his lessons that caused most of his trouble at school. Of course he liked to play pranks, yet I must say that secretly I found them quite amusing and original."

His grades were bad, and sometimes he would sign his own report card, or tell his father he had lost it, stratagems that the teachers knew about. Young John disliked both regular school and Sunday school. Yet Mrs. Elsa Ellsbury, who taught the Sunday-school class at the Hillside Avenue Disciples of Christ Church, later remembered him fondly. "All boys are like that," she said. "They tear up their lessons or lose them and are always thinking up some prank to distract attention. Johnnie was mischievous like the rest of them, but he was such a healthy normal specimen of boy that you couldn't help liking him. One thing about him I'll never forget: he always tipped his hat to me."

School was something John could do without, however, and when he was sixteen he quit and got a job in the veneer mill, where he was a good worker and—because of his willingness to help his fellows—a "right guy." But the veneer works grew boring, too, and after five months he became an errand boy at the Indianapolis Board of Trade, where he stayed for four months.

Then he moved on to the Reliance Specialty Company, on the West Side, a machine shop owned by James P. Burcham. He worked there several years, but not regularly. Three or four months of steady work seemed about his limit. But while he worked he was "very fast and accurate," according to Burcham, who added, "We liked John very much personally, besides . . . we found him sober, honest and very industrious. His main trouble . . . he would not stay long."

It was in March, 1920, a year after John quit school, that his father decided to sell his Indianapolis properties and move to a farm just west of Mooresville, his wife's home town. By now the family included John's half brother Hubert, born in 1914, and half sister

Doris, born in 1916. Mooresville was a sleepy little Hoosier hamlet nestled in rolling countryside off the main highway, 15 miles southwest of Indianapolis.

Hendrixson assisted with the moving and visited John in Mooresville once or twice, helping to spray the fruit trees, then lost track of his friend until he later read about his exploits. The Dillingers soon moved to another farm, one of sixty acres on Highway 267, half a mile north of Mooresville.

His father admitted, years later, that John failed to inherit the family love of farming: "My people have been farmers for generations, both on my father's and mother's side. John's mother even was the daughter of a farmer. I liked the land. John never did. Said it was too slow. He was born and raised in Indianapolis, and I guess the city kind of got a hold on him. He never did take to school. Said he'd rather be earning his own way. . . .

"When he wasn't playing baseball he was generally out hunting. He was handy with a gun and a dead shot. We always had plenty of rabbits, squirrels and possums during the open season. John got his love of hunting from me. There's nothing I'd rather do."

The fact that John suffered from hay fever undoubtedly aggravated his dislike for the farm, and although he considered resuming his schooling in Mooresville, he decided to keep on working in Indianapolis—when he was in the mood to work at all. For a time he rode back and forth on a motorcycle. Then, when he had saved enough money, he bought a secondhand Chevrolet, which led to his first known brush with the law (not a very serious one): in 1920 he was arrested in Indianapolis for speeding and paid an eleven-dollar fine.

Mooresville was a tight conservative little community consisting in good part of Quakers who minded their own business and had respect for their neighbors. In addition to the Friends Church, the village of 1,000 supported three others: Lutheran, Methodist, and Christian, which the elder Dillinger attended; he had been a deacon of the Hillside Christian Church in Indianapolis. Oddfellows and Masons had fine halls there, but the Martinsville newspaper observed, "The [Mooresville] public school building is a dilapidated affair not worth noticing except to condemn." The town's only attractions for the growing Dillinger were a poolroom, a movie theater called the Idle Hour, and the sandlot baseball team on which he played second base with a skill that some observers felt might presage a major league career.

John spent as much of his spare time as possible in Martinsville, the county seat, about 15 miles south on the White River. He and a friend often had dates there, using the friend's Model T for transportation. When they lacked money for gas, they would stop on the way back to "borrow" kerosene from the railroad signal station near town.

Martinsville, being a metropolis of 6,000, offered other kinds of excitement than dates. It was known for its many violations of the Prohibition law, which the local WCTU vainly protested, and the KKK was popular. John played pool there, and Robert (Bob) Humphreys, who later covered his funeral for the International News Service, recalled watching him at "Big John" Gebhardt's pool hall.

"John would come in," Humphreys said, "hang up his hat and play pool at a quarter a game. He wasn't very good, and he frequently lost. When he would lose two dollars, he'd put back the cue, get his cap, and walk out without a word. Never gave anybody any trouble and never said much."

During his late teens he was known to stay out late at night, and he sometimes failed to come home at all. About this time, too, he began seeking the friendship of older men, whom he met in the poolrooms of both Mooresville and Martinsville. But until he was twenty, although he showed no great ambition to get on in the world, he displayed no notable talent for finding real trouble.

The year 1923, however, marked a new trend in his career, one which occurred shortly after he was refused permission to marry the girl he was in love with. Although he had known Frances Thornton, the very pretty stepdaughter of his uncle Everett Dillinger, for a long time, the affair suddenly grew serious. Frances was seventeen, and her stepfather—who may also have had other doubts about his would-be son-in-law—said they were too young to get married. Actually, Uncle Everett favored a well-to-do Greencastle farm boy as a suitable husband for his stepdaughter. When Frances obeyed the parental order to stop seeing him, John grew sullen and resentful.

On the evening of July 21, 1923—John had eleven years and one day to live—Mr. and Mrs. Oliver P. Macy of Mooresville drove to the Friends Church, which young Dillinger had occasionally attended. They parked their new car and went in to the service. When they came out, the car was gone. John, brooding over his disappointment and tempted by the thrill of driving a new car, had appropriated it and headed for the road. Macy reported it stolen, and he and his wife were driven home by neighbors.

A few hours later the car was recovered in Indianapolis, and there seemed little doubt who had driven it there. An Indianapolis policeman, patrolling a downtown beat, noticed a young man walking along the street shortly after midnight and asked what he was doing. The man gave his name as John Dillinger and said he had driven in from Mooresville. He led the officer to a parked car. When the policeman went to a call box to check the license number, however, the suspect broke loose and fled.

The car was returned to Macy, who refused to press charges, and only a few persons in Mooresville ever knew of the incident. But Dillinger panicked. He went to a Navy recruiting office in Indianapolis early Monday morning and signed up, giving his own name but a false address in St. Louis. He was sent to the Naval training station at Great Lakes, Illinois, from which he wrote a letter to Macy, offering to prove (by the word of a Mooresville girl he said he had been dating) that the charge of his having stolen the car was false. Macy did not answer.

When Dillinger's basic training ended on October 4, 1923, he was assigned as a fireman third class to the *U.S.S. Utah*, a battleship that was to become famous for her spectacular end at Pearl Harbor. Known details of his naval career are few. But it is a matter of record that on October 28 he was absent without leave for almost a full day, and on November 7 was sentenced by a deck court-martial to ten days' solitary confinement on bread and water with full ration every third day, and a loss of eighteen dollars in pay.

Two days after the court-martial, Dillinger disappeared again and when caught was sentenced to five extra days of solitary confinement, a sentence he served without incident. A month later the *Utah* anchored in Boston harbor, and on December 4, 1923, John Herbert Dillinger, fireman third class, bade the Navy a silent farewell. He was listed as a deserter, with a price of fifty dollars on his head.

He was soon back in Mooresville—certainly no later than March of 1924. He told people he hadn't cared for the navy, and his family believed he had received an honorable discharge because of illness. He seemed to settle back in his old groove—the poolroom, baseball, late hours. His skill at baseball brought a new romance, this time in the person of Beryl Hovious, sixteen and pretty, who saw him play in Martinsville, her home town. They were married there on April 12, 1924. For a while they lived on the Dillinger farm and with the Hovious family in Martinsville.

Later the young couple had their own apartment in Martinsville. Ivy Knipstine, who lived next door, recalls that Dillinger used to stay out late and Beryl would go hunting for him.

It was reputedly in a Mooresville poolroom that Dillinger met Edgar Singleton, thirty-one, a former convict, who was married and the father of several children. The two became friends, then accomplices in crime. Dillinger's family maintained that John's complicity was due to Singleton's influence, a belief that is plausible in view of the older man's previous experience.

So far as is known, their first criminal venture was their last, but it rearranged the private world of John Dillinger in such fashion that it became easier for him to go bad than to make good. How their plans were laid, and why Frank Morgan, a sixty-five-year-old Mooresville grocer, was chosen as the victim, has never been set forth. The only ones who could clear up the points are dead. What is known, however, occurred on a Saturday night, September 6, 1924, between ten and eleven o'clock. While Morgan was walking home from uptown, John Dillinger was hiding in a recess next to the side steps of the Mooresville Christian Church, and Singleton waited in Broad Alley behind the church in a parked car. As Morgan passed the church steps, Dillinger leaped out and struck without warning, swinging a heavy bolt wrapped in a handkerchief, which hit the grocer on the head. Dillinger swung again and Morgan went down. He was old, but a man of courage, and promptly got up. Dillinger showed a revolver, which Morgan knocked from his hand. The gun was discharged, and the sound of a shot in the quiet residential street, added to the Masonic distress signal, which Morgan began to give, frightened Dillinger, who took to his heels. Singleton—it is believed—had already started the car and left without his bungling accomplice.

Porch lights began flashing on, and neighbors rushed to the aid of the dazed Morgan. Dillinger reached a restaurant in the downtown section of Mooresville, a few blocks distant, and promptly qualified as an amateur by asking whether Frank Morgan had been shot. Since this was the first anyone in the restaurant had heard of the holdup attempt, Dillinger became a natural suspect.

Not realizing this, however, he set out for home, and if the thought of the assault worried him he failed to show it. Two teen-age girls, Reva Comer and Frances Keller, were sitting on the steps of the Keller home opposite the Mooresville High School when Dillinger came past in the warm fall evening. They heard him whistling a gay tune. Another neighbor, farther up the road, also heard the twenty-one-year-old farm youth go past his house singing, some time before midnight.

Authorities questioned several persons around town Sunday, getting information that seemed to implicate Dillinger. A local youth said that John had talked to him several times about "an easy way to make money," and had also inquired how much money Morgan was in the habit of carrying.

On Monday Deputy Sheriff John Hayworth went to the Dillinger farm and picked up John. He was taken to face Morgan, whose head wound had required eleven stitches. Morgan was reluctant to believe that Dillinger, a frequent visitor to his store, was his assailant.

"Why, John, you wouldn't hurt me, would you?" he asked.

"No, Mr. Morgan," said Dillinger.

On the basis of the other information, however, Dillinger was taken to the county jail at Martinsville, and on Tuesday morning, September 9, was bound over to the Morgan County grand jury after a brief hearing before a justice of the peace.

The elder Dillinger and a friend, James Latta, then visited John, and the youth broke down and admitted the holdup attempt. The father promptly urged the son to tell the truth and John did so, making a full confession to Fred Steiger, the county prosecutor. The confession implicated Singleton, who was arrested on September 15. Dillinger's father later maintained that he had been told his son would be given leniency if he pleaded guilty. If there was such a promise it was not kept.

Judge Joseph Williams of Martinsville was considered by far the most severe in the area, and it was before Judge Williams that the twenty-year-old Dillinger, who had no lawyer, pleaded guilty to conspiracy to commit a felony and assault with intent to rob. He received concurrent sentences of two to fourteen years and ten to twenty years on the two charges. He was also fined one hundred dollars on each charge and disfranchised for twelve years.

Singleton was then arraigned before Judge Williams and pleaded not guilty. He was taken to jail in lieu of $4,000 bond, and on September 23, through his attorney Don McKahan, asked for a change of judge, which was granted.

Singleton's trial began on October 15 before a jury in the court in Martinsville. He had been free on bond since September 27. Dillinger was brought from the Indiana State Reformatory at Pendleton to testify against Singleton (a courtesy to the prosecution which usually means a lesser sentence for the witness), and it took only a day for a guilty verdict to be brought in. Judge Fremont Miller sentenced Singleton to two to fourteen years in the Indiana State Prison at Michigan City on a charge of conspiracy to commit a felony, fined him twenty-five dollars, and took away his civil rights for one year.

Deputy Sheriff Russell Peterson, who was given the job of escorting Dillinger to and from the trial, found the assignment rather harrowing. When he picked up the prisoner at Pendleton, he was told that Dillinger had already distinguished himself by trying to escape. He had managed to slip away from the other inmates during the daily march from the foundry to the washroom and disappear. All lights were turned on and a two-hour search was made. Finally one of the prison officials spotted Dillinger in a large pile of excelsior. Through the expedient of setting fire to the excelsior, the official persuaded the prisoner to come out of hiding. For this escapade Dillinger was given eight days in solitary confinement, and six months were added to his sentence.

On the way back to Pendleton via interurban after Singleton's trial, Dillinger offered Peterson a peach and, later, some candy, but the deputy sheriff declined both, suspecting they were doped. At the carbarn in Indianapolis, Peterson took Dillinger to a nearby soft-drink place and they sat down at a table. Suddenly Dillinger placed his feet against the table, tipped it over on his guard, and fled. Peterson followed him as he ran south along Washington Street, west across the Capitol lawn, then across Senate Avenue into a slum area. Here Peterson fired at the runaway with a .25-caliber automatic, and Dillinger, who found himself in a blind alley, surrendered. Back they went to the carbarn, and onto the interurban again.

At Pendleton the deputy agreed to tell the warden of the incident only after being assured that the young prisoner would receive no extra punishment: he considered Dillinger "just a kid." He knew and respected the elder Dillingers and thought their son had gotten "a raw deal." He still says, "You just can't take ten years from a kid's life."

At Pendleton Dillinger was known as a difficult prisoner from the start. Records show that a comparison of fingerprints was made with those in the Navy's files, and the Navy then issued a dishonorable discharge to Dillinger, promising to waive any claim to him after his sentence was served. Pendleton authorities were also warned, in a letter from Marshal T. H. Greeson of Mooresville, that Dillinger had made threats to "rough up" the guards at the reformatory and boasted he would soon escape. Greeson also told them that Dillinger had voiced threats against some of the citizens of Mooresville. His letter mentioned the theft of Macy's car, said that Dillinger had not been home much just before the Morgan robbery attempt, and that he had been under suspicion for other (unspecified) crimes. It concluded: "From information regarding this young man there is very little I can say in his favor."

Not long after Dillinger's first abortive attempt to escape—just after Christmas the same year—another apparent escape attempt earned him a second six-month addition to his term. On January 31, 1925, he was accused of being "disorderly," but escaped with a reprimand. For a time he seemed to be settling into the routine. But on February 25, 1926, he was caught gambling, an offense which added thirty more days to his sentence, and in August he was again disorderly, and again his sentence was lengthened by thirty days.

When Singleton was paroled after serving two years, Dillinger's disposition did not improve. Warden A. F. Miles later described him as sullen and brooding when he heard the news. He was sent to the guardhouse on December 27, 1926 (Christmastime seemingly increased his bitterness), and when he was released, promptly got into a fistfight and was back in confinement on December 31—hardly an auspicious way to start the new year.

This was almost his final offense at Pendleton, however, and he remained on good behavior until October 17, 1928, when he was given another thirty-day extension of sentence for destroying prison property. Despite this string of rules infractions, Warden Miles later was quoted as saying that Dillinger had not been a "bad prisoner," since he remained aloof from the more vicious inmates.

The image Dillinger established within the walls and the one he created outside, through the medium of letters home, were very dissimilar. His two favorite correspondents during this period were his young wife, who lived with her own folks part of the time and with the Hancocks on occasion, and his niece Mary, who was nine years old when her favorite uncle went to prison.

"The thing I remember most vividly before that," Mary says, "was how we used to go to the little grocery store in Maywood and buy chewing gum at a penny a pack. I remember lying flat on the floor, our heads together, trying to see who could chew the most gum. And I remember Johnnie's constant love of baseball. We used to play catch when I was seven or eight, because I was a tomboy. We used to Indian-wrestle—he was more like my own brother than an uncle. And he had no violent temper, although he had definite likes and dislikes. If he didn't like some food he wouldn't try it. He was generous to a fault and had a wonderful smile as a youngster, although later it was something of a cynical expression. But he was *made* into that type of person."

Mary and her uncle corresponded regularly during his stay behind bars. "He knew when I had my first lipstick and went to my first party and had my first date," Mary says. "I wrote him every week. They would remember those long letters they used to have to read at the prison. I wrote ten, twelve, fifteen pages. When I visited him he used to ask me what I intended to do when I got out of school and I told him open a beauty salon.

"He kidded me about getting his fingernails fixed and keeping his hair from thinning; told me he'd be a good customer and drum up business for me. But his life was very much routine. He never discussed what *he* wanted to do when he got out. I don't think he ever had any intention of living the kind of life he did. If only some one person had cared enough to say, 'I'll take him into business with me,' or had given him a chance—given him a feeling he would be useful!"

Dillinger, who had been married less than five months when he was sentenced, received frequent visits from his wife during the first three years he was in the reformatory. Once—according to Mrs. Hancock—Beryl sold a sweater to raise enough money for interurban fare to Pendleton. But Ivy Knipstine recalls that when Dillinger sent Beryl a beautiful scarf he had made, she refused to wear it. And eventually her visits became fewer and fewer.

On August 18, 1928—when he had been behind bars for almost four years—Dillinger wrote:

My dearest wife:
Received your sweet letter Tuesday eve, the only one this week, and I'm still waiting for that interview. Gee honey I would like to see you. Hubert wrote to me last week I would sure like to see him if he wants to come see me let me know and I will send him the car fare.

After reprimanding her for growing angry because he hadn't written ("You ought to have known that I would have wrote if I could"), he went on:

Dearest we will be so happy when I can come home to you and chase your sorrows away. . . . I wonder if I will get an interview Monday. I sure hope so for I am dying to see you, darling have some pictures taken every time I see you you look dearer and sweeter to me so I want late pictures now say rassberries but honey it's the truth. . . . You can imagine what a disappointment it was to me when you didn't come on your birthday I've been cross as a bear ever since. . . . Lots of love and kisses to the sweetest little wife in the world.

His eloquence was wasted, for on April 9, 1929, his wife filed suit for a divorce, which was granted two months later. He makes no mention of the action, however, in a letter dated May 11, 1929 (Mother's Day) shortly before his twenty-sixth birthday:

Dear Mom and All,
I hope this letter finds you all well, wish I could be home with all of you tomorrow. . . . If Sis can't come this week or next, maybe Dad will have a chance to come and bring Doris or Frances. . . . We had our second ball game today and won 12 to 9. It wasn't a very good day for a game though. . . . I am feeling good and getting

along okay. I am trying hard to make my time clear so I can come home sure will make Dad hustle to feed me enough chicken rassberry pie and cake. What do you think, I am going to school 2 hours a day. I don't mind it though it has been so long since I left school it won't do a bit of harm to go over some of the studies. I wish I had listened to Dad and went to Tech. . . . I suppose Dad is working pretty hard now maybe I will be out and can help him some next year. . . . Lots and lots of love to you all.

Johnnie.

His hopes of going home soon were dashed, however, when he appeared before the parole board early in July, 1929. The board was composed of John Hoy of Lebanon, Warden Miles, and Harry G. Leslie, governor of Indiana. In view of Dillinger's spotty record, his application for parole was denied. But Governor Leslie and the others did accede to an unusual request then made by Dillinger: that he be transferred to Michigan City.

His professed reason was that the penitentiary at Michigan City had a better ball team. But it seems unlikely that this consideration could have outweighed the fact that at Michigan City—about a hundred miles farther from Mooresville than Pendleton—he would have fewer visits from his family.

A possible true reason—admittedly conjectural—can be offered. His wife had been granted a divorce a few days before, and this may conceivably have increased the bitterness he already felt because Singleton had been out on parole more than two years and his own parole had been denied. If this is true, it is possible that the request for a transfer marks the moment when Dillinger definitely made up his mind *not* to go straight when he finally won his freedom. Because at Michigan City he would find the elite of the Indiana criminal world—bank robbers, murderers, and holdup men who were artists in their line. If, indeed, he wished an education for a criminal future, the state penitentiary at Michigan City was an excellent school to attend.

In any event, Dillinger never played baseball at the penitentiary—although he later insisted that the transfer had been made because the Michigan City authorties wished him to play on the baseball team, and that he had not asked for it himself.

While he was at Michigan City, his letters home improved in tone and maturity and gave the impression that he really intended to give honesty and hard work a try when he got out. Whether or not he was merely writing with one eye on the possibility of parole, no one knows.

In September he was given solitary confinement, second grade, for a minor offense—cooking in the dormitory—but on Christmas Day, 1929, he wrote to his niece Mary, and said, in part:

> I am so glad you like school so well for if you don't go their are plenty of times you wish you had. I am sure glad to see you make such fine grades.... Well, how is everyone: I hope all of you are well and having a nice Christmas. Wouldn't it be swell if I was spending Christmas with you? But don't you worry I will be out sometime and believe me I am going to stay out....
>
> Sis wants me to pray for her to get better but I am not very strong for praying; I think it will take more than prayers for her to get well or for me to get out of here. Now don't think I am an athiest for I am not, I do believe in God, but his ways seem strange to me sometimes; for if anyone deserves health and happiness it is your dear mother who is the best and sweetest woman in the world. I will try to pray for Sis, though not that I think it will do her any good. But I would do anything for her.
>
> I know right from wrong and I intend to do right when I get out. I suppose you think that I do not try to make my time clear but honey I do try, and a lot of times when I want to do something or start something that might get me into trouble I think of Sis and don't do it.... Well it is nearly dinner time we had a show this morning. We get a cigar, candy, apples, chicken and all the fixings today. I sure hope Santa treats all of you real good....

Dillinger's spirits were still remarkably high on March 2, 1930, almost six years after he was sentenced, when he again wrote his niece:

> ... The main reason I am writing you so much is because you are going to save your money this summer for me, so I thought I had better kid you along Ha! Ha! I wrote Dad last time and I told him to tell Clarice and Hubert that Ben Davis would sure wallop M.H.S. and now they are giving me the Ha! ha! ... I sure would like to take in the finals this year for there sure are some fast teams in the state this year. What do you think of Purdue's team this year? I am picking McLarnin to whip Sammy Mandell last night but the papers

won't be in for an hour yet. My papers ran out and I guess I will order the Chicago Herald and Examiner this month. . . . It has an exceptionally good sport sheet so that is the reason I like it. Well baseball season is nearly hear but I don't care to try for the team hear although I love to play, if I hadn't played on the team at the reformatory I don't think I would have been sent up hear; and I am sure I would have made a parole there this winter, so you can understand why I am not enthusiastic about making this team. . . .

It is nearly church time I go every Sunday sure am steady huh? Of course I have to go that explains it ha! ha! well sweetheart be a good girl and give my love to all and keep writing your letters for they certainly cheer me up and if you stick real good I will blow you to a now let's see I was going to say a new dress but that's pretty steep so I will make it a box of candy that is if I can find any on sale ha! ha! Lots and lots of love to all.

Johnnie.

That same month—on March 29—he was caught gambling and given a mild punishment, but on May 12 he was ordered to solitary confinement, first grade, for his most serious breach of prison discipline. On that day he sawed the bars of his own cell and was found in the cell of another inmate, again working with the saw.

Despite this obviously unpleasant punishment, he failed to become docile. On March 28, 1931, he was caught in the prison factory defying regulations by making a shirt— for a friend whom he refused to name—and again went to the solitary cell. Five months later he committed a "crime" which must have brought back memories of his boyhood: he broke into the prison garden house and stole all the tomatoes stored there, and smuggled a whole watermelon back to his cell. The result was another trip to solitary. Undaunted, he flouted the rules again on October 10, when he was caught hiding a razor in his cell. Back to the "hole" he went.

During this period he stopped writing letters. He explained the hiatus on January 17, 1932, when he told Hubert:

. . . The reason I didn't write all last summer and fall was I was in checks all the time and wasn't in the humor to write. I graded up a couple days before Christmas but I suppose I'll lose out again right away. It just seems like I can't keep out of trouble here, of course it was just as bad at the reformatory or nearly so anyway. I guess I am just incorigible. I wish I was back at the reformatory for

I know I could get out in six months there, and besides its closer to home and I could see you oftener. . . . Sorry I couldn't send you anything for Xmas we got our pay cut and only make ten cents a day and by the time you pay for your toothpaste, soap, papers and magazines you haven't much left. . . . Don't know when I'll write again for I got in a little trouble yesterday eve so I'll probably lose my grade tomorrow but don't worry kid I'll get out of here sometime and it will all come out in the wash. . . .

Sure wish baseball season would hurry up and come I only seen four or five games last year because I was in checks. I hope Dad, Sis, and George can get me transferred back to the reformatory this spring believe me if they do I'll sure watch my step so I can get out next fall. . . . well kid tell everyone hello for me and I hope all of you are well. So long from Johnnie.

The "little trouble" he spoke of—being caught with cigarettes and a lighter in his possession—brought yet another taste of solitary. But this was his final gesture of rebellion. Something or someone must have persuaded him that the way to a parole lay in conforming to prison regulations. And he was a model prisoner thereafter.

After more than a year of good behavior, he wrote his niece Mary, on March 5, 1933, a letter that is full of the feeling that release is imminent, and he issued orders to his family with the alert assurance of a general directing his troops:

I am quite pleased over the progress Dad is making on my case. Tell Emmett [Hancock] to see that party right away although I don't think he can do me any good because I am pretty sure there will be a new pardon and parole board. The bill for the change is before the legislature now and has all ready been passed by the House. It will be a three man board of trustees, and Mr. Coy, the governor's secretary, and they will meet at Indianapolis every quarter for a period of thirty days. I want Sis to go with Dad before the board when my case comes up and make a plea for me and don't take no for an answer, if Sis will just argue with the board like she does with Emmett I will be planting my dogs under her table this Spring Ha! Ha! . . . I got a letter from Bud a few days ago and he said Mr. Morgan was one of the first to sign my papers. Honey, I wish you would write to Dad and have him see Mr. Morgan about writing a recommendation to the board for me. . . . Dad is going to sign my papers and if I am lucky enough to make it you can all drive up right away to get me.... And say are you keeping in practice making coconut cream pie and coconut cream cake. Oh! Boy! I mean is Sis keeping in practice not you I'm not like those beaus of yours that can exist on love Ha! Ha! ... I have asked Dad several times why he doesn't see Howard Phillips and Reverend Fillmore and get there help. But he doesn't say anything about them and I am sure they would help me out. People like them are the ones that count and we can't afford to miss any opportunity.... Love and kisses from Johnnie.

Late in April the Dillinger family petitioned for a pardon for John Herbert Dillinger, inmate 13225 at Michigan City. The petition said that John was needed to help his father on the farm, and that his stepmother was ill and wanted him home. The plea was signed by the clerk, auditor, treasurer, recorder, assessor and sheriff of Morgan County, as well as by former Judge Joseph Williams and by Frank Morgan, victim of the robbery nine years before.

Judge Williams, writing the parole board, said in part, "I have read the petition ... in behalf of J. H. Dillinger for clemency. I see that B. F. Morgan signs the petition. He was the party that was assaulted. I join in the recommendation for clemency petitioned for. Mr. Singleton, his partner, only received a sentence of from 2 to 14 years and has been out of prison for about six years. As the trial judge I am entirely free to say that I think he should receive clemency as you in your judgment may see fit to grant, and trust that he may without delay be paroled to his father who will act, if appointed, as his parole officer.... The father of this prisoner is getting up in years and needs the assistance of his son on the farm.... I believe the prisoner has learned his lesson and that he will go straight in the future and make a useful and honorable citizen."

Judge Chester Vernon, a member of the legal firm which had obtained the divorce for Beryl Hovious, was also among the 180 signers. The petition was sent to Governor Paul McNutt and turned over to the parole board, which met in May. Present were Delos Dean, J. Tom Arbuckle, and Wayne Coy.

After a study of the petition and Dillinger's record, Dean suggested that the parole be granted and Arbuckle agreed. Coy abstained from voting. The board's recommendation reached Governor McNutt's office May 9, and an order for Dillinger's release was issued

May 10. But through some error the order was not implemented at the prison.

Mrs. Dillinger, meanwhile, had suffered a stroke. She was critically ill, and John Wilson Dillinger sent a telegram to the prison May 20 asking why the release was being held up. Dillinger was freed May 22, and Hubert drove from Mooresville to Michigan City to bring him home. They pulled into the farmyard just before undertaker Harvey arrived. Lizzie Dillinger had died less than an hour before.

His family saw that Dillinger was depressed because he had not reached home before his stepmother died. They found him more reserved than he had been before he went away, and when he joked at all, he had "a twisted smile."

He seemed to sense that Mrs. Hancock was uneasy about him. "Now, Sis," he said, "don't worry about me. I'll be all right."

After the funeral John seemed—briefly—to settle down as if he meant what he so often had said about not going back to prison. He had several confidential talks with Mrs. Gertude M. Reinier, pastor of the Friends Church in Mooresville. He attended church on Father's Day about a month after his release.

"I preached on the Prodigal Son," Mrs. Reinier said later, "and throughout the sermon young John sat there beside his father, crying. Afterwards he came to me and said, 'You will never know how much good that sermon has done me.'"

But whatever may have moved Dillinger to tears on this occasion, it was not shame for his past misdeeds, for already—less than two weeks after his release from Michigan City—he had gone to Indianapolis in search of action.

THREE

● ● ●   "THERE WAS A COUPLE OF OTHER KIDS I WOULD HAVE
PICKED TO WENT THAT WAY. BUT I WOULDN'T OF NEVER
PICKED HIM."   —SCHOOLMATE OF DILLINGER

The life to which Dillinger returned in the spring of 1933 was
not the same one he had left in the fall of 1924. During his eight
and a half years behind bars, the newspaper whose "exceptionally
good sport sheet" he followed so diligently also was reporting the
story of a changing world.

In 1925—the year he read that Red Grange, the Galloping Ghost
from the University of Illinois, had turned professional—the New
York Central Railroad's Twentieth Century Limited inaugurated its
New York-to-Chicago run: 960 miles in 960 minutes. In 1926, when
Gene Tunney knocked out Jack Dempsey for the heavyweight cham-
pionship and Gertrude Ederle swam the English Channel, United
States Marines were sent into Nicaragua and a devastating tropical
hurricane struck Florida and the Gulf states. In 1927 Babe Ruth hit
sixty home runs, and Charles Lindbergh made the first solo flight
across the Atlantic. . . .

And Americans were growing rich.

But three months after John Dillinger had been moved from Pendleton to Michigan City—on Black Tuesday, October 29, 1929—the stock market crashed with the roar that reverberated around the world; and for the last four years of his imprisonment headlines flashed images of the headlong plunge into the Great Depression. Although readers still followed the sports pages, they were uneasily aware of economic disaster. Twenty thousand businesses failed in 1930, twenty-nine thousand in 1931. By 1933 the Depression had hit bottom: banks had closed in thirty-eight states, farmers were forestalling foreclosures with pitchforks, one-quarter of the country's civilian labor force was unemployed, and there were bread lines in almost every city. Indiana had 100,284 on relief in March, when Roosevelt was inaugurated as President.

During these years crime too had been making news. Prohibition had brought the gangsters, of whom the Capone mobsters were the most notorious, and the St. Valentine's Day Massacre in 1929 had been only the worst of the 500 gang murders in Chicago during the twenties. A rash of bank robberies had broken out in 1930, when in Illinois alone 85 banks were held up for a total of $300,000, and in 1932, the year before Dillinger was released, there had been 631 bank robberies throughout the country, 516 of them in daylight, with a loss of $3,562,371.

A number of freelance desperadoes were terrorizing various sections of the country. In 1925 Charles "Pretty Boy" Floyd had begun his career, which included robberies, kidnapings, and murders in Oklahoma, Missouri, and Ohio. Floyd had escaped once from prison and once from the custody of a guard on the way to prison. An Oklahoma newspaper called him the "most notorious" outlaw the state had known since the days of Al Jennings and the Dalton Brothers. Clyde Barrow of Dallas, known as the Texas Rattlesnake, also specialized in holdups in which he did not hesitate to kill, and engaged in numerous machine gun battles with police. Verne Miller of South Dakota and Alvin "Old Creepy" Karpis of Kansas were other freelance criminals of the period who were addicted to kidnaping and armed robbery. Karpis had escaped from prison in 1929 only to resume his chosen profession with greater violence.

In Indianapolis, during the spring of 1933 the police were plagued by the daring raids of a holdup gang whose fondness for such headgear earned them the sobriquet of the White Cap Trio. Actually, the makeup of the threesome, which specialized in drugstores and super-markets varied from job to job but usually included a nineteen-year-old Indianapolis resident, William Shaw.

The group had begun operations while John Dillinger was still imprisoned, but early in June, less than two weeks after Dillinger's parole, Shaw was playing softball in one of the city parks when a friend drove up and called to him. Shaw approached and the friend, whose name was Sam, asked whether he would like to "work" with a stranger who was just out of jail and in need of money. The stranger—seated beside him in the car—was Dillinger.

Shaw hesitated, reluctant to become involved with a partner of unknown quality, and asked his friend to walk to the drugstore with him. When out of earshot, Sam said he had known the stranger in prison and that he was a "swell fellow." On the basis of this sterling recommendation, Shaw agreed to try out the stranger if Sam would join them. Sam suggested that Shaw steal a car and promised to meet the two at a neighborhood poolroom.

They then returned to the car, where Dillinger surprised Shaw by saying, with obvious approval, "I like you, kid. You're smart to check on a guy like me."

They told Dillinger the arrangements, and Shaw asked what name to call him by. "Just call me Dan," Dillinger responded.

Sam left, and Shaw and his new acquaintance went downtown and began looking for an unlocked car worth stealing. At last they discovered one—a Dodge—in front of the Apollo Theater. Dillinger nonchalantly climbed in, and Shaw lifted the hood and expertly installed a "jumper," which permitted starting the car without a key.

While they had been walking, Dillinger had asked about guns, which Shaw told him could be had on a rental basis from a tavern owner he knew. So they drove the Dodge to the tavern, where Shaw pocketed his regular weapon, a .45 automatic, and Dillinger chose a long-barreled 32.30 revolver from the saloonkeeper's illegal arsenal. They picked up Sam, who rode in the back seat. Their first stop was near the Tivoli Theater, where they stole some Indiana license plates to replace the more distinctive out-of-state plates on the Dodge. But two policemen in a cruising squad car noticed Shaw at the task and chased the trio for a short distance before Shaw gave them the slip.

The three then pulled into an alley near Tacoma and St. Clair and had just finished switching plates when another prowl car turned in behind them. Shaw leaped into the driver's seat and threw the car into gear. The tires screamed as he took off, without headlights. A split second later there was a sharp explosive sound. The car veered to the right, then straightened out as Shaw jerked the wheel. Shaw thought the car had been hit by a bullet. He cast a quick glance over his shoulder at Sam, and saw him trying to hold the right rear door shut.

Again Shaw outdistanced his pursuer, while Sam explained that the fast takeoff had caught him by surprise and the half-opened door had hit a telephone pole and was almost ripped from its hinges.

Despite this inauspicious beginning, the three decided to carry on. They found some wire and fastened the door, then drove east on Nineteenth Street to an all-night supermarket.

They circled the store two or three times, looking it over and watching for police cars. Satisfied with the "feel" of things, Shaw double-parked on Drexel near Tenth and told "Dan" he would go in first, and get close enough to the office door to stop anyone from locking it when they showed their guns. Sam stayed in the car.

Both were inside and Shaw was nearing the office when a girl clerk noticed Dillinger's gun, whose length made concealment difficult, and screamed the alarm. Shaw pushed his way into the office and, menacing the occupants with his gun, herded them into the store. He then rifled the cash register.

Dillinger, meantime, was having trouble with the manager, who was too frightened or too stubborn to move to the back of the store when ordered to do so. After four or five such commands were ignored, Dillinger lost his temper and swung the gun, smashing the man in the mouth.

Shaw, who had emptied the register, covered Dillinger as he left the store, and Dillinger, in turn, waited outside to guard Shaw's retreat. They drove to the tavern without pursuit and split the loot. Dillinger left for home.

"As I recall it," Shaw says, "he had to report to his parole officer."

Dillinger returned to Indianapolis a few days later, and this time he and Shaw and a friend of Shaw's named Lefty borrowed a car from the friendly saloonkeeper and drove to a drugstore at Audubon

Road and Washington Street. Lefty, reputedly a fine driver, double-parked and remained at the wheel as Shaw and Dillinger, wearing white caps and colored glasses, went into the store.

Shaw began rifling the main cash register and Dillinger the one at the soda fountain. Suddenly Shaw realized that everyone in the place was watching and he ordered them to turn around, only to have Dillinger, who had not heard Shaw's command, gruffly tell them to look the other way. Aside from this small mixup the holdup went smoothly.

When they fled, however, they found to their dismay that Lefty, a new hand at the trade, had moved the car into a vacant place at the curb and it was wedged between two other cars. He managed to extricate it "after a few nervous minutes."

His two companions gave Lefty an angry lecture on getaway procedure while they headed for a supermarket on College Street. As they drove, Dillinger asked Shaw if the mob had "hit" this place before and Shaw said no, although he and Sam had held it up a few weeks earlier. Lefty parked half a block away, after a stern injunction to keep the motor running and his eyes open, and to start driving slowly toward the store the moment either Shaw or Dillinger appeared.

The two strode into the store, weapons in hand, and as soon as the manager saw the white caps he called out, "Here they are again folks." Shaw went directly to the familiar cash register, but the manager shook his head and said almost apologetically, "I'm sorry, but you guys have started the company collecting and the collector just left."

Shaw scooped up the small amount in the drawer and grabbed some tins of cigarettes, and he and Dillinger hurried out. Lefty pulled up with commendable promptness, and Dillinger stepped in. The excited Lefty then took off, leaving Shaw standing in the street. Shaw started running after the car, and Lefty, suddenly aware that the third partner was missing, stopped and backed up. They started off again, and Lefty sped through a stop sign and made a sharp turn into a cross street. When his companions cursed, he immediately slowed down—so much that they still felt conspicuous.

This drew a snarled protest from Dillinger: "If you can't drive, let the kid take over."

So Shaw drove them back to the tavern, without further blunders.

Dillinger refused to work with Lefty again, but did come back to see Shaw after a few days. This time he asked the younger man whether he were interested in "some big money." Shaw said he was. Dillinger pulled from his pocket a map and a list of holdup prospects, which his friends at Michigan City had given him as a sort of going-away present.

After studying the notes, the two drove to the first of two Indianapolis places listed. This was a bank at Belmont and Washington, and they found it out of business. Then they stopped at a gambling joint on Oliver Avenue, but were refused admission because the doorman didn't know them. So they searched the list once more and decided to rob the thread factory at Monticello, some 75 miles north —timing their arrival with that of the payroll, which Dillinger's notes indicated was due the following day.

After they had made their plans, Dillinger left to go to an afternoon movie—one of his favorite forms of entertainment—and said he would see Shaw about seven o'clock. They met on schedule and drove to a small town near Monticello, where they spent the night. They reached Monticello early the next morning, June 24, and parked a couple of blocks from their destination. Then they walked down the railroad tracks to a highway bridge, where they stood and watched the factory.

In a short while a man came out and headed for town. His appearance matched the description given in Dillinger's notes of Fred Fisher, the plant manager. The watchers left the bridge and drove to the local bank, where they expected to see Fisher withdrawing the payroll money. They missed him somehow and returned to the vicinity of the factory, where they sat under a tree in a vacant lot.

Soon a sedan went by, and both were convinced they saw Fisher in it. Dillinger walked to the plant and applied for a job (which he failed to get) as a ruse to obtain a look at the floor plan. He returned to tell Shaw he was sure he had seen Fisher.

It was decided that Shaw should go into the plant alone, and when the receptionist came out, draw a gun and back her into the office. Shaw would bang the office door as a signal to Dillinger to join him. The two got into their car and parked it near the building. Shaw went in.

To his surprise, the girl came out a different door from the one Dillinger had told him about. Shaw said he wanted to see the manager, and when the girl turned to lead him, pulled out his .45 and told her to act natural, a difficult feat under the circumstances.

As they entered a large room with seven or eight persons in it, Shaw slammed the door to signal Dillinger. Then he discovered that he could not watch everyone at once. While his head was turned, Fisher grabbed the .45 and forced it up under his own chin.

While Fisher was jerking at the gun, Shaw kept trying to pull it away because he didn't want the man to be hurt. Dillinger, unaccountably, failed to appear. At last, with no choice except to let go or pull the trigger and shoot Fisher, Shaw snapped the safety into position and released his hold on the weapon. He darted out the door and down the hallway, just as Dillinger, who had failed to hear the signal, was coming in. Shaw shouted that the man had his gun, and both raced for the car.

They piled in, and Shaw had driven a short distance when Dillinger yelled for him to stop. Thinking his companion had dropped his gun, Shaw did so. Dillinger got out and ran to the rear of the car, where he placed one foot on the bumper, steadied his elbow on a knee, and took careful aim at Fisher, who had just stepped from the factory door, Shaw's .45 in his hand. Dillinger fired, and Fisher reeled back out of sight, shot in the leg. Dillinger got into the car once more and said with gleeful satisfaction; "I either got him or scared him half to death."

Shaw, using dirt roads to avoid observation, became hopelessly lost; the two soon circled back into the vicinity of Monticello, where they turned a corner to find themselves cruising behind an ambulance, which, they were sure, was taking Fisher to the hospital. Shaw sped past and finally found the proper road.

As they headed toward Indianapolis, Dillinger suggested they stop in nearby Logansport to rob a bank, but the weaponless Shaw objected. Not wanting to waste the trip entirely, however, they went out of their way to Muncie to check on a bakery mentioned on Dillinger's list. It, too, was out of business. So they continued to Indianapolis. There they bought a newspaper. Although it contained no account of their luckless Monticello venture, Shaw did find a story about a $5,000 holdup by two young gunmen of a place he had suggested to Dillinger.

"We had a good laugh," Shaw reports, "since we had drove all over northern Indiana and hadn't made a penny."

The partners sat in the park for a time, browsing through the papers. Dillinger said he thought it would be wise thereafter if Shaw picked the spots instead of using his list, which apparently was out of date. They decided to rob an open-air fruit market that night, largely in hopes of obtaining some guns, among them a Thompson submachine gun, which were rumored to be on the premises.

After agreeing to meet about 8 P.M. in Spade's Park, Shaw dropped Dillinger at the bus terminal. The younger man then went home, ate, changed clothes, and picked up a .38 to replace the missing .45. He was back at the park playing ball when Dillinger arrived. The two went at once to the market, which was at the corner of Tenth and Bellfountain.

When they walked into the store, guns in hand, Shaw saw a boy who lived near him, and in order to avoid recognition, ducked his head and told Dillinger they had to leave as soon as possible. They took what money they could find and fled without searching for the weapons.

As they neared their car, someone threw a milk bottle at them. Dillinger replied with a single high shot, which discouraged further pursuit.

They split their take at the saloon. Dillinger was highly amused when Shaw had to pay for the .45 Fisher had wrested from him. As they parted, he told Shaw to try to find "something good" and said he would be back in a few days.

During Dillinger's absence, Shaw scouted a sandwich shop on East 28th Street. When Dillinger showed up on June 29, the two drove past the place and decided it was worth a try. They wore sailor straws for the occasion, since the white caps were becoming too well known. They drove a stolen car, which Shaw parked a block west of the shop.

Shaw approached the manager at the cash register and displayed a pistol. At the same time, Dillinger, just a step or so behind his partner, also showed a gun. One of the waitresses, seeing Dillinger's pistol, put her hand to her mouth and walked outdoors. She was leaning against the building in a state of shock when the two gunmen left with the money.

While they were dividing the profits in the alley behind Shaw's house, Dillinger asked if he could take the car—a 1931 or 1932 De-Soto—to Kentucky, where he wanted to visit some friends. Shaw agreed to let him have it. Just after Dillinger drove off, he ran into a fence at the top of the street, and apparently because he did not know how to back up, Shaw had to extricate the car for him before he could resume the trip.

He was away several days. He returned to Indianapolis on July 7 and explained that he had gone from Kentucky to the World's Fair in Chicago and that he had left the car with friends. Shaw, who had been married during Dillinger's absence, now invited his partner into his home for the first time and introduced him to his mother and his bride. Earlier Shaw had told his mother he was running whiskey; now he told her Dillinger was his employer. Dillinger accepted Mrs. Shaw's invitation to stay to dinner, and Shaw noticed that their guest refused to let his briefcase out of sight.

When the meal was over, the two men retired to Shaw's room, where Dillinger used a sharp knife to rip the briefcase open. His explanation was that he had lost the key. Shaw decided at once that his partner must have robbed a bank, for the case was packed with greenbacks. Dillinger tossed Shaw some of the money and asked where he could buy a car. Shaw himself had just bought one; he had given his father the money and instructed him to act as if he were purchasing a wedding present for his son.

Shaw warned Dillinger of the danger of buying a new car with "hot" money. Three bank robbers, he said, had been picked up within the month for making that mistake. He then accompanied Dillinger to a number of places where they looked over the stock of secondhand cars.

At the Jones-Maley Agency, where Shaw's car had been bought, Dillinger found a maroon 1928 Chevrolet sport coupé with red wire wheels, priced at $250. It suited him, and he said he would take it. Then he asked the salesman whether he would have trouble getting a driver's license, since he was just out of prison. This sent Shaw into a near panic. He abruptly told Dillinger he would wait outside.

Dillinger appeared shortly, with the deal concluded, and followed Shaw to his home. There he explained that he needed more money immediately because he wanted to help some friends get out of jail. They talked over several possible jobs, including one Shaw and Sam had been planning for weeks: the holdup of a woman collector for the Haag drug chain. Shaw found Sam, and the three went to Spade's Park, where it was decided to take in a fourth man to help. Preparations began at once.

Dillinger wanted to rent an apartment, so while he was off on his own business, Sam and Shaw rented a garage on Park Avenue, then went downtown to steal a car. They watched a man park his Chrysler Imperial roadster and followed him until he bought a ticket for the Apollo Theater. They returned to the roadster, Shaw hooked up a "jumper," and the Imperial ownership changed hands. Sam followed in the other car while Shaw stopped to fill the Chrysler with gas and then drove it to the newly rented garage.

The next day Dillinger and the fourth man came to Shaw's house to plan the actual holdup. Shaw told them the collector's last stop was at the northwest corner of Ninth and Penn, that she would park her maroon 1932 Chevrolet, a two-door, on Ninth, that she was redheaded, and that the collection money would be in the shopping bag she carried. The holdup was planned for the next morning, and Dillinger and his companion would have tear gas for use if necessary.

Shaw picked up the stolen Chrysler, and Sam drove Shaw's car. The newcomer was to pilot the Chrysler for Dillinger during the holdup. Shaw warned him not to stop the motor, since this would burn out the jumper, and showed them where to park on Ninth, with the car headed east for a quick departure.

Shaw and Sam were to give a signal by driving past and waving to the other two when the collector left Sixteenth and Illinois, her preceding stop. They did so, saw Dillinger and the other man standing in the street, and drove on to wait at Dillinger's new apartment in the 1100 block of North New Jersey Street.

Time went by. Shaw and Sam grew alarmed when the others failed to appear. They hurried back to Ninth Street and found Dillinger and his driver on the corner. The latter said he couldn't start the Chrysler because it was out of gas, and that after the collector had gone into the store to make her pickup, he and Dillinger had abandoned the project.

Shaw, of course, knew the tank had been filled after the car was stolen. Upon investigation, he discovered that the jumper was burned out as a result of the motor's having been stopped. When he put on a new jumper, the Chrysler started at once. Disgruntled by the failure of their plans, they drove the car to the rented garage and left it.

Dillinger was eager for action, and when Shaw and Sam told him they had cased the Massachusetts Avenue State Bank in Indianapolis, he said he would look it over. Before he could report, however, both Shaw and Sam had left town; they had become aware of a sudden police interest in them in connection with a payroll robbery they had pulled before Dillinger joined them, and with Shaw's bride and Lefty had fled to Muncie in the stolen Imperial.

There they looked up Harry Copeland, a parolee, who showed them where to rent a couple of apartments, and that evening played the genial host at some of the town's better bootleg joints. The next night Shaw, Sam and Lefty drove back to Indianapolis, where Lefty telephoned his parents and learned that police had raided the house looking for him. They called the fourth man who had taken part in the collector fiasco and asked that he let Dillinger know where they were.

Then they stole a DeSoto, put the Imperial back in the Park Avenue garage, and returned to Muncie, pausing long enough, on the way out of town, to rob a place at 28th and Meridian.

When Dillinger received the message, he left for Muncie and arrived on the morning of July 15. He and Sam and Copeland drove to nearby Daleville to investigate the tiny Bank of Daleville, which looked like a soft touch. It was decided that they would rob this on Monday. Copeland was to wait near the bank and drive them over back roads to Muncie. Dillinger, though, wanted to pick up some high-powered rifles first, for use in case they were pursued. A telephone call to Fort Wayne resulted in an appointment that evening with a man who promised to supply the rifles.

While the others were in Daleville, Shaw and Lefty went to a beer parlor near the apartment. The two gambled for a while, and then Shaw retired to a back room with a willing "waitress." He was still there when the others dropped in on their return from Daleville. Lefty had gone to the apartment.

After repeated urgings from Dillinger, Shaw reluctantly left the girl and accompanied the rest home, where they discussed plans for the Daleville robbery. These settled, Shaw went upstairs to his own apartment and found his bride in a sulky mood. When he asked the trouble, she said Lefty had told her about the waitress. She added that she didn't see how she could keep Shaw the rest of her life if he couldn't even remain faithful for two weeks.

As they argued, Sam and Dillinger came in. Shaw, in a rage, asked Sam to bring Lefty upstairs. After Sam left, Shaw told Dillinger he intended to shoot Lefty for having told his wife about the beer parlor episode.

Then, Shaw adds, "I will never forget the picture Dillinger left in my mind at this time. I had an automatic in my pocket. Dillinger was leaning on the mantelpiece over the fireplace. He said, 'Kid, if you miss him, I'll get him.' His gun was in his hand. I think that snapped my mind back to what was really going on. Lefty came in with Sam behind him. I told Lefty when I had sent for him I had intended to kill him, but had changed my mind."

Things finally quieted down, and all the men but Lefty went to Fort Wayne. Lefty was told to take Mrs. Shaw to the movies. She, in turn, was instructed to keep close watch on him in case fright or anger induced him to telephone the police. The Fort Wayne trip was wasted, since the man who had promised the rifles failed to show up. But the rest of the evening was profitable.

After the return to Muncie, Dillinger, Copeland and Shaw got the DeSoto out of the garage, and Copeland drove to a roadhouse he knew—the Bide-a-Wee—that did a thriving business. He got out of the car and waited half a mile up the road while Shaw and the others drove back. Dillinger and Sam went in, held up the place, and emerged a few minutes later. As they backed out, guns in hand, two couples were entering. Dillinger, for reasons Shaw never learned, slugged one of the men.

The three then picked up Copeland, who drove them home. Shaw left his pistol and a sawed-off shotgun in the car, which was placed in the garage. After breakfast the next morning, Dillinger said he wanted to put up the Chevrolet he had just bought, since they were not going to use it on the Daleville job.

Shaw, who wanted to talk with his wife privately to see if she were still angry, suggested that Copeland go with Dillinger. He never saw Dillinger to speak to again.

After the two men left the apartment, Shaw realized he would have to move the DeSoto to make room for the Chevrolet. Sam and Lefty went out with him. They were approaching the garage when they heard someone shout an order to put their hands up. Police were all over the place.

Just at this moment Dillinger and Copeland, who were in the Chevrolet, spotted the police. Without hesitation Dillinger stopped the car, reversed gears, and shot backwards out of the trap, Shaw remembers, "faster than some people drive forwards."

"I thought," Shaw says, still savoring that high-key moment, "that he couldn't drive. He did better than I could have."

The Shaws, Sam, and Lefty were arrested. Mrs. Shaw was freed when the others said she was ignorant of their activities. Shaw, however, was identified in the Monticello and Bide-a-Wee holdups and admitted about twenty others. He was sent to the reformatory. Dillinger later tried to give Shaw's parents some money to use in trying to have him freed. But they were so shocked at learning what their son had been doing that they refused the offer.

"I have," Shaw concludes, "heard many stories about Dillinger. But one thing is sure, nothing was too good for his friends."

The personnel of "the Dillinger gang" is sometimes assumed to have been constant during the fifteen months in which Dillinger pursued his violent career. Instead, the makeup of the gang changed as members were killed or arrested, or drifted away. With the loss of Shaw, Sam and Lefty, one "Dillinger gang" ended. But Dillinger himself kept rolling along, unrepentant and always ready to go.

Daleville was not shelved. On July 17, shortly before 1 P.M., twenty-two-year-old Margaret Good was alone in the Bank of Daleville, a red brick structure about twenty-five feet deep. Dillinger walked in, showed a gun, and said, with unexpected courtesy, "This is a stickup, honey."

He then vaulted the railing separating the outer area from the working quarters (and the cash) and asked where the money was. The trembling girl pointed to the vault. Dillinger stepped inside and began taking anything portable, including a collection of old coins, and two diamond rings belonging to the daughter of the bank's owner, J. N. Barnard. She had taken them off to play tennis and had put them in the vault for safekeeping.

Copeland followed Dillinger inside, leaving the getaway car parked in front of the door. As customers entered, Copeland covered them with his pistol and ordered them to join Miss Good against the rear wall. The first one was Linley Hall, a young filling station proprietor, who needed some change. Then came Frank Mowrey, a fifty-three-year-old farmer, who parked so close behind the bandit car that he felt the exhaust as he walked between the two vehicles on his way to the bank.

Before entering, Mowrey glanced into the dimly lit interior and saw Miss Good with her hands high above her head. She was so immobile he thought she was a painting.

"If I'd had a thimbleful of brains," say Mowrey, still angry with himself, "I'd have known something was going on."

As Mowrey entered, Copeland ordered him to the back.

"I thought he was kidding," Mowrey says. "I had three checks to cash because I was going to Indianapolis to pay off a note. Then he pulled a gun and put it in my belly and said, 'This is a stickup.' So I went in. The girl was standing there with her hands as high as she could reach, and tears running down her face.

"I remember when I went in, seeing Wes Cox, the barber, on his porch, and he waved to me. A moment later he came in to the bank to see about the change Hall was after, because the customers were waiting.

"They had us all in the back room with our hands in the air. But Cox was a tall man and his hands showed above the latticework. So he [Copeland] told us to put our hands down.

"The other fellow was in the vault getting the money, and the second one told us to stand with our faces to the wall. I suppose Dillinger gave him the signal that he was ready to come out. Then they both went out, and I went out right behind them. But I didn't follow them. I went to Indianapolis and paid the note."

Before leaving, Dillinger and Copeland ordered everyone into the vault and shut the door. Miss Good quickly opened it from the inside. The robbers took about $3,500, and the young woman later said of Dillinger, "I think he knew I was a kid and was sorry to scare me. He didn't want to scare me any worse than he had to."

The holdup, of course, created great excitement in tiny Daleville, and is an event of which the townsfolk even today seem strangely proud. The bank is long gone, and the building houses a law office, but a sign, carved on a split log, still hangs above the old vault. It reads:

DILLENGER [sic] WAS HERE.

The ex-farmboy crammed an amazing amount of activity into the last months of his life, almost as if he realized that time was not available to him in the same generous amount allotted to most people.

Not long after his parole, and possibly late in June, when he may have helped rob the bank at New Carlisle, Ohio, Dillinger made the acquaintance of Mary Longnaker, of Dayton, married sister of James Jenkins, one of his prisonmates at Michigan City. A day or so after the Daleville job he turned up in Dayton once more to visit Mary.

The two were together when they met Mary Ann Bucholz, twenty, a friend of Mrs. Longnaker, in front of Vargo's Restaurant on Riverview Avenue. Dillinger, his pockets filled with money from Daleville, invited both girls to see the World's Fair in Chicago as his guests, and they accepted.

They left that evening in Dillinger's car, and on the way stopped in Mooresville long enough for a drink of water at the Dillinger home, and again at a gas station where John left ten dollars for Hubert. They reached Chicago about 3 A.M., checking in at the Crillon Hotel. The two girls shared a room; Dillinger had his own. The second night they had a suite of adjoining rooms, and Mary Ann saw a pistol on Dillinger's dresser. Mary Longnaker also showed her Dillinger's wallet, which was bulging with fifty-dollar bills.

During their stay the three seem to have enjoyed themselves. Dillinger took photographs at the fair—numerous ones of the girls, and at least one of a policeman—and he posed with Mary. He also became very friendly with a dancer at the Island Queen nightclub in South Chicago.

On their way back to Dayton, Mary asked if they might stop in Michigan City to visit her brother, and Dillinger showed no reluctance to do so, although he had robbed a bank only a few days before and was being hunted for the bungled Monticello holdup.

They reached the prison about 1 P.M., after stopping to have lunch on the way. They had bought some bananas, plums, apples, oranges and grapes to take to Jenkins, and before entering the gates, Dillinger carefully pulled down the skin of one of the bananas and opened a neat hole in the top with a knife. Then he rolled a fifty-dollar bill in paper, inserted it in the opening, concealed it with some of the pulp, and replaced the banana in the basket. He told Mary to instruct Jenkins to give ten dollars to "certain people," and wrote a message for her to read to him.

Mary delivered the basket of fruit, and as she talked with Jenkins, read to him from a piece of paper, lying in front of her, a few words at a time. The message ended with an admonition to "sit tight." Before leaving, she suggested to Jenkins that he eat the banana first. As they departed, Dillinger handed someone at the gate fifty dollars with instructions to have Jenkins's teeth fixed. Dillinger dropped the two young women in Dayton, then headed for Indiana.

Three days later, having learned that Mrs. Longnaker had filed suit for divorce, Dillinger sent her a letter from Fort Wayne which said, in part. "I only hope you seen the kids yesterday. [*Mrs. Longnaker had two young daughters.*] I'm just crazy to see them. I only wish I had you and two or three sweet kids and was in South America. If that lousy husband of yours bothers you any more just let me know and he will never bother you again."

The reference to South America is interesting, in view of recurrent rumors during the next twelve months that Dillinger was trying to build his bankroll to the point where he could escape to South America with enough to live on. Nor was his mention of Longnaker just idle chatter. About a month earlier he had engaged in an inconclusive battle with Mary's twenty-four-year-old husband Howard; Dillinger and Mary had driven to Pleasant Hill, Ohio, a town of 1,000 not far from Dayton, to see him.

Ellis Cecil, in charge of the village pumping station, remembers Dillinger and Mary driving down the dirt road to the plant, where Dillinger asked Cecil if Longnaker were around. Told that he was, Dillinger asked to talk with him.

Cecil called the other man, and, as he remembers it, the conversation went like this:

"Your name is Howard Longnaker?"

"Yes."

"You've been treating Mary like a dog. She wants to know where the children are."

"It's none of your God-damned business," Longnaker retorted.

"You just come out here a piece and I'll show you whether it is or not."

"Don't need to go out a piece," Longnaker replied. "I'll take care of you right here!"

Dillinger sprang from the car, and the two began to tussle. Cecil ran for the town constable, Orth Stocker, who also worked on the grounds. Stocker and some of the other men separated the two battlers. Stocker stepped onto the running board of the car and ordered Dillinger to drive uptown, where he planned to put him under arrest.

Dillinger pretended to comply, but once the main street was reached, continued to the outskirts of town at high speed. There he slowed down and ordered the surprised marshal to get off. He then drove away with Mary, leaving behind as souvenirs several articles he had dropped during the fight: his hat, fifty or sixty cents in change, and a fountain pen with the name "D. M. Dillinger" on it, which is still treasured by a Pleasant Hill resident.

Late in July, probably about the twenty-second, Frank Hope, parole officer for Marion, Morgan, and Monroe Counties, received a telephone call telling him that Dillinger had broken parole (the Daleville job) and should be picked up. (Dillinger had earlier written Hope asking to have his parole sponsor changed to a man in St. Matthews, Kentucky.) Hope drove at once to the Dillinger farm, where the elder Dillinger said his son had gone to Maywood, the Indianapolis suburb where the Hancocks then lived. Hope drove the seven or eight miles to the Hancock home, and was told that John had taken two of his nieces to Hubert's gas station in Indianapolis.

Hope went to the sheriff's office, sent two deputies to Maywood, then continued to the gas station. He was told that Dillinger had been there and had gone. He returned to Maywood only to find the deputies sleeping under a tree. Mrs. Hancock told him that Dillinger had returned, dropped off the two girls, and gone home. The weary parole officer again went to the farm. The elder Dillinger said he had not seen John. Captain Matt Leach of the Indiana State Police later told Hope that Dillinger, at the time of his second visit, had been standing in the orchard with a gun trained on Hope.

By early August, Dillinger had been identified as having taken part in both the Monticello and Daleville holdups. While the general public knew little about him—he'd been out of prison for only a couple of months—the police of several states were beginning to develop an intense desire to catch up with him. Their next chance came August 4, about 2:30 P.M., when Dillinger, Copeland, and a third man—probably a fellow ex-convict—drove up to the First National Bank of Montpelier, Indiana, in a dark-blue Dodge.

Dillinger and Copeland went in, while the other man stayed at the wheel. Dillinger promptly leaped the guard rail—a characteristic action which had become his hallmark—and began scooping up cash into what looked like a sugar sack turned inside out. Copeland, chewing gum, kept order with a .38. When two customers entered, Copeland added them to the lineup of employees and other customers. He and Dillinger finally left with $10,110 in currency and coin and a .45 belonging to the bank; they were apparently satisfied with the explanation of M. D. Tewksberry, bank president, that government bonds were kept in a vault in Fort Wayne.

There had been little conversation during the holdup. The man later identified as Dillinger said to Copeland, with some satisfaction, "This is a good haul," and later, on finding the .45, "This is a good gun." About $3,900 of the haul was on the counters. The rest was in the corner safe, which the cashier was forced to open.

Police from the nearby towns of Hartford City and Marion set up roadblocks but not, unfortunately, on the roads the bandits seem to have used. Albert Stoll, a farmer, saw them changing license plates near Hartford City, less than ten miles from the scene of the crime; otherwise their getaway was clean, although the holdup trio probably never knew just how lucky it had been. Chief of Police E. R. Coleman shared an office above the bank with an attorney and Mayor H. L. Kelly, and rifles were kept there against just such an emergency. In a holdup attempt two years before, one bandit had been killed and the rest captured because of this very precaution.

This day, however, Chief Coleman was repairing a street two blocks south, the attorney was out of town, and the Mayor was racing a horse.

The theft was extremely annoying to the American Surety Company, which had to repay the Montpelier loss. The firm ordered Forrest Huntington, a former Pinkerton detective, to take up the search for the bandits. For the next four months no one was more closely or consistently on Dillinger's wayward heels than Huntington, who had been one of the original members of the Indiana Crime Bureau, the forerunner of the detective division of the Indiana State Police. His private file of data on criminals was one of the most complete in the Middle West.

Huntington went immediately to Montpelier and found that Dillinger had already been identified as the gunman who leaped the railing. He also learned that a former convict, living in Montpelier, had witnessed the robbery from the front door of Engle's Poolroom nearby—thus giving rise to the suspicion that the bandits may have had the advantage of some local knowledge—and that Opal Jones, a waitress in Barr's Restaurant, had been shown a photograph of Dillinger and said it resembled one of the three men who had eaten lunch there the day of the robbery. One of the gang had worn a Panama hat, and a man in such a hat had been seen visiting the ex-convict three days before the holdup.

Huntington also discovered that four men with two cars had stayed at a camp on the Salamonie River near Montpelier for a few days before the robbery. But the men were gone and the trail was cold, so Huntington headed for Muncie, Copeland's home town.

The police there told him the Muncie friends of the wanted men included two prostitutes and a gambler, but all three were believed to have moved to Fort Wayne. The police informant said the gambler was able to warn his friends when they were being sought, because he received this information from a Fort Wayne detective with whom he was familiar.

Huntington went to Fort Wayne, where the police told him it was true that the gangsters he was trailing had, in the past, been warned when they were being hunted, but that the warnings had not come from a Fort Wayne detective; they were ascribed to a Muncie detective. However, they agreed that Copeland and Dillinger knew the two prostitutes, and said Copeland's girl was a friend of the Muncie man.

One of the Fort Wayne detectives took Huntington to a house of prostitution, where the madam, who said she had formerly operated in Muncie, admitted that both Copeland and Dillinger had paid her several visits, including one on July 30. On that day she overheard one of her girls tell Dillinger that "the heat is on" and he had better get out of Fort Wayne. She named Copeland's girl, but said she was no longer with her and denied knowing her whereabouts. The detective warned the madam to let him know when the girl turned up again or he would close down the house.

Huntington then went to the reformatory at Pendleton for a chat with Shaw. Shaw, hoping that Huntington would put in a word for him with the parole board when the time came, admitted that Dillinger and Copeland had been within a few seconds of capture at Muncie when he, Sam and Lefty were caught. He said that Dillinger could well be in Kentucky, where—Shaw said—he had robbed a bank early in July. He added that a gambler friend of Copeland's in Fort Wayne had supplied guns for the mob.

Huntington, still looking for the prostitute who knew Copeland, also visited Logansport. But the detective could not find the girl.

While Huntington was following up leads, scouring the countryside for Dillinger and Copeland, state police were keeping the Indianapolis home of one of the duo's ex-convict associates under surveillance; the Muncie police had told Huntington that Copeland and Dillinger spent much time there. They also picked up Singleton for questioning. But after photographing him and taking fingerprints, they released him with a warning to let them know if he learned Dillinger's whereabouts. The state police, meanwhile, had instructed the postmasters at Mooresville and Maywood to make tracings of addresses on all first-class mail received by Dillinger's relatives. Huntington had managed to get a sample of Dillinger's handwriting for use in comparison.

Huntington's tips now took him to Bluffton, Ohio (a town Dillinger was to visit later on business), where he learned that Copeland and another man—who fitted Dillinger's description—had been staying with a former convict until a week or so earlier, when all three left for Muncie.

Acting on other information, Huntington picked up a deputy sheriff and two state policemen, and drove to English Lake, in northeastern Indiana, where the four lawmen met with Sheriff Fred Hinz. They checked numerous bars and resorts in the area. Dillinger and two other men were identified from photographs as having been frequent patrons during the past month.

Further legwork supplied a direct link between the English Lake area and the Montpelier holdup gang. Deputy Sheriff Cecil Rowe of nearby Medaryville told Huntington and the others that about dusk on August 4—the day the Montpelier bank was robbed—a farmer had found an abandoned blue-green Dodge five miles north of town.

It carried no license plates and the rear window was smashed out —presumably to permit firing at possible pursuers. A five-dollar bill, fifteen cents, a lipstick, and eight pounds of roofing nails were on the back seat. The nails, another Dillinger touch, were for tossing on the road in case of a chase. (The $5.15 was spent by a farm youth to buy beer for his friends.) A torn paper, apparently part of an escape route, was also found. It read:

Fleetwood.
Hy. 65.
M B on L.
house on R.
1 M B on R.
1 big post on big refiners.

Other farmers in the neighborhood said two men had parked the Dodge, taken the plates off, and left in a dark-colored coupé with wire wheels and a rumble seat, probably Dillinger's "legal" car, which had followed the Dodge to the spot. The Dodge, investigation disclosed, had been stolen in Chicago on July 19. At that time, the odometer showed 300 miles. When the car was abandoned the mileage had climbed to 3,284.

After hearing this, the state police issued an "all points" bulletin calling for the arrest of Dillinger, Copeland and three other men who had been seen in their company.

On August 12, Kentucky police arrested a man in a DeSoto sedan believed to have been used in several Kentucky bank holdups. Huntington questioned Shaw once more, and learned that the DeSoto was the one he had stolen for Dillinger, who had given it to the Kentucky man after having had it repainted and the serial numbers changed. Shaw added that he had stolen several cars for Dillinger, the latest a 1932 Chrysler. He told Huntington the garage where these stolen cars were usually hidden was at Thirteenth and Central in Indianapolis.

The talkative Shaw also gave Huntington the name of a Chicago "contact" of Dillinger's and told him that a Negro dope peddler and saloonkeeper in Indianapolis was the source of Dillinger's guns.

Huntington then left for Louisville, stopping in Indianapolis long enough to learn from the owner of the garage at Thirteenth and Central that it had been rented by a man giving the name of "Mr. Monahan," whose handwriting closely resembled Dillinger's.

In Louisville, Huntington questioned the prisoner who had been seized in the DeSoto. He had been identified as one of the men who held up a bank at Gravel Switch, Kentucky, on August 8—a distinction he denied. But he did identify photographs of Dillinger as the man known as "Johnnie" who had been in Lebanon some weeks before and had boasted of being wanted in Indiana and Illinois.

A closer tie-up between Dillinger and the Kentucky gang came when Huntington learned that the same license plates had been reported on bandit cars during a bank holdup at Paragon, Indiana, May 11, 1933 (while Dillinger was still in jail), at the Monticello thread mill, and at Gravel Switch—which meant the plates were passed from car to car.

A second Kentucky man, named by the one arrested, was picked up with his brother and brought to Indianapolis, where he was questioned at length. He finally admitted having known both Dillinger and Copeland while a prisoner at Michigan City. Dillinger, he said, had driven to his home in Lebanon, Kentucky, late in June or early in July.

"I told Johnnie that I'd married and was trying to go straight," said the man. He also admitted that he told Dillinger where he could have the maroon DeSoto repainted black. When the job was done, the informant said, Dillinger invited him and his new wife to visit the World's Fair. Dillinger displayed a large amount of money and said the trip would be "on him." The three left Lebanon July 3, and stopped twice en route, once in Fort Wayne and once in East Chicago; on each occasion Dillinger looked up a former convict. After visiting the fair, where he was a free spender, Dillinger took his guests home by way of Champaign and southern Illinois. This time he made only one stop—again to visit a former convict.

The prisoner insisted he hadn't seen Dillinger since that time, but believed he had been in Lebanon on August 6, two days after the Montpelier holdup. He said two men in a Chevrolet coupé, whose descriptions fitted Dillinger and Copeland, had come to Lebanon on that date and stopped at his house to ask for him, but he had

45

been away. A few days later, he said, he received a letter from Dillinger saying the parole officer was after him. There was no return address on the letter.

This informant and his brother were later turned loose for lack of evidence.

The yearning for publicity on the part of some of those directing the hunt became obvious in mid-August, when the Muncie papers carried a story naming Dillinger, Copeland, and an ex-convict, Glen "Big Foot" Zoll, as being sought. Two of the prostitutes also were named.

"This," Huntington's reports noted, "was very harmful."

FOUR

●●●● **"IT WAS NOT THE WORK OF AMATEURS."**
—BLUFFTON NEWS, AUGUST 17, 1933

The epidemic of holdups throughout the Middle West gave Elmer G. Romey, cashier of the Citizens National Bank of Bluffton, Ohio, the haunted feeling that the Bluffton institution was on somebody's list.

Early in August he ordered the big safe kept under a time lock day and night, as a precaution. His hunch was sound. About noon on Monday, August 14, a large green sedan, carrying muddy Indiana license plates, pulled up beside the bank, facing the wrong way on Church Street; five men got out, leaving the motor running.

Two well-dressed men about thirty years old, wearing gray suits and straw hats, entered the bank. A third one in a neat blue suit loitered just inside the front door, and the two other men stood on the sidewalk.

One of the men inside walked up to the third window—farthest from the street—where Roscoe Klingler, the assistant teller, was stationed. The customer asked for change for a five-dollar bill: three singles, a dollar in nickels and another in dimes. Klingler made the change, and the man, as he pocketed it, drew a gun and said in the voice of one imparting confidential information, "Stand back. This is a stickup!"

Meanwhile a customer—Charles Burkholder, an employee of the Farmers Grain Company—had approached the same window. The gunman took him by the shoulder and led him behind the counter. There the bandit covered Burkholder and Klingler with a pair of revolvers.

At the same time the other invader, who had been leaning on the glass-topped table opposite the second window, vaulted over the grillwork and landed behind Romey, who was working on some papers. He ordered Romey and Oliver Locher, the bookkeeper, to put up their hands. All four, the three employees and the lone customer, were then told to lie down on the floor.

Dillinger, the vaulter, holding his revolver in readiness, began gathering up money from the drawers and stuffing it into a large sack. He was disappointed in the amount, however, and said sharply to Locher, "You've got more money in here. Where is it?"

Locher pointed to the great safe, just as the alarm on the Church Street wall of the bank began sounding. The clamor upset the other gunman, who urged immediate flight, saying, "They're after us. Let's go!"

Dillinger remained calm, assured his nervous companion there was plenty of time, and continued searching, pausing once while the waterworks whistle was sounding in the distance to ask Romey and Locher, "Where the hell's the drawer to this window?"

His calmness was not shared by the rest of the gang, however. As the alarm continued to clang, one of the lookouts started firing at random, apparently to keep a throng of curious citizens at a distance. Two of the bullets drilled the Church Street window of Peter Gratz's drygoods store and others chipped stone from the wall of the Hauenstein Drugstore and Fred Gratz's clothing store, a block up North Main Street.

The two men outside were joined by the man in the blue suit and the jittery one in gray, and in all more than twenty revolver shots were fired. One of the bandits, a short-sleeved fellow who resembled the movie conception of a gangster, swung a submachine gun menacingly at the crowd but did not fire it. Dr. Gordon Bixel, who had an office on the second floor above the bank, was on his hands and knees on the floor, peering down at the scene.

The waterworks whistle continued to add its bansheelike wail to the uproar, but despite this some of the residents of Bluffton later said that while they had heard shots, they thought it was simply members of the American Legion setting off noisemaking devices as they came through town on their way home from a state convention in Lima.

The wild shooting continued for a moment or two longer. The Hardwick pool hall, next to the Town Hall, was hit, and a bullet knocked the gas gauge off the rear of a car owned by Robert Maxwell, a mail carrier. It was parked near the post office on South Main. Another bullet struck the Patterson barbershop.

Ralph Badertscher of the Bluffton *News* walked out to the front steps of the office, but a shot sent him back indoors. Anothers *News* man, reporter Red Biery, was crossing Main Street about a hundred feet from the bank when he saw the gunmen. Biery promptly ducked behind a car, later explaining, "Good men are scarce. I decided to preserve one."

Sidney Garau, a merchant policeman, ran into Greding's Hardware Store, shouting, "Let's get out the shotguns and get them!" But the bandits were gone before a posse could be organized. Postmaster Dode Murray also had ideas. He stood in ambush behind a large brick post in front of the post-office building on Main Street, armed with either a shotgun or a .45. The bandits went the other way.

Dillinger, in leaving the bank with about $2,100, had snatched a .32-caliber revolver from the cashier's cage. The driver was at the wheel of the getaway car as the bandit dashed forth, and the other four swiftly piled in. They went roaring down Church, then north on Jackson, with a machine gun protruding from the rear window for use if needed. The car was variously identified as an Essex, a Buick, a Chrysler, a Pontiac, and a Chevrolet—this in a day when it was easily possible to tell cars apart—which will give a fair idea of the panic that had come to town. Police finally took the word of a gas station operator, who saw the car skid into Riley Street from Jackson, that it was a Chevrolet.

Gideon Luginbihl, the town marshal, was home eating dinner when the holdup began and got to the bank after the smoke had cleared, a forgivable circumstance since witnesses said the whole thing—arrival, holdup and departure—had taken less than five minutes.

Deputies arrived from Lima—fifteen miles away—fifteen minutes after being notified, and Sheriff Jess Sarber set up roadblocks in the Lima area. Sheriff Lyle Harvitt and Deputy James Holden did the same near Bluffton. The getaway, however, was a clean one.

The *Morning Republican* in nearby Findlay carried this memorable paragraph on August 15: "One of the shots fired by the bandits before they fled crashed through the window of the apartment of Mrs. Lou Eaton above the Siefield bakery and sped near a chair in which Mrs. Eaton frequently sat. She was in Lima at the time."

While Dillinger and his men were busy in Bluffton, Huntington was still in Kentucky, and the Indiana State Police were questioning several men picked up that same day (August 14) in East Chicago —in an apartment whose address Huntington had obtained in Lebanon, Kentucky. Among those arrested was the brother of a Kentucky suspect in the Gravel Switch holdup. Another was Clarence "Whitey" Mohler, a parole violator from the Michigan City prison, who, by drinking shellac, had duped prison authorities into believing he had tuberculosis—thus winning a temporary parole for treatment.

Captain Matt Leach offered Mohler a deal. If Whitey gave him information, Leach would send him to Kentucky to stand trial as a robbery suspect instead of returning him to Michigan City to complete his life sentence. Mohler made the best of a bad bargain. He told Leach that the third man in the Montpelier holdup was Sam Goldstine, and that Homer Van Meter, twenty-seven, another Michigan City alumnus, was also associated with Dillinger and had been in Kentucky recently. (Van Meter, a holdup man and machine-gun expert, had been given a parole a few weeks before Dillinger. There is evidence to show that Dillinger went to St. Paul in a successful search for Van Meter shortly after his own parole.)

A bank in Grand Haven, Michigan, was held up on August 18. Michigan State Police found in the abandoned getaway car a driver's license in the name of Fred Monahan, one of Dillinger's aliases, and also the inevitable roofing nails.

Mohler told Leach that Dillinger, Copeland, Goldstine, and Van Meter had held up both the Grand Haven and the New Carlisle, Ohio, banks. He also said the gang had pulled more than twenty-four bank robberies during the previous sixty days. On August 22 he gave Leach the address of a $75-a-week apartment in Gary, which the gang had rented two weeks before.

Leach quickly left for the state police barracks to organize a raiding party. A Gary police lieutenant, who had been helping to question Mohler, went to the apartment mentioned by the informant to await Leach and his troopers. As he watched the place, he saw Goldstine come out and arrested him. Goldstine swiftly admitted that he and Dillinger had been sharing the apartment. He said they had stayed there with a couple of blondes on August 18 and had left the next day. He also said Dillinger was using the alias John Donovan. Goldstine added that the gang had still another apartment in nearby Hammond.

The raiders swooped on that hideout, and the woman owner of the apartment was arrested when two .45 automatics were found on the premises. The garage at the rear yielded a new Pontiac (rear window broken out, roofing nails on the back seat), which was found to be stolen. A boy living nearby, who was keeping a watchful eye on the place for the police, told Leach that several men in a Terraplane had driven up shortly before the raiders arrived and asked him to tell Goldstine they would see him at a Gary resort. The descriptions fitted Dillinger, Copeland, and Van Meter. The boy said he telephoned this information to the Gary police but the policeman he spoke to hung up. By the time police finally reached the resort rendezvous, the gang was not there.

Huntington, questioning one of the other men arrested by Leach, learned that Dillinger, Copeland, Van Meter, and a fourth man had been using the East Chicago area as a base of operations, and that they had a fleet of three Terraplanes—a fast car favored by Dillinger —which Dillinger had bought in South Bend. Huntington sent this and other information to the Pinkerton Detective Agency in Indianapolis. They, in turn, relayed it to their Ohio branch, which represented the Ohio Bankers' Association.

The police weren't the only ones who couldn't keep track of the elusive Dillinger. Mary Longnaker was having her troubles, too. She wrote, on an undetermined date—probably early in August— to give him her address and told him to walk in but not to ask for her because she was not known by her right name. She said if she was not at home he should leave a note or wait for her return.

On August 25 she again wrote him, expressing regret at having missed him on the evenings he had called (August 17 and 24) and saying she had heard from her brother Jim the day before and had seen her husband, Howard Longnaker, at the Greenville fair. She said that apparently Howard was not going to contest the divorce. Mary urged Dillinger to visit her on Sunday, saying she had some things she wanted to take to Jenkins.

This letter, however, was remailed later with a footnote saying it had been returned unclaimed and asking why Dillinger didn't stay home.

On August 25 the divisional manager for Pinkerton's in Cincinnati wrote a letter to Inspector C. E. Yendes of the Dayton, Ohio, police department, telling him what the Pinkerton investigation of Dillinger had turned up. The letter said:

Dear Inspector Yendes:
RE CITIZENS NATIONAL BANK, BLUFFTON, OHIO, HOLDUP.

John Dillinger, alias John Hall, is wanted in connection with some of the holdups in various towns in Ohio. . . . I enclose circular containing his fingerprints, description, etc. Will you please return it to this office after it has served your purpose?

Recently the Indiana State Police arrested Sam Goldstine, Fred Berman and Clifford Mohler at East Chicago, Indiana.

John Dillinger has a female friend at Dayton, Ohio, whose given name is unknown, but her maiden name is Jenkins. She has a brother, James Jenkins, serving a life sentence at Michigan City, Indiana, State Prison for murder. This woman is suing for divorce from her husband at Dayton, Ohio, and Dillinger is paying the expense of the divorce action. Dillinger calls upon this woman regularly and, no doubt, can be apprehended at Dayton, Ohio. He is driving a new Essex Terraplane "8" sedan, black color and probably is using Indiana license 418-673, 512-979, 703-736 or 86-927. On July 8, 1933, Indiana license 86-927 was issued to John Dillinger for a 1928 Chevrolet coupe. . . .

Sam Goldstine has been identified by Carl Enochs, cashier, New Carlisle National Bank, New Carlisle, Ohio, as the bandit who threatened to kill him when the bank was held up in June, 1933. Unfortunately the following day when Enochs returned with Horace Grisso, and [Grisso] could not make a positive identification of Goldstine, Enochs became doubtful, although he had previously picked him out of a line of eight men.

Dillinger has been known to take a 1931 Indiana license plate and change one number to make it appear that it is a 1933 plate.

You will note by the circulars I am enclosing for Copeland and Dillinger that they are wanted. The thought is that considering Dillinger is contacting with the woman in Dayton, you could have the police be on the watch for these license numbers, or probably they could get some information concerning this woman and cause the arrest of Dillinger and in all probability, Copeland, as they spend considerable of their time together. . . .

The "thought" was a good one. Detective Sergeants Russell K. Pfauhl and Charles E. Gross of the Dayton force were assigned to hunt for Dillinger. They found that Mary Longnaker (whose name had been supplied by the warden of the Michigan City prison) was living in a "plush rooming house" at 325 West First Street in Dayton. The two detectives made a quiet search of her room and found a letter from Dillinger saying he would see her soon.

So Pfauhl and Gross moved into the house, bringing shotguns and machine guns with them. They lived there several weeks on the ground floor; Mary's room was on the floor above. The cooperative landlady, at the request of the police, kept a front room vacant so Dillinger would have a place to stay if he showed up; from time to time the detectives got a look at letters from the outlaw to Mary in which he kept promising he would "see you soon."

They were still watching the apartment on September 6, when Dillinger and another man entered the Massachusetts Avenue State Bank in Indianapolis while Hilton Crouch, a former dirt-track race driver, remained outside in the car. A. S. Krueger and L. W. Reinhart, cashiers, were waiting on customers when the two gunmen ordered them to raise their hands, and Dillinger vaulted the railing and went into the teller's cage while his companion stood in the doorway, a handkerchief over his face, and covered everyone with a machine gun.

Dillinger went swiftly from cage to cage, sweeping the money—including $500 in half dollars—into a white sack. The other man, obviously jittery, kept yelling at his companion to hurry, and finally both ran out and jumped into the car, which Crouch wheeled away at top speed. Witnesses said it was a DeSoto, bearing Ohio plates. The loot was something over $24,000, which made the holdup the second largest in Indianapolis history.

By this time Dillinger had moved his headquarters to Chicago. On September 15, he had an Essex Terraplane repaired in a garage at 3034 Lawrence Avenue, Chicago, giving his name as Donovan and his address as 2649 Kedzie Avenue. He had the car washed, tappets adjusted, fenders straightened and painted—and the total bill was $5.85.

Six days later—on the evening of September 21—Pfauhl and Gross decided to sleep in their own homes for the night, only to have a telephone call from the rooming house proprietor announcing that Dillinger had come. A large number of Dayton police surrounded the house. Gross and Pfauhl, who were better acquainted with the place than anyone else, went in, stationing another sergeant downstairs.

Pfauhl and Gross went quietly upstairs with the landlady, who knocked on the door and stepped quickly aside as Mary opened it. The two detectives burst into the room—Pfauhl with a sawed-off shotgun and Gross with a submachine gun—to find the desperado in his undershirt showing Mary some of the photographs taken during their World's Fair trip.

"Stick 'em up, John. We're police officers," one of the raiders said.

Dillinger dropped the photos and raised his hands shoulder high, then slowly began to lower them. Pfauhl thrust the shotgun toward Dillinger and warned that he would shoot if the hands were not kept up. Mary also tried to help Dillinger by "fainting," but Pfauhl, refusing to be taken in, ordered her to crawl out of the way on hands and knees, so that she wouldn't be between Dillinger and the police guns—an order which enraged Dillinger.

The detectives found a .38 automatic between the cushions of a sofa and several other guns in Dillinger's luggage. There also were a large supply of ammunition and some roofing nails in his 1933 Terraplane. He was carrying $2,604 in cash.

When Dillinger was convinced that he was caught, he became philosophical. "When you fellows came in," he said, "I didn't know if you were part of another gang or not. I know uniformed police, but not plainclothesmen. I thought you were somebody else."

As for Mary Longnaker, she demonstrated soon afterward that

this sort of excitement was not to her taste—by marrying another man, presumably a quieter fellow.

A more thorough search of Dillinger at the County Jail, where he was ordered taken for safekeeping, resulted in the discovery of a diagram which Dayton police thought was of a prison. It had cross-marks on it, and Pfauhl later tried to tell Matt Leach that it might be a diagram of the Indiana State Prison at Michigan City, marked with a break in mind. Leach professed amusement, according to Pfauhl, and replied, "You've been reading too many detective novels. He ain't that big. They couldn't get out of there if they tried."

Dillinger was arrested on September 22. Ten convicts broke out of the "big house" at Michigan City four days later.

Word of Dillinger's apprehension was sent to all law enforcement bodies concerned, and Dillinger himself was questioned by Dayton's Inspector Yendes but said very little except that he wished to talk with Jack Egan, a Dayton attorney. So nonchalant was Dillinger in his talks with Yendes, in fact, that the veteran police officer had a feeling that Dillinger wasn't much worried and might be expecting a rescue party.

There was only one warrant out for Dillinger at the time, and that was for the Daleville robbery. But instead of returning him to Muncie, where Sheriff Fred Puckett would have held him for trial on the Daleville charge, Yendes decided to keep Dillinger in Dayton until witnesses had a chance to view him in connection with other hold-ups.

Among those who came were Matt Leach, Claude Dozier and Harvey Hire of the Indiana State Police. They asked about his actions since he was paroled, but got nothing from Dillinger other than the rueful remark that one of his former prison mates "must have talked a lot" to provide them with so much information.

Chief of Police Frank Massie of Muncie identified Dillinger as having taken part in a mid-June holdup there. There were unconfirmed stories that he had also been fingered in the $24,000 holdup of a bank in Farrell, Pennsylvania, September 12. Attorney Egan filed a petition for a writ of habeas corpus. Before this petition could be heard, however, Dillinger had been sent to Lima.

Huntington, notified in Indianapolis that Dillinger had been caught, prepared to leave for Dayton at once. But just before he left his office the telephone rang, and Arthur McGinnis, a minor underworld character who had served time, told him he had something to talk over with him. Huntington said he was about to leave for Dayton, but McGinnis mentioned the Massachusetts Avenue Bank holdup, and the detective decided to meet with him.

Half an hour later, McGinnis told Huntington he had been in prison with Dillinger and they were paroled about the same time. He had read of Dillinger's arrest, McGinnis said, and was sure he could turn up the rest of the gang for a suitable reward, plus a percentage of any money or bonds recovered. McGinnis named Dillinger, Crouch and a third man as the trio that had held up the Massachusetts Avenue Bank; he was certain of this since he had been running errands for Dillinger the week of the robbery.

The story was impressive enough so that Huntington told McGinnis he might be able to work out an agreement if McGinnis would repeat the tale to Inspector Fred Simon of the Indianapolis police—an arrangement which could be a sort of insurance policy for McGinnis in case he were seen or caught with the gang. McGinnis agreed, and told his story once more at police headquarters. Huntington told Simon he would seek permission from his clients to "use" McGinnis. Simon agreed to the plan but urged complete secrecy as a safeguard for the informer. Huntington then dropped McGinnis off near his home in Indianapolis and drove to Dayton.

The Dayton authorities were cooperative, and Huntington was allowed to question Dillinger in his cell. The prisoner was friendly but uncommunicative.

"We talked to Dillinger a few minutes," Huntington said in his report, "and though he was pleasant, he did not admit any robberies."

Huntington finally gave up and went to police headquarters to see Inspector Yendes. He told Yendes that Dillinger was wanted for the Massachusetts Avenue Bank holdup, and that 10 per cent of any loot recovered would probably be offered by the insurance company as a reward.

Yendes replied that the Dayton police were not permitted to accept such payments, and suggested that any reward should go to the landlady who had tipped off his men. Yendes added that if Indiana police wanted Dillinger for the Massachusetts Avenue Bank robbery, they should send an officer to Dayton with a warrant.

Huntington passed on this information to his friend, Inspector

Simon, and began wondering once more about the wisdom of using McGinnis as a spy. When he learned that McGinnis had flown to Dayton with Hubert Dillinger to visit the jail the day after Huntington was there, he decided it might be worth taking a chance with the informer. The American Surety Company authorized Huntington to give McGinnis money enough to set himself up in Chicago in order to make the necessary gang contacts. McGinnis promptly left for Chicago.

Since McGinnis was on parole from an Indiana prison, and would be looked for if he vanished without explanation, there was nothing for Huntington to do but let Leach in on the scheme. Huntington did this reluctantly, since he believed Leach gave out too much information to the press. Leach approved the plan and assigned Detective Gene Ryan to accompany Huntington to Chicago the following day to meet McGinnis.

At this meeting McGinnis told the two lawmen that Dillinger, while in Chicago, had been associating with an ex-convict, and that Hilton Crouch, also wanted for the Massachusetts Avenue Bank holdup, was living in Chicago, unaware that he was being sought. Copeland had been in Chicago also, McGinnis said, living with a couple on Montrose Avenue.

Copeland, McGinnis added, had just gone to a place near Hamilton, Ohio, and had recently visited Dewey and Pearl Elliott in Kokomo. Pearl, McGinnis said, had called on Dillinger in Dayton and received some money from him. McGinnis said he did not know what the money was for.

Meanwhile plans to extradite Dillinger to Indiana continued. Prosecutor Herbert Wilson obtained an indictment September 25 in Indianapolis charging Dillinger with taking part in the holdup of the Massachusetts Avenue Bank. The next day Governor Paul McNutt, who four months before had signed Dillinger's parole, signed the extradition request.

But Dillinger himself had other plans, and these became much brighter that very day, with the carrying out of a project he had helped formulate before his release from the prison at Michigan City.

FIVE

●●●●● "MAYBE I'LL LEARN SOMEDAY, DAD, THAT YOU
CAN'T WIN IN THIS GAME."
—LETTER FROM JOHN DILLINGER TO HIS FATHER

Early in September John Dillinger had stopped at the Indianapolis home of Mary Kinder to give her some money and some instructions. He told her that a group of men would be coming to see her at some not too distant date, and that the money was to buy clothes to replace those they would be wearing.

Mary asked some eager questions, and Dillinger gave her a sketchy fill-in. There should be fourteen men, he said, including her brother Earl Northern, and her sweetheart Harry Pierpont, both then serving time in Michigan City. Mary asked no further questions, and agreed to help.

A few days later someone (Dillinger himself seems a likely nominee) tossed a package over the wall into the exercise yard of the Michigan City prison. It contained three automatics—for which Dillinger had paid forty-eight dollars apiece—and eighteen cartridges, muffled in cotton and wrapped with a Chicago newspaper.

The "wrong" inmate found it, however, and turned it over to a guard.

Warden Louis Kunkel failed to connect Pierpont—for whom it was intended—with the package, and instead ordered three Chicago convicts, Daniel McGeoghagen, Jack Gray and Edward Murphy, placed in solitary confinement. Curiously, these three were among those involved in the plot.

Later the same month, probably on September 24, three automatic pistols were successfully smuggled into the prison. The weapons came by truck with a shipment of thread for the prison shirt factory. Walter Detrick, twenty-eight-year-old convict also in on the escape plan, was assigned to the unloading platform and quickly spotted the marked carton with the guns in it. He hid them in a button box in the factory. Detrick, who had served two years of a life term for bank robbery, then spread the word to Pierpont and the others.

Pierpont, thirty-one, had been an inmate of the prison since 1925. He was 6 feet 1, weighed 162 pounds, had light chestnut hair and gray-blue eyes. His nickname was "Handsome Harry"; he had a soft and pleasant voice, and was known as a ladies' man. He was also considered a potential killer; he had been arrested in Terre Haute in March, 1922, for assault with intent to kill. He was paroled after two years and in 1925 was arrested in Detroit for the holdup of a Kokomo, Indiana, bank. Convicted, he was given a sentence of ten to twenty-one years and served a brief portion of that time with Dillinger at the Pendleton reformatory before being transferred to Michigan City.

His record inside bore out his reputation. Between 1925 and 1931 it included not only the minor offense of talking in dining room and chapel but also attempting to plan escapes with aid from New York and Chicago, assaulting a guard, binding him and trying to escape, writing requests for guns and saws to be smuggled in, making a key for his cell door, possession of a handcuff key, and other not-so-boyish pranks. Pierpont was a man who just didn't like being locked up.

Another in the escape plot was the Canadian-born John Hamilton, who was serving a twenty-five-year term for auto banditry. He was sentenced from St. Joseph County, Michigan, in 1927. Hamilton, a frowning, chunky man of thirty-four, had the index and middle fingers of his right hand missing, and was known as "Three Finger

Jack." Despite his reputation as a "tough guy," Hamilton's only inside offenses were for being noisy in 1927 and for skipping rope in the shop five years later!

Another of the crash-out gang was forty-four-year-old Charles "Fat Charley" Makley. Makley, born in Ohio, was first arrested in 1921 while working as a railroad switchman in Detroit, on a charge of receiving stolen property, and again in 1922 in St. Louis, for questioning. He was freed both times. In July, 1924, he was arrested by the Wichita, Kansas, police and turned over to Kansas City authorities, who wanted him for robbery. He was given a fifteen-year sentence, but was freed on parole in June, 1928. That same month he was rearrested in Hammond, Indiana, for a bank robbery and sent to Michigan City prison for ten to twenty years.

Makley, a former auto salesman who walked with a slight limp, was described as "rotund and slow-moving." But he was also quick-witted and amusing—the court jester type. His inside offenses were minor: possession of contraband cigarette papers, possession of a five-dollar bill, possession of an electric stove, and changing his clothes from "second grade" to "first grade" in order to attend a prison baseball game.

The other major figure in the plot was Russell Lee Clark, large, strong, unobtrusive, who was serving a twenty-year sentence, imposed in 1927, for bank robbery. His home was Detroit, and his prison record was a bad one. It included taking part in a strike, refusing to work, trying to foment a revolt, trying to escape, and trying to kill his guards while being returned from New Castle, Indiana, where he was tried.

The others invited to the coming-out party, in addition to the three whom Kunkel had ordered to solitary after the first guns were found, were Joseph Burns, a former Chicagoan serving life for murder; Joseph Fox, sentenced to life for bank robbery; Edward Shouse, with twenty-two years left of a robbery term; James Clark, no relation to Russell, serving life for robbery; James Jenkins, brother of Mary Longnaker, a murderer serving a life sentence; and Mary Kinder's brother Earl Northern, who failed to reach the rendezvous in time and was left behind.

About 1:30 on the afternoon of September 26, Pierpont quietly approached those in on the plot and said, "All right, boys, if you want to go and take a chance, we will go now." Pierpont and Russell

Clark then approached G. H. Stevens, superintendent of the shirt factory, and told him he was needed in the basement. Stevens went down and was made prisoner by the other plotters, then threatened by the armed Pierpont. A moment later Albert Evans, the assistant warden, entered the basement—having been told by Detrick that a jug of wine had been found there—and was seized.

The convicts, with the two officials in front, then walked casually out of the building and across the yard. Three of the escaping men carried automatics concealed under piles of shirts and those without guns had iron bars hidden under the bundles. Although they passed scores of their fellow convicts, no one saw anything unusual in what looked like a routine work patrol. Nor were the guards on the walls suspicious.

Marching in regulation step behind Evans and Stevens, the convicts reached the first steel gate, where Evans whispered to the guard, Frank Swanson, "They've got guns. Open the gate or they'll kill us." Swanson unlocked the old-fashioned open-bar gate and was added to the procession. At the second gate the convicts showed guns to the guard, Guy Burklow, who opened the door without argument and also fell in line.

But at the third barrier, Fred Wellnitz, the gatekeeper, was slugged and knocked unconscious when he started to reach for his rifle. Evans, remonstrating with the convicts for this violence, also was slugged. The keys were taken from Wellnitz and the gate opened. The entire group then marched into the administration building, where the convicts saw Lawrence Mutch, superintendent of prison industries.

"Let's get Mutch!" one of them shouted, and two of the prisoners leaped on him, then led him off toward the prison arsenal. When he bravely refused to open the door to the storehouse where machine guns and rifles were kept in quantity, Mutch was beaten to the floor.

The other prisoners went into the large office and began herding eight clerks, two of them women, into the vault. Finley Carson, seventy-two, moved too slowly, and one of the convicts, cursing, shot him in the stomach. Warden Kunkel, who happened to be in the office at the time, was not recognized. He wisely refrained from identifying himself and was shoved into the vault with the others.

The escaping ten rushed out the main entrance, meeting Sheriff Charles Neel of Harrison County, who had just delivered a prisoner.

Neel was grabbed by Detrick, Burns, Fox and James Clark, and pushed into his own car. The other six halted a passing auto, driven by Herbert Van Valkenberg of Oswego. They forced the driver and his passengers—his wife, and Mrs. Minnie Schultz, eighty-nine, a relative—out of the vehicle and drove it away.

Tuesday evening, shortly after the breakout, Captain Leach sent his finest troopers into Michigan City to keep an eye on things until he had time to do some investigating. He then called Huntington and told him he thought the ten might be headed for Elliott's place in Kokomo, in view of the information McGinnis had given Huntington earlier. Leach asked that the detective bring McGinnis to state police headquarters.

Huntington refused to do this, but said he would telephone Mc-Ginnis, who had returned from Chicago, and question him, if Leach would delay the planned Kokomo raid, which would probably place suspicion on McGinnis. Huntington then drove quickly to McGinnis's house and took him to Indianapolis police headquarters, where they conferred with Inspector Simon and Chief Mike Morrissey; McGinnis told them he had arranged to meet Copeland at Elliott's, but that the meeting had not taken place and he knew nothing of the escape.

The two Indianapolis officers agreed with Huntington that it would be unwise for Leach to be allowed to confer with McGinnis; they shared Huntington's view that Leach talked too much to the press. Huntington, after advising McGinnis not to go near Elliott's place, telephoned Leach and told him his informant had no knowledge of the Michigan City escape. He urged Leach to make the raid whenever he wished, but Leach said he would delay it because he had several other good tips.

On Wednesday, September 27, McGinnis gave Huntington further details of his Chicago visit. He had talked with Crouch, he said, who was living with a girl in an apartment whose address he did not know. Crouch had given McGinnis a note to take to his mother in Indianapolis, telling her to forward his parole papers. He signed the note "Bob" but gave no address. McGinnis said Crouch had about $8,000—his share of the Massachusetts Avenue Bank job—in a Chicago bank vault and was paying for "protection" in Chicago.

Copeland, McGinnis went on, lived in the 800 block on Montrose Avenue, not far from the lake, and frequented gambling places on

Broadway, West Ontario and East Huron Street. Copeland had visited the roadhouse in Kokomo two days before the Michigan City escape. He was driving a late-model Oldsmobile and was at present, McGinnis said, in either Chicago, Kokomo, or Hamilton, Ohio.

McGinnis also arranged for Mrs. Crouch to wire a request to her son to meet the informer in Chicago, simply so that the police could ascertain the address from the wire. She did so, and as a result a trap was laid for Crouch at Sheridan Road and Ainslie Avenue, the evening of September 28. Nothing came of this, quite possibly because the area was packed with policemen that evening. Captain Leach, Deputy Warden Claudy and both Indiana and Chicago police were in the same neighborhood at the same time on a tip that Joseph Burns and Detrick were to meet an ex-convict there; the former convict had told the police that he had promised to drive Burns and Detrick to New Orleans for $1,500. However, his passengers failed to arrive.

The Michigan City escape brought from Leach the charge, published in the Wednesday morning papers, that he had not been permitted to examine the documents found in Dillinger's possession when he was arrested, even though these contained information connected with the Michigan City break. Yendes gave Leach the lie on this, saying that not only had the Indianapolis State Police official been told of the papers and warned of their possible significance, but he had also been urged to copy them if he wished.

Huntington told Simon and Morrissey that he had been present when Leach saw the documents and could verify Yendes's account. The Indianapolis officers told Huntington they were afraid the argument might result in refusal by Ohio to turn over Dillinger. Within the hour there was a telegram from Dayton saying that Dillinger had been remanded to the custody of Allen County officials and would be removed to Lima to await trial for the Bluffton robbery.

Both cars in which the prisoners were escaping went west on State Route 12 toward Chicago, but in a few miles Neel's car turned south into a side road, where the driver lost control and ran it into a ditch. The four, taking Neel along, walked to a farm owned by Carl Spanier. They forced Spanier at gunpoint to get his car and drive the whole party south. His machine was low on gas, and Spanier managed to escape when they stopped to refuel.

Shortly thereafter, out of gas, Spanier's car was abandoned; the fugitives, still accompanied by Neel, cut across the fields southwest of Michigan City and spent the night in the thick underbrush. All wore prison clothes—regulation blue shirts and trousers—but they were in an area with thousands of acres of timberland and their principal problem was food. It rained intermittently throughout the night.

On Wednesday they set out once more, in the general direction of Gary, but again retreated into the woods when it became obvious they were lost. At nightfall on Thursday, it was suggested that they tie Neel in the brush near the road, but Clark argued against it, saying that leaving the elderly man in the rain, which was falling again, might result in his death.

The others—Burns, Fox, and Detrick—agreed this was a possibility, and told Clark that since he was worried about the sheriff's health he could stay with him. The group separated near Hobart, Indiana, about 3 A.M.

Neel and Clark walked for several hours until they reached Highway 6, where they caught a ride into Hobart. There Neel bought food for Clark and himself and gave Clark a topcoat. Both then caught an interurban for Gary, where Neel went directly to the police station. His arrival caused a sensation. Three companies of state militia had been unable to find him and he had been presumed dead. Neel was questioned but gave a vague account of his adventures, probably from a combination of exhaustion and an understandable feeling of gratitude toward Clark who was still in the area.

Clark, who had gone on to Hammond, was traced through a taxi he had hired, and was picked up later in the day. He was brought to police headquarters at Gary, where Neel greeted him in friendly fashion and gave him five dollars as he was taken off to be returned to Michigan City. Clark had been free for three days. Neel changed some parts of his story after Clark was caught.

The group of six, in the meantime, had headed for Indianapolis. About three in the morning on September 27, they were knocking at Mary Kinder's door. Dillinger's capture in Dayton four days before the prison break had prevented his arranging for a hideout as planned, and Pierpont calmly told Mary it was up to her to find them a safe place. Mary explained that her parents were in the apartment; she then took the six fugitives—still in prison blues—to the home of Ralph Saffel, a young man whose part in the affair was involuntary and completely innocent. Saffel had had a few dates with Mary, and in return he was forced to give temporary refuge to the six convicts. When Mary went downtown to obtain clothes for them, Saffel was made to accompany her.

When the two returned, they found that Pearl Elliott had arrived from Kokomo with more money. She was an associate of the gang, who had come in response to an earlier telephone call from Mary. The six fugitives washed, shaved, changed clothes, divided the money, and waited. Jenkins sang most of the morning, Mary remembers, and had a "wonderful voice." The gang kept the hapless Saffel on edge until late that night, when Harry Copeland arrived. Then all of them left, having warned Saffel to keep his mouth shut.

The morning after the jail break Captain Leach gave Chief of Detectives Simon a letter sent to Dillinger in Dayton, Ohio, which bore Mary Kinder's address. Simon sent two detectives to the Kinder apartment. They talked with her sister, Mrs. Margaret Behrens, who said that someone had come to the Green Lantern Resort (a tavern) the night before to get Mary, and she hadn't been home since—a story which may have been a cover-up for Mary.

According to the Indianapolis police, the six convicts spent September 28 at the home of an Indianapolis blonde, against whom no charges were placed even though money wrappers were later found in her home. Police picked up Mrs. Behrens, who was also known as Silent Sadie—because of her refusal to talk after the bank holdup for which her husband had gone to jail in 1927. She was released after a short time, although police were sure she had seen the fugitives for a while on the twenty-eighth.

It was not until the evening of the twenty-ninth that the fugitives came into the spotlight once more. This time they abandoned a getaway car at Brownstown, south of Indianapolis, in which prison jackets belonging to Shouse and Makley were found. Witnesses said the men had gone east on Route 31 in a second car about 7 P.M. Two hours later they were a hundred miles northwest of Brownstown at Terre Haute, where they halted a Franklin sedan driven by Frank M. Ratcliffe. They made him drive to a point several miles east of Terre Haute, where he was forced from the car. They then drove away, using both cars.

At approximately 8:45, 32 miles east of Terre Haute on U.S. 40 at Brazil, Indiana, the police spotted Ratcliffe's stolen car but were outrun. The Indiana State Police, although greatly hampered by the lack of a two-way radio system, were also scouring the roads for the Franklin. At 1:30, Sergeant Bert Davis of the state police, sitting in his patrol car several miles east of Indianapolis on Route 40, saw an Oldsmobile with Illinois license plates flash by. He took after it, heading for the city. He switched on his siren and red warning light and pushed the Ford speedometer to 80. Soon he was closing the gap.

When he was only a few hundred feet behind the fugitives' car, it suddenly screeched to a halt at High School Road, in Ben Davis, a western suburb of Indianapolis. As the police car shot by, the bandits broke the rear window of the Olds and poked a submachine gun out, training it on some Ben Davis residents standing at the intersection. The driver of the Olds then tried a sweeping turn into High School Road, striking a light pole in the process. James Jenkins either jumped or fell from the car, and as he fled into the night, a local jeweler, Edward Watts, got off one shot at him. The damaged Olds sped west. Ratcliffe's Franklin was found abandoned in Greencastle the next day.

When word of the incident reached the Indianapolis police, they made no secret of their annoyance. They had set up a trap for the fugitives on Route 40 at Mickleyville, nearer town, and Sergeant Davis's precipitate action had disrupted their plans.

Early on the morning of the thirtieth, Victor Lyle, twenty-four, was leaving Ben Davis for his home in Indianapolis after a date. About to enter his car, he was approached by Jenkins who asked for a lift, explaining his disheveled look as the result of a fight "over on Route 40." Lyle invited him into the car and headed for Route 40, only to have Jenkins pull a gun and order him to drive south and keep away from the state route.

Lyle went south, eventually reaching the downtown section of Bloomington, where Jenkins ordered him to change his route. He then headed east to Nashville, where he ran low on gas. While Jenkins was trying to rouse a filling station operator, Lyle drove away and went at once to the police station at Bloomington. Although it was then 3 A.M., a posse was soon formed, made up of deputies, state police, farmers with shotguns and rifles, and men from the new Civilian Conservation Corps camp near Bloomington.

Marie Poling, telephone operator, kept the exchange open throughout the night for emergency calls.

Despite the small army now hunting him, Jenkins managed to reach the village of Bean Blossom later in the day. Apparently to allay suspicion, he asked a local resident, Will Altop, where he could get some parts for his broken-down car. Altop, suspicious, walked away. He then rallied three friends—Herbert McDonald, a storekeeper; Ivan Bond, and Benjamin Kanter, a farmer—and the group went hunting for Jenkins.

They came upon him on the main road and said they would help him if a search showed that he was unarmed. McDonald started to get out of their car, shotgun in hand. Saying, "Don't get out!" Jenkins promptly pulled a revolver and shot the thirty-five-year-old grocer in the right shoulder. As he shot again, Kanter, fifty-five, standing nearby with a double-barreled shotgun held out of sight along his right leg, raised it and fired from ten feet away.

The first charge missed, but the second caught Jenkins in the side of the head and he fell in the weeds beside the highway. He was taken by Sheriff Fremont Weddle to the office of Dr. L. R. Crabtree in Nashville, where he died. Identification was made by the state police, and by Jenkins's father, the Reverend George Jenkins, a Pentecostal minister, who prayed for McDonald's recovery as he knelt beside the body of his son. Said the Reverend Mr. Jenkins, "I'm glad it's like this. Better this than that he'd killed somebody else."

Back at Michigan City, authorities admitted having heard through the grapevine that a jail delivery was planned. They excused their failure to prevent it by explaining that their information indicated the breakout date was about October 1.

Similarly in Dayton, authorities heard reports that Dillinger was to be freed, and men with machine guns were stationed on the roofs of buildings near the County Jail on Fourth Street. As an added precaution a policeman at the central station was instructed to take the license number of all suspicious cars cruising the area. He soon reported the number of one car from Ohio and another from Michigan which made several trips past the station.

While still in Dayton, Dillinger was identified in the Massachusetts Avenue Bank holdup by five men, and "partially" identified by Cashier Enochs of New Carlisle, Ohio. After the Michigan City escape, Sheriff Eugene Frick kept the front door of the jail locked and allowed no one to see Dillinger. His deputies were heavily armed and the night force was doubled.

A day or so after his arrest Dillinger pleaded guilty to the holdup of the Bluffton bank, although neither Romey nor Locher had identified him. He was ordered transferred to the Allen County Jail in Lima—which, later events indicated, was exactly what he had hoped for. The Lima jail was an old one, and chances of a delivery were far better there than in either Dayton or Indianapolis.

Sheriff Sarber sent three deputies to pick up the prisoner, but when Dayton authorities said they felt that the force was too small, he ordered more men to go. The Dayton police had such respect for Dillinger's importance that they transferred him to the county line in an armored car. But Sarber, who met them at Piqua, refused to take Dillinger seriously, according to Pfauhl. The Dayton detective says Sarber was warned of the probable tieup between Dillinger and the ten who escaped from Michigan City, but refused to believe it, calling his prisoner "just another punk." Huntington, however, shared the feeling that a delivery was planned.

"I am strongly of the opinion," he said in a report written September 27, "that Dillinger's associates will make an effort to effect his release. I telephoned Mr. Ackerman, superintendent of the Pinkerton Detective Agency that has the protection of the Ohio Bankers' Association, and advised him that an effort might be made to free Dillinger in Ohio."

The first day he was in Lima, Dillinger wrote his father a penitent letter which said:

Dear Dad.

Hope this letter finds you well and not worrying too much over me. Maybe I'll learn someday Dad that you can't win in this game. I know I have been a big disappointment to you but I guess I did to [sic] much time for where I went in a carefree boy I came out bitter toward everything in general. Of course Dad most of the blame lies with me for my environment was of the best but if I had gotten off more leniently when I made my first mistake this would never have happened. How is Doris and Frances? I preferred to stand trial here in Lima because there isn't as much prejudice against me here and I am sure I will get a square deal here. Dad don't believe all that the newspapers say about me for I am not guilty of half of the things I am charged with and I've never hurt anyone. Well Dad I guess this is all for this time just wanted you to know I am well and treated fine.

From Johnnie.

On October 4 he wrote again, this time to his niece Mary, and—significantly—he again spoke of how well he was being treated by Sheriff Sarber, a perhaps too-pleasant host:

About the only time I ever get any letters from you is when I'm in jail, ha, ha. . . . My trial will probably be the week after next. Visiting day is Wednesday and of course you can't come then, but I think the Sheriff will let you in if you come on Sunday. I would love to see you before they send me to Columbus. The Sheriff has treated me just fine and if you explain to him you are working and going to school I am sure he will let you see me for a few minutes. I would sure love to have seen the World Series. I was intending to drive to New York and see the first two games, then go on to Washington to see the rest. Wouldn't that have been a nice trip? . . . I am well and getting along fine so don't worry about me. I'm not guilty of everything they have against me. . . . Lots of love,

Uncle Johnnie

While Dillinger waited in the Lima jail, his friends were far from idle. After Jenkins was slain at Bean Blossom, the others hid out at the farm home of Pierpont's father and mother near Leipsic, Ohio. The group, which included Pierpont, Makley, Russell Clark, Detrick, Shouse and Copeland, also had a hideaway at Hamilton, Ohio, and Mary Kinder was with them. Their immediate aim was to get Dillinger out of jail, but for this they needed operating money. They decided to raid the First National Bank of St. Mary's, Ohio. This scheme almost certainly was suggested by Makley, since St. Mary's was his home town.

Many a banking institution had closed its doors during this period, and a circumstance which Makley may not have known was that St. Mary's was now in the hands of a conservator, W. O. Smith, with whom Makley was acquainted.

Five members of the gang—Pierpont, Makley, Hamilton, Russell Clark and Shouse—left Hamilton, Ohio, by auto on October 3, driving behind another car with Pierpont's brother Fred at the wheel and his mother as a passenger. Pierpont had given the car to his brother, presumably because it had been used since the Michigan City getaway and was too "hot" for the gang to be seen in.

The five said goodbye to Fred near Springfield, and he continued toward his home near Leipsic, while they went on to St. Mary's, which they reached in time to park on Front Street, near the bank, shortly before the 3 P.M. closing time. One man remained in the car, one loitered in a doorway near the bank as a lookout, and the other three entered.

Teller Roland Clausing was the first to realize that a holdup was in progress. He approached his window to wait on a man who seemed to be reading a road map. As the map was lowered, Clausing found himself staring into the barrel of Pierpont's .45 automatic. Pierpont said, "Just stand still!" He then went behind the cage, while a fellow gunmen kept Clausing covered.

At that moment W. Clarence Young, assistant treasurer of the Union Building and Loan Company, and W. L. Noggle, owner of the Fort Barbee Hotel, were approaching the front door of the bank. There was no reason for them to suspect that anything was wrong. Scores of their fellow townsmen were standing across the street from the bank, listening to the World Series broadcast. One policeman was standing in front of the station on Front Street, not far from the bandit car, and Young and Noggle said hello to another officer as they neared the bank.

When they entered, Makley, who was standing out of sight beside the door, walked with them to the window where Clausing was standing, apparently waiting to serve them. As Young reached the opening, however, Pierpont arose from a crouching position and covered him. Makley also drew a gun, and took both customers to the directors' room, where the third bandit was already holding three other employees and a customer, Clarence Wagner. Makley then returned to the front door.

After removing all the money from the counter, Pierpont—apparently believing that Young was a bank official—ordered him to open the small safe in the vault. Clausing and Young finally persuaded Pierpont the latter was a customer and that no one but Smith, who was absent, could open the safe. Just then Smith walked in. While he was explaining that the safe was protected by a time lock, the lock clicked off and he was forced to open it.

The bandits herded the eight into a vault, partially closed the door, and were preparing to leave when Makley suddenly called out, "Wait a minute—here's another one." He brought back Roscoe Turner, a patron who had just entered, and ushered him into the vault with the others. Pierpont warned that if there were any outcry from the gathering before the gang left, they would "blow the side of the building in with submachine-gun fire."

The three, with the lookout, then strolled in leisurely fashion to their car, taking with them more than $14,000 in currency, and drawing no notice whatever from the baseball fans across the street, who still listened to the game Dillinger had once planned to attend.

The sortie, the first since the breakout at Michigan City, got what the gang undoubtedly regarded as a rave notice. The St. Mary's *Evening Leader* for October 4, after describing the raid, said, "Officials believe the bandits were all professionals. They worked quickly and with a nonchalance which amazed their victims."

Shortly after the holdup, E. L. Ramsey, a farmer living near St. Mary's, told police that a green Hudson sedan and a black Oldsmobile, both traveling very fast, had stopped near his farm. Two men, one carrying a satchel, got out of the Hudson and into the Olds, which was driven by a woman. The cars then sped down Route 210 toward State Route 127.

Whether this was the St. Mary's gang or not, the five were soon back in Hamilton, where Pierpont, who either had been named leader or had assumed that position, told the others to remain until sent for. He and Mary Kinder then left for Leipsic. Smith, meanwhile, who had failed to recognize Makley and refused to believe he was one of the gang, picked out Fat Charley's photo from a rogue's gallery selection without knowing it was Makley until after the identification.

Within a few days after the escape from Michigan City a board of inquiry found that a shortage of guards and the way in which outside material was delivered to the prison were jointly responsible for the escapes. Governor McNutt, however, told newsmen he would have an independent investigation made by Captain Leach. McNutt also petitioned the state legislature for $4,000 for the purchase of an armored car, light cars, red lights, sirens and guns, explaining that a lack of such equipment had hampered the chase after the fleeing convicts.

By early October, despite the raid at St. Mary's, the police seemed without a solid clue to the whereabouts of the missing men. On October 7 the first of several raids was made on the home of Mary Kinder. Police seized a diary of Mary's in which there were numerous names, including that of John Dillinger.

On the following day, Pierpont, Makley, Hamilton, Russell Clark and Shouse arrived at the home of Pierpont's brother near Leipsic to spend the night. They had stopped in Lima on the way to case the jail where Dillinger was held, but decided to delay the rescue attempt for twenty-four hours. They told Fred Pierpont they wanted to leave some cars in his barn, but he told them there was no room. They then went to the elder Pierpont's place, which was nearby, and hid the cars there.

✴

SIX

●●●●●● "HE SAID HE EXPECTED THEY WOULD BE HERE
AFTER HIM, BUT SINCE JENKINS GOT KILLED HE
SAID HE DIDN'T KNOW IF THEY WOULD OR NOT."
—ART MILLER, CELLMATE OF DILLINGER

It was Columbus Day, and things had been quieter than usual
around the Allen County Jail in Lima all afternoon. Sheriff Sarber
took a prisoner to the dentist to have an aching tooth fixed, and at
five o'clock, in response to a request, visited an old lady on her
deathbed who had business to discuss with him. Still later a youngster brought some articles for one of the inmates, and Sarber took
them back to the cell.

Now it was drawing on toward twilight. Supper was over, and
Mrs. Lucy Sarber and a servant had finished the dishes. Sarber read
a letter, then took up the newspaper as he sat behind his desk in the
jail office. His wife sat near him, her back to the door, working a
crossword puzzle. Deputy Wilbur Sharp lounged on the davenport
against the south wall, playing with Brownie, the sheriff's dog. The
time was 6:25.

An hour or so before, two hard-eyed strangers had called on
Attorney Chester M. Cable and tried to persuade him to get per-

mission for a woman—who was not with them—to visit Dillinger. The woman was Dillinger's sister, the men told Cable, and had something important to talk over with the outlaw. Cable, after telling the men that Dillinger had left fingerprints in the Bluffton bank, and that his clients, the Fidelity and Casualty Company of New York, would recommend a lighter sentence for him if the loot were recovered, promised to see what he could do the following day about arranging an audience for the woman.

Cable, reportedly, then telephoned to warn Sarber about the men who had visited him, but if he did so, Sarber paid little heed to the warning, still probably believing that Dillinger was "just another punk." He sat in vest and shirt-sleeves, his gun in the middle desk drawer. Sharp was also unarmed.

Back in the cellblock Dillinger was playing pinochle on a large dining-room table with Art Miller, awaiting sentence for second-degree murder, and two other prisoners, Claude Euclid and George Young. In earlier conversations, which Miller later said he remembered clearly "because John was more important than the rest of the prisoners," Dillinger had spoken of his friends from Michigan City and said he had been "going with" Jenkins's sister and thought it probable the gang would try to "spring" him. After Jenkins's death, Miller added, his cellmate seemed less confident.

Outside, things were shaping up for the rescue attempt. Pierpont and Russell Clark, who had just left Cable's office after their unsuccessful effort to get Dillinger's "sister" (actually Pierpont's mistress, Mary Kinder) inside the building so that access to Dillinger would be easier, were walking toward the jail.

Four others were also in the neighborhood: Makley, Copeland, Hamilton and Shouse. They had left the Pierpont farm near Leipsic about an hour after Pierpont and Clark, and parked their Chrysler a block away from the jail. The Terraplane in which Pierpont and Clark had come to town was immediately in front of the prison.

There seems to have been no thoroughly thought-out plan, rather an agreement to play it by ear. Their objective was to "free Dillinger and stick together and help each other if we could, and if we couldn't, why, make a break for it and go for ourself." This was the explanation later given by Shouse, who added that Pierpont, the appointed spokesman for the evening, had been urged to avoid shooting unless it was inevitable.

All six met in front of the courthouse, and Operation Johnnie began. Pierpont, Makley and Clark (or Copeland—later testimony on the identity of the third man was contradictory) went up the steps and into the office. Copeland (or Clark) sat in the Terraplane. Shouse stood by the monument not far from the walk leading to the jail, and Hamilton was near the theater behind the jail.

The trio entered the office and approached the desk where Sarber sat. The sheriff looked up and asked what was wanted. Pierpont said they were officers from the prison at Michigan City and wished to question Dillinger. Sarber, still friendly and polite, requested their credentials—a routine precaution. Pierpont's face tightened and he whipped a .38 revolver from beneath his coat.

"These are our credentials," he said harshly. Sarber uttered one protesting sentence—"Oh, you can't do that!"—and Pierpont fired twice. The sheriff had just started to get up. The first shot struck him in the lower abdomen, driving him backward to the floor. The second shot went wild and into the wall.

A femoral artery was severed, and Sarber was bleeding badly. But he made a gallant effort to rise, apparently with the idea of reaching for his own gun. As he pushed up on one elbow, he was felled by Makley, who lifted a pistol high above his head and brought the barrel down with such force that Sarber's scalp was laid open to the bone. Pierpont hit the dying sheriff once or twice more, stopping only when Mrs. Sarber screamed a protest and promised to bring the keys.

Pierpont followed her to a hallway cupboard, where the keys hung on a nail. He took them and started for the cells, but returned to remove Sarber's pistol from the desk. Then he unlocked the first two doors leading to the cellblock, and when he had trouble working the final lock, tossed the keys to Sharp, who opened the door. Dillinger, who had gone calmly to his cell for his coat when the shooting began, stepped out at once.

As he did so, Pierpont handed him the sheriff's gun and at the same time fired a single shot, which ricocheted along the jail corridor. There were about fifteen other prisoners in the block, and Pierpont shouted, "You other bastards get back. We want John."

Dillinger, who had invited Miller to accompany him, shook hands and said goodbye when the other refused. He walked into the office with Pierpont. When he saw the dying Sarber, he paused and gazed down at the sheriff but remained silent. He avoided Mrs. Sarber's gaze.

Sarber's mind was still clear. He said weakly, "Men, why did you do this to me?" Then, "Mother, I believe I am going to have to go."

Mrs. Sarber begged to be allowed to remain with her husband, but Pierpont refused. He herded the hysterical woman and Sharp to the cellblock, holding his gun in his right hand. He pushed Mrs. Sarber through, behind the deputy, then locked the doors.

Outside the jail, the first two shots were heard by Mr. and Mrs. Fay Carter, an elderly couple walking along North Street on their way to dinner at the Loyal Order of Moose lodge hall. They stopped when they heard the reports, and the watchful Shouse stepped up to assure them he also had heard something and would investigate. He went up the stairs and opened the office door wide enough to see Sarber lying near the desk. Then he came hurrying out, a smile on his face, to assure the Carters that some heavy files were being moved and a couple of drawers had slid out and fallen to the floor.

Just then the third shot sounded, and Mrs. Carter said, "Why, that sounds like they are killing each other."

All three of them looked up, but Shouse remained calm. "Oh, that was another drawer that fell," he said.

Mrs. Carter still was uneasy. "Well," she said uncertainly, "there's so darn many crooks around nowadays, when you hear a noise you don't know what to think."

Shouse smoothly changed the subject. "There's a big time going on at the lodge tonight, isn't there?" he asked. As he spoke he took Mrs. Carter politely by the arm and began walking the couple away from the jail, explaining that he himself was on the way to the drugstore for some medicine.

As they strolled on, after bidding Shouse good night, Mrs. Carter said to her husband, "He must be a Moose. Did you ever see him?"

"No I don't believe I ever saw him," Carter replied.

Shortly after reaching the lodge hall, the Carters heard an ambulance go past, and a little later learned that Sarber had been shot.

By the time the Carters were gone, Dillinger and Pierpont had come out through the kitchen and the other two by different doors. Dillinger, Clark and Pierpont got into the Terraplane, which Copeland drove to where the Chrysler was parked. Copeland then joined Hamilton, Shouse, and Makley in the bigger car, and the two groups left town in the gathering dusk, heading for their hideout in Hamilton.

Locked in the cellblock, and knowing that her husband was dying unattended a few feet away, Mrs. Sarber continued to be hysterical. Miller, an ex-bootlegger and slot-machine racketeer from Toledo, was unexpectedly kind. He found Mrs. Sarber a chair, asked her to sit down, and tried to talk her into calming down. Sharp, unable to open one of the windows over the alley, smashed it with a chair.

Policeman William Houtz saw Pierpont leave the front door, but thought he was someone who had been visiting the sheriff. An eighteen-year-old boy, Lowell Cheney, heard the glass break as he got out of a friend's car on North Street. He ran into the alley, passing Dillinger and the others as they came out. Cheney shouted up to ask what was happening, and Sharp yelled that the sheriff had been shot.

Cheney ran back to the front of the jail and into the office. There he telephoned the Lima police for aid. An ambulance came swiftly, and Sarber was taken to the Memorial Hospital, where he died at 8:05 after telling his son Don that his killers were all "big men."

The sheriff was in the hospital before his wife and Sharp were freed, since the raiding party had gone away with the keys. Two locked doors had to be opened. The first was battered down and the second burned through with an acetylene torch, an operation which took about half an hour.

The cold daring of the attack on the jail and the callous way in which Sarber was murdered stirred Lima's civic temper to a high pitch. Six motorized posses raced through the night in a fruitless search for Dillinger and his friends. About midnight a raid was made on the Pierpont home near Leipsic, but none of the mob was found.

On the following day, Sharp and Mrs. Sarber identified Pierpont, through a photograph, as the one who shot Sarber. Fred Pierpont was arrested when a new Oldsmobile, without license plates, was found in the barn of his farm near Leipsic. Two days later Fred admitted that his brother, Copeland, Clark, Shouse, Makley and Hamilton had stayed at the farm. And he said the Oldsmobile had been given him October 3.

"Harry gave me the car because of a lot of trouble he got me into when he was sent up in Indiana," Fred explained. "I was in a dozen different jails and they held me a long time before they turned me loose. Harry wanted to pay me back, and gave me the car."

The car was apparently bought in Detroit by Copeland, before the Michigan City break, for use by the gang. It may have been used in the St. Mary's bank holdup, although Fred said it was not, and was probably the one chased by the state police at Nashville before it was driven to Hamilton and given to Fred there. The gift may not have been a completely altruistic one, however. If police theories on where the car had been and who had seen it were correct, it was a pretty hot vehicle. It must have seemed sensible to the gang to be disassociated from it.

John Dillinger wasted precious little time taking advantage of his unearned freedom. Late in the evening of October 14—the same day that three thousand persons attended Sarber's funeral at the Trinity Methodist Church in Lima—two well-dressed men walked briskly into the Auburn, Indiana, police station, which occupied the corner of Ninth and Cedar Streets, across from the courthouse.

Officer Henry West was at his desk. Officer Fred Krueger, who had come in a moment or so before with a bag of popcorn, sat eating it, with his back to the door. Sheriff John P. Hoff and Chief of Police Charles Davis had left the city hall, which housed the police station, a few minutes earlier.

Each visitor held a revolver. One of the two walked up to West and said, "You might as well sit still. We don't want to kill anyone unless we have to. Have you got any guns?"

Krueger stood up and said, "Yes." Then he reached for his hip pocket.

"Oh, no," the bandit said sharply. "I'll get it!" He removed Krueger's revolver from the officer's hip. West also was disarmed, and the keys to the gun cabinet were surrendered. Krueger, who had been peering out the front window, was ordered to stand against the wall to prevent his catching a glimpse of the bandit's car.

The first load of guns had been carried out, when one of the raiders suggested putting the two policemen in a cell. This was done, and as they turned the key, one of the gunmen said to Krueger, "I have heard of you for thirty years."

The visitors made two trips with their booty, which included a

Thompson submachine gun, two .38 revolvers, a .30-caliber Spring-field rifle, a Winchester automatic rifle, a shotgun, a Colt .45, a Smith and Wesson .44, a Spanish .25, a German Luger, three bullet-proof vests and a large quantity of ammunition. The two policemen had a fleeting glimpse of a third man, apparently serving as a look-out in the corridor.

After the gang—believed to include Dillinger, Pierpont and Mak-ley—had fled, the imprisoned officers shouted across the street to George Anderson, a restaurant owner, who got another cell key and released them.

That same day Indiana and Ohio state police joined forces to search an apartment at Hamilton, Ohio, where the gang was be-lieved to have stayed. No one was found. After this sortie Al Feeney, safety director for Indiana—who had gone to Ohio to investigate the denial of Indiana's extradition request—returned to his home state. He denied rumors that a shakeup was planned in the Indiana State Police force. But after mystery cars, believed to contain armed men, were seen near the Michigan City prison, Feeney admitted that some shifts were planned, but said Leach would remain in com-mand.

Seemingly fearing an attempt at a wholesale delivery from Michi-gan City, Feeney announced also that a six-man mobile squad would be formed whose sole duty would be to ransack Indiana for the Dillinger mob. Feeney took that occasion to point out that there were only sixty-eight state troopers in all, less than one for each of the state's ninety-two counties.

By now all of Indiana was on edge. Even the Mooresville *Times,* which had been omitting all mention of its most infamous son, took notice of Sarber's murder with a story in the October 19 issue:

> Stopping in the midst of sawing wood for Winter use, John W. Dillinger, farmer living on the Mooresville Pike, told a representative of the Times Thursday he believed his son John, paroled gunman who was liberated last week from the Lima, Ohio jail at the cost of a sheriff's life, would never have figured in major crimes had the judge who sentenced him for the first offense been more lenient.
>
> The father, who has been besieged by squads of police, deputy sheriffs, constables and newspaper men since a report spread that his son was taking refuge at the Mooresville home, has gone quietly

about his work—for he says despite all the trouble that can come to a family, he realizes that corn must be shucked and wood must be cut.

The next day, October 20, the police station at Peru, Indiana, was the target, and this time two machine guns, six bulletproof vests—a choice sartorial item for the gang—two sawed-off shotguns, four .38-caliber police specials, two 30.30 Winchester rifles, three police badges and ammunition were taken.

Leo "Red" Eakins, porter from the Model Restaurant two doors east of the station, walked into police headquarters about 11 P.M. and was greeted by a stranger with a gun, who took him by the arm and said, "Come back here, I want to show you something."

Eakins, thinking it a joke of some kind, went to the office of the Chief of Police, where another stranger was pointing a submachine gun at Patrolmen Eldon Chittun and Eddie Roberts, and Ambrose Clark, a merchant policeman.

"I still thought they were in fun," Eakins later explained, "until I noticed the cops' knees shaking. Then I knew it was a holdup."

During the holdup one of the gunmen, later identified as Pierpont, said in a cheerless voice, "I haven't killed anybody for a week, and I'd just as soon shoot one of you as not. Go ahead and get funny."

The three policemen, already relieved of their guns, holsters and badges, showed no desire to test Pierpont's sincerity.

The gangsters lined up their four victims against the wall, spread a robe on the floor, dumped the weapons into it for easier carrying, ordered the policemen and Eakins into the basement, and walked out with the haul.

The bandit car pulled away just as Deputy Robert Tillett of Miami County arrived. He said he thought the vehicle was a Hudson with Indiana plates.

The second police station robbery in a week spread something akin to hysteria throughout the ranks of Hoosier lawmen. Sheriff Buck Sumner of Marion County asked commission approval for an appropriation of $1,000 to build a steel-plated cage in the prisoner runway at the Marion County Jail in Indianapolis, in which he proposed to mount a twenty-four-hour watch. Sumner offered the theory that the mob was trying to collect enough weapons and ammunition for a pitched battle with the guards at either Pendleton or Michigan City, in hopes of effecting a wholesale delivery. It was an excellent guess.

The police of Fort Wayne planned to install bars on the station windows—to keep people out, as well as to give added protection to the station arsenal.

But the panic was not confined to police circles. The Indiana American Legion offered to arm thirty thousand of its members as vigilantes to patrol Hoosier highways, and the National Guard said it was prepared to use tanks, poison gas and airplanes, if necessary, to aid the police.

Armored cars, with machine guns mounted, were on twenty-four-hour duty in Indianapolis, and the Indiana Bankers' Association, headed by Felix McWhirter of that city's People's Bank, began a drive for funds to create a statewide one-way radio network. It had become disturbingly obvious that the lack of such a warning system was a major factor in the ease with which the Dillinger gang kept disappearing.

The Indianapolis *Times* made a civic gesture too, sending a telegram to Homer Cummings to inform the United States Attorney General that the situation in Indiana seemed to be too much for state authorities to handle.

While this could hardly be considered a formal request for Federal aid, since it did not come from Governor McNutt, Cummings directed J. Edgar Hoover to look into the situation. Hoover and his staff had already started a file on the nation's outlaws—products, for the most part, of the twin evils of the Depression and of Prohibition. Hoover instructed the special agent in charge of the Cincinnati office of the Bureau to offer Federal help to the Indiana police if they wished it.

By this time the investigation into the Michigan City breakout had been completed, and both Harry D. Claudy, the deputy warden, and Albert Evans, the assistant deputy, were discharged. The report of the prison trustees showed that prisoners were allowed to handle without supervision shipments arriving from the outside, and that two of those who escaped had opened a shipment from a Chicago firm just prior to the break. The report also said that the prison was seriously understaffed—at least twelve men short—and gave Warden Kunkel a vote of confidence.

Governor McNutt supplemented the report by adding that the

guards taken advantage of during the escape were left over from the previous administration, not new political appointees. Captain Leach, never one to overlook publicity, had conducted his own investigation of the break—at McNutt's request—and told newsmen he thought the ten had bought their way out, an allegation no one seems to have taken seriously.

With Indiana so aroused, distance must have seemed the better part of valor to Dillinger and his companions. They all moved to Chicago, and quickly provided themselves with all the comforts of home, including women.

Mary Kinder shared an apartment with Pierpont. Makley was living with a girl named Patricia Long (also known as Pat Cherrington), whose sister Opal was paired off with Russell Clark. Marie Conforti, one of the pretty ones, was Homer Van Meter's moll, and John Hamilton, the taciturn older man with the two fingers missing, had somehow acquired a girl with a splendid assortment of names: Elaine Sullivan Dent Burton DeKant.

Dillinger, too, who less than six months before had boasted to William Shaw that he was going to keep away from two things— women and automatic pistols—had changed his mind on both counts. He had fallen head over heels for Evelyn (Billie) Frechette, a French-Indian beauty. And he had forsaken his 32.30 revolver for the .38 and .45 automatic pistols.

Miss Frechette, who was also known as Billie Sparks, had come to Chicago from the Chippewa Indian Reservation at Neopit, Wisconsin, at the age of eighteen. She had black hair and sparkling brown eyes, was 5 feet 2 inches tall and weighed 120 pounds. Her husband was serving time for mail theft, and she had been working as a hatcheck girl in a Chicago nightclub when Pat Long, one of the entertainers, introduced her to Dillinger.

SEVEN

"JOHNNIE'S JUST AN ORDINARY FELLOW. OF
COURSE HE GOES OUT AND HOLDS UP BANKS AND
THINGS, BUT HE'S REALLY JUST LIKE ANY OTHER
FELLOW, ASIDE FROM THAT."

—MARY KINDER

A black Studebaker sedan with Ohio license plates moved sedately
along Jackson Street and double-parked next to the Central National Bank of Greencastle, Indiana, at 2:45 Monday afternoon,
October 23. Four men got out, leaving the car empty, and three
walked to the corner and went into the bank's Washington Street
entrance. The fourth stayed outside.

The bank was crowded, and Harry Pierpont approached the fifth
window, where Ward Mayhall, assistant trust officer, was working.
He handed him a twenty-dollar bill, and asked for change. Mayhall
told him to take it to Harry Wells at the second window. Instead,
Pierpont opened his overcoat and pointed a machine gun at Mayhall's chest.

At the same time Dillinger vaulted into the railed-off area at the
front of the bank, smashed the lock of the door leading to the
cashier's cage, and walked in. There were a dozen employees and
eight or ten customers present, but none dared take action. Virtually

the first words uttered by the bandits after the holdup began were a warning to everyone not to "press anything."

So well planned was the raid that it did not start until Leo Ratcliff, the elderly bank guard, had come down from his steel cage above the front door, inside the bank, and gone to the basement to stoke the furnace. Less than a minute after entering the bank, Dillinger was filling a sugar sack with money. Pierpont, who had also gone behind the cages, was doing the same. Makley, meanwhile, kept the patrons and employees under control, herding them at gunpoint back into the vault room.

The two collectors worked swiftly and methodically, taking everything they could find except pennies and nickels, even to $400 in halves, $200 in quarters, and eighteen silver dollars lying in a tray on the counter. They then ordered Wells to open the inside door of the vault—a task accomplished on the first try, although normally he had to work the combination several times before getting it right.

During the excitement, one of the employees, William Stiles, slipped to the rear door without being seen and went down the basement steps and out an exit there. He tried in vain to find some large tacks to place under the tires of the waiting Studebaker, then called the police station and was told to remain where he was. Before the police arrived, the robbery was over. No one, apparently, thought to telephone the sheriff's office across the street, where—as it happened—a deputy, a state policeman and some high-powered rifles could have been found.

As soon as Dillinger and Pierpont had picked up $18,428 in cash, and bonds valued at $56,300, the three bandits left as quietly as they had come, or almost as quietly. Rex Thorlton, manager of the A & P store a block east, was just entering the bank to make a deposit. He was reaching toward his back pocket for his bankbook and money as he came in.

Unfortunately for Thorlton, Makley and Pierpont, who were coming out at the time, saw and misinterpreted the gesture—which was like that of a man reaching for a gun—and one of them slugged him with a pistol. Thorlton went down, got up again in a dazed condition (there is a legend that he knocked Dillinger's hat off as he fell and politely picked it up and handed it back), staggered to the grocery, and collapsed in the back room.

The three bandits, one with a bulging bag over his shoulder, walked to the car without excitement or apparent haste, got in, and drove to the corner, where they stopped to pick up Copeland (or possibly Clark), who had been serving as lookout. They headed east on Washington, turned south on Route 43 to the Pennsylvania Railroad tracks, found a freight train blocking the way, and doubled west, following a dirt road which took them, finally, to the city limits. Here they disappeared without a trace. Charles Crawley, a poolroom proprietor, gave chase in his car but was quickly outdistanced.

Telephones began jangling, and all roads were blocked. Both Indianapolis and state police were alerted, along with guards from the Indiana State Farm, but no one sighted the black Studebaker again as it sped to Terre Haute.

Although it seems unlikely, Pierpont was reported seen the evening of the day the bank was robbed, traveling by interurban from Terre Haute to Indianapolis; two men who had once worked with him at the sand plant in nearby Fern thought they saw him. One reason the Greencastle bank was chosen may have been that Pierpont had at one time worked at the plant and quite probably knew the countryside.

The attitude of the victims after the holdup serves to illustrate the prevailing fear of the gang's violence. Instead of voicing indignation at the robbery, the bank officials expressed relief.

"There was a metal guard cage over the door," one of the bank officials said, "but the guard wasn't there at the time, thank goodness!"

The same man said that a filling station owner across the street had seen hands being raised all over the bank, and had telephoned the police. "But thank goodness they didn't come, or somebody would have been killed!"

This resignation in the face of what the newspapers were beginning to call the Terror Gang was widespread. Many of the banks robbed seemed willing to lose their money so long as no lives were lost. In one town at this period, the night patrolman was stopped on the street by a citizen who told him that a holdup by the Dillinger gang was in progress less than two blocks away. The patrolman was not eager. "I don't give a damn," he said. "I ain't on duty."

Huntington was on the Greencastle job quickly and found that a man whose description fitted Makley had been in town early in the morning on the day of the holdup. He said he was a former sailor and wanted a permit to peddle Oriental rugs. Authorities referred him to the local American Legion commander, who was suspicious of his credentials. The permit was not given.

Huntington also showed photographs of the mob to bank employees, and both Dillinger and Pierpont were identified as probable participants.

Huntington went to Louisville on Tuesday to see McGinnis. He told him the insurance company had authorized payments for information leading to the apprehension of the bandits: $1,000 each for Dillinger and Pierpont and $500 for each of the others, and also was willing to pay 10 per cent of any money or bonds recovered. McGinnis said he was keeping for Dillinger a shotgun and a rifle that Dillinger wanted back, and felt that he could safely get in touch with him for this reason. Huntington gave McGinnis fifty dollars for expenses.

The Greencastle robbery had some salutary effects. Governor McNutt was moved to agree to Feeney's plea for more money for state police use. Subsequently $10,000 worth of equipment was bought, including bulletproof vests, machine guns and riot guns, and ten fast squad cars with sirens and flares.

Sheriff Sumner asked the Governor for a detachment of National Guardsmen to protect the county jail at Indianapolis from possible assault. The county commissioners granted his request that the jail be reinforced with sheet armor. They also authorized him to buy a machine gun and erect a bulletproof cage against the possibility of a visit from the Terror Gang.

The uneasiness spread to the penitentiary at Michigan City, where Warden Kunkel formed a special squad of fifteen guards, to be on duty day and night, and also bought extra machine guns. At Marion, fifty firemen were armed and sworn in as special police officers, and Mayor Jack Edwards asked the board of public works for permission to turn the police station into a fort.

It was during October that the Indianapolis News carried a cartoon which many felt summed up the situation with admirable succinctness. The drawing showed a gunman chasing a group of policemen and citizens out of the state. The caption read, "Happy Hunting Ground." An accompanying editorial suggested rather plainly that Indiana law enforcement bodies were not up to the task of controlling Dillinger and his fellows.

By this time virtually any bank robbery was automatically ascribed to the Terror Gang. On October 24 three men held up the Western State Bank of South Bend and escaped with $5,000. Dillinger and Company were suspected of this until the actual holdup men were caught a short while later.

Two other holdups took place on the twenty-fifth, but Dillinger escaped blame for these, probably because of the insignificance of the haul. The Fillmore State Bank yielded $130 and the People's Loan and Trust Company at Modoc $400—hardly jobs for Dillinger and his crew.

But each additional holdup added to the official panic. McNutt instructed all sheriffs to deputize anyone willing to take up arms against the desperadoes. Roadblocks sprouted like ragweed across the state, many of them amateur affairs, guarded by motley groups armed with rifles, shotguns and little know-how. One of these is said to have uncovered "a load of stolen chickens, several kegs of illegal liquor, a youth who burglarized the Franklin High School, and a gang of armed Negroes."

Curiously enough, and unfortunately for the public peace of mind, the Dillinger gang seemed to have little trouble with these barriers. Pierpont confided to a friend late in October that he himself had gone through such roadblocks near Indianapolis more than thirty times.

On October 26, 765 of the most expert marksmen among the Indiana Guardsmen were stationed at armories throughout Indiana with instructions to take orders from Feeney. Guardsmen also served at the barricades. So high was the tension, and so jumpy were the police, that Feeney issued a warning to Halloween celebrants, advising them not to do anything that might lead police to believe they were members of the Dillinger gang.

The guardsmen were replaced at the barricades by state troopers early in November, when Feeney announced that the roadblocks had stopped Dillinger and his mob and would become a permanent part of the Indiana scenery. J. Edgar Hoover, Feeney said, had written for information on the system. Feeney added that "Indiana banks have tempted bandits until they can no longer resist the temptation to come and get it."

The meaning of this statement was never very clear, although there were rumors—probably started by irate depositors who had lost their savings when some institutions closed—that at least a few of the holdups throughout the Middle West were welcomed by bankers with shortages to conceal, a story which seems cut from whole cloth but does indicate the temper of the times. Also indicative are a couple of later letters to the Voice of the Reader columns in an Indianapolis paper, which seem apropos here. One writer said:

> I am for John Dillinger. Not that I am upholding him in any of his crimes; that is, if he did any.
> Why should the law have wanted John Dillinger for bank robbery? He wasn't any worse than bankers and politicians who took the poor people's money.
> Dillinger did not rob poor people. He robbed those who became rich by robbing the poor. I am for Johnnie. . . .

The other, a reply to an editorial castigating Dillinger, said in part:

> This person [the editorial writer] calls Dillinger cheap. He isn't half as cheap as a crooked banker or a crooked politician because he did give the bankers a chance to fight, and they never gave the people a chance.

Fuzzy attitudes like this helped the Dillinger gang survive as long as it did. Although some persons who could have aided the police with information failed to do so because they were afraid, others, obviously, withheld information because of a misplaced admiration for and sympathy with the hunted men.

The day after Halloween, Leach came to his office in the State House to find that someone had mailed him a copy of a paperback book, *How To Be a Detective*, published in 1896. Leach believed until his death that the sender was Dillinger. The joke actually was the work of two veteran Indianapolis newsmen, who figured that the state police chief was in a proper state of mind to be taken in by such a jest.

Early in November, Huntington finally persuaded officials of the Greencastle bank to sign complaints naming Dillinger, Pierpont, Makley, and Copeland as the holdup men, despite expressed fears of false identification. Huntington had sought such complaints so that if any of the lost assets were recovered, he would have a legal basis for claiming them in behalf of his client, the insurance company which made up the loss.

But Huntington's efforts elsewhere were less fruitful. In Chicago, the newly formed and hush-hush Secret Squad, directed by Lieutenant John Howe, whose headquarters were in the LaSalle Hotel, had discovered that McGinnis was working as an informant against Dillinger, a security leak Huntington blamed on Leach, who had intercepted a telegram from Huntington to McGinnis. Huntington soon learned that Howe's men were keeping McGinnis under surveillance, a circumstance which made the job of spying on Dillinger far more dangerous than necessary.

At this time Huntington wrote in his official report:

> I would like to explain . . . that I have tried to work with Captain Leach and confided information to him two months ago that, had it been handled properly, would have resulted in the arrest of John Dillinger, Harry Copeland, Homer Van Meter and Sam Goldstine in Gary, Indiana, and in East Chicago. . . . Leach, by his indiscreet methods of sensationalizing criminal information to the press, by his domineering attitude toward city and county officers and by other irrational and erratic acts, has antagonized the majority of police officials of the state and they will not cooperate with him. To disclose confidential information to him is to jeopardize the success of any important investigation. This condition has reached a state where I feel that it is dangerous to my client's interests and the public welfare to confide confidential criminal information to Leach or officers subject to his orders.

Huntington, alarmed for McGinnis's safety, warned his "pigeon" of the intercepted telegram and urged that he cease trying to ingratiate himself with Dillinger in Chicago. But McGinnis, eager for the promised reward, refused to quit.

He told Huntington of the gang's grandiose plans to increase their growing arsenal still further. On October 24 and 25, McGinnis said, Dillinger, Copeland and Joseph Burns stopped at Fort Harrison, near Indianapolis, posing as Oriental rug salesmen, and talked with the base commander, a Colonel Robinson, and Chaplain Alfred C. Oliver.

Incredible as it seems, McGinnis assured Huntington that the outlaws were looking over the fort preparatory to a raid to get heavy machine guns and mortars, as well as army uniforms, after which a wholesale delivery was planned at nearby Pendleton reformatory. McGinnis said his information came from a former convict and acquaintance of Dillinger.

Huntington drove at once to Fort Harrison, where Colonel Robinson confirmed that a trio resembling the suspected three had visited the post. Huntington told the Colonel who his visitors had been, and the commander ordered the doubling of his security force and the searching of all vehicles entering or leaving the fort.

Further verification of the possible plot came from Warden A. F. Miles of the Pendleton reformatory, located a few miles east of the fort. Miles told Huntington that a prison guard and a truck driver who brought supplies into the reformatory had been caught that very week in the theft of almost $1,000 worth of prison-made clothing, which had been taken away and stored in an empty house in Indianapolis. The cache was next door to the home of the same ex-convict who had told McGinnis of the plan to raid Fort Harrison.

The guard, trucker and former inmate all were arrested, and the guard and truck driver admitted the clothing thefts, but denied any knowledge of a wholesale jail delivery plot.

On November 3, Pierpont, Hamilton, Copeland, Shouse and Joseph Burns were indicted in Lima for the murder of Sheriff Sarber, although Joe Burns was not one of the raiders. On November 6, McGinnis telephoned Huntington and told him he had been in touch with the mob and was trying to persuade them he could fence the stolen Greencastle bonds for them.

Two days later there was evidence that despite Feeney's hopes, the Dillinger gang had not been driven out of the state for good. The morning of the eighth a speeding Chrysler sedan slid into a ditch near Avon, and four men walked from the car to a nearby farm. They paid Edgar Lovell to go to town and arrange with a garageman to tow the car in and repair it, saying they would return to pick it up. Lovell came back to say the garage was not open, and the men then went into Avon on foot.

There, after talking to the garageman, they hired another farmer, Paul Walton, to drive them to Terre Haute. As soon as they left, the garageman telephoned the sheriff's office in Danville to report the incident. He said all the men were carrying guns with blankets wrapped around them. The sheriff notified Terre Haute authorities and Leach. Leach, in turn, telephoned Huntington. The two then drove to Avon, where they found Walton back from his fifty-mile trip.

The farmer said he had dropped the men in a residential area in Terre Haute. Both he and the garage owner identified photographs of Clark, Makley, Shouse and Copeland. (Shouse supposedly had quit the gang by this time and his identification was probably an error.) Leach told the mechanic to repair the car, and summoned one of his men from Indianapolis to watch for anyone coming after it. He and Huntington then drove to Terre Haute with Walton.

The farmer pointed out where he had left the quartet. Leach called on the Terre Haute police, who were apologetic because the gang had managed to enter town in spite of the blockade set up at its east end after Leach's call. The police raided the homes of several known associates of Copeland but found nothing. So Leach and Huntington went back to the Avon garage, where they learned that the licenses on the damaged Chrysler had been issued to Pearl Elliott, a fact which made the identification of its occupants look better than ever.

As the two detectives left the garage, Huntington saw a car parked across the street and thought he recognized the driver. Walking across, he found a brother of the ex-convict who had been arrested in connection with the theft of clothing—the one who had told McGinnis of the plan to raid Fort Harrison. The driver, also a former convict, gave Huntington an unconvincing explanation for his presence; the detective, however, pretended to believe him. Huntington still hoped the gang would return for the car, which he suspected the ex-convict had been sent to check on. He did not tell Leach who the man was, and the car was never called for.

On November 9, however, Leach and two Terre Haute detectives found the rooming house where the four convicts had gone after being let out by Walton; they had left again on foot, carrying their luggage. The rooming house was run by a man with a prison record, who had known Shouse. He was not arrested since it could not be proved that he knew who his guests were. They had first arrived Monday, the sixth, and left Wednesday about 6 A.M., returning at 11 A.M. after the wreck. They left again about 3 P.M. The landlord told investigators that one of the men had a badge and claimed to be a Federal officer.

During this or any other period of Dillinger's last few months on earth it is possible to keep track of his whereabouts only when he surfaced, so to speak, long enough to perform some deed of violence, or when (rarely) he was behind bars.

One such occasion, if the belief of Detective Pfauhl, who arrested him at Dayton, is correct, came at approximately this time. Pfauhl's daughter, Mrs. Ruth Hetzler, answered a knock at the Pfauhl door, and a man asked for her father. When she inquired his name, he said he was a lawyer from Springfield and added that Pfauhl "will know me when he sees me." Mrs. Hetzler was suspicious. She said her father was not at home and the stranger left. A short while later he appeared at the home of Sergeant Gross, who was away. The stranger never returned.

Some months later, after Dillinger was dead, Pfauhl talked with Evelyn Frechette, who came to Dayton with a traveling carnival. She told him, he says, that Dillinger had been in search of the two detectives in hopes of shooting them both.

One night during the late fall or early winter, after Mr. and Mrs. Hancock had retired, Mary, who was then a student at Butler College in Indianapolis, was studying when the back door opened and Dillinger walked in.

"She jumped up and about tore the house down," Mrs. Hancock says. "We were in bed, but we all fell out at the same time. Clark came in, too, and the only thing I remember about him is that he said he'd been to see his folks in Detroit and Johnnie wanted to come by and see me. Both were wearing heavy winter overcoats."

After a brief visit, Dillinger invited Mary to go with them to the farm at Mooresville and she eagerly accepted.

"You would never have known what circumstances existed," Mary said. "Clark drove about eighty or ninety, and Johnnie and I were just two people who were fond of each other, talking. I suppose he made some comment like: 'I see you have your nose to the grindstone again,' and he probably kidded me about working so hard. I held the machine gun in my lap. I even remember holding it up and pretending to shoot. It was silly. Kid stuff, as one is apt to do.

"Grandpa retired early. I remember very clearly when we got there. I don't know what month it was, but the stove in the living room was going and Johnnie said, 'Pile a little wood on. Warm things up a bit.'

"The conversation was relaxed. We stayed away from what they had been doing—it wouldn't have done any good to talk about it."

A short while later the two visitors and Mary left. They drove her back to Maywood and then drove off in the night toward a destination they were careful not to mention.

"I don't know when I next saw him," Mary concluded.

On November 11, Huntington went to Chicago with Lieutenant Chester Butler of the Indiana State Police for a conference with Lieutenant Howe of the Secret Squad, who told them his unit was responsible only to Police Commissioner James Allman and Mayor Edward Kelly.

Howe said much of his information came from the Scotland Yard section of his squad, whose duties included wire-tapping of telephones of known gangsters. He said his men had followed McGinnis and knew he was living with another former convict on Irving Park Boulevard. When Huntington expressed irritation at this, Howe promised to take the "tail" off McGinnis, but urged Huntington to keep a wary eye on his contact man.

Huntington met with McGinnis at the Morrison Hotel that night and took a long statement. McGinnis gave him a detailed account of his actions since he had arrived in Chicago on October 22, visiting friends of mob members in search of specific information. One man had been uncooperative and suggested that McGinnis was "trying to cross up this bunch."

"I have been making an effort to locate and contact John Dillinger and Harry Pierpont," McGinnis told Huntington. "My pretext to persons whom I knew and met in the underworld, principally ex-convicts, was that I had facilities for fencing the bonds they had in their possession. To support my pretext I contacted a bond broker who served time in Leavenworth and a banker who served time in the same prison. . . . I can locate their offices on downtown LaSalle Street. I told them I had some 'hot' bonds and they offered to take them off my hands at a good price."

McGinnis said he had driven past a building in the 800 block on Montrose Avenue several times, where he knew Copeland still maintained an apartment, "looking for cars that the mob might be driving."

He also said he had learned that Joseph Burns had been in town during the week, staying on the near West Side. He himself, he said, was using the assumed name of Jack Costello and a mail-drop address at an office building. He had given this information to a source close to Dillinger in Indianapolis, he told Huntington.

McGinnis continued, according to Huntington's typewritten report: "I received two letters at this place addressed to Costello which were turned over to me. These letters purported to be from John Dillinger and another whose name I cannot reveal without exposing this party. Both these letters referred to handling the bonds and I was to meet someone in the Loop who would go with me to . . . the offices where I had arranged to sell them. Each time I was to meet this party I had two men with me . . . one named Curley, whom I had got out of jail in Chicago by paying a fine of $6.50. The man who was to meet me did not keep his appointment. I do not know who this man would be, but it was to be a member of the mob that would know me.

"After my failure to meet this man, I was in the Loop several mornings early on a tip that I could see some member of the mob. I usually waited from one to two hours and did not see anyone I knew. I had a telephone call from a woman yesterday [November 11] about 9:30 A.M., asking for me and when informed I was out, said she would call back at 12 o'clock. I was there at 12 o'clock but no one called . . . I think this was Dillinger's girl. She has a peculiar voice and [the woman who answered the phone] said this was true of the girl who called. I do not know Dillinger's girl's name. She uses several . . . I can find out who she is as I know a party who knows her.

"Crouch gave me a card to his mother signed Bob. This is the name he is known by in Chicago. He received his mail through a girl whose first name is Jean. I do not know her last name or present address. She did live in the 900 block on Ainslie Avenue in an apartment on the first floor.

"I got Dillinger's guns, an automatic rifle and shotgun from . . . Montrose Avenue several weeks ago. I also got a .45 caliber Colt revolver . . . that belonged to Dillinger and was stolen in a holdup by him in Indiana." McGinnis reported that he left this gun at a house on Warren Boulevard, the home of a former convict who was a friend of Dillinger's, and Copeland came and got it when McGinnis was away. "I stayed [there] about six weeks ago and paid $15.00 board bill. Dillinger gave me $100 in Indianapolis the day before he was arrested at Dayton. His girl was with him then. He had just left Copeland. A week later I was in Chicago and stopped at [the Warren Boulevard place] and [the lady of the house] wanted me to give her $100 and did not like it because I did not.

"I have Dillinger's automatic rifle and shotgun hidden out in Chicago waiting word from Dillinger. I can produce them in an hour's time. These guns were used on the Massachusetts Avenue Bank robbery in Indianapolis. Dillinger shot a man with the rifle in a holdup at Monticello." (Dillinger's partner in this holdup said Dillinger used a revolver.)

McGinnis also said that Dillinger had told him he bought the three guns thrown over the wall at Michigan City for $48 apiece, and that he (Dillinger) had thrown them over personally—which seems an unnecessary risk. When those were found, McGinnis said, Dillinger arranged for the others to be smuggled in.

McGinnis added that he had not yet been able to find either Dillinger or Pierpont in Chicago and had "no idea" where they were. And, Huntington's report said, he concluded, "Dillinger has cased two jobs in Indianapolis to my knowledge and may hold up these places anytime:

"Haag Drug Company—collections from stores. Collections made by woman and man. Money out in basket. Amount guessed at $4,000. Cohen's Dry Goods Company—Brightwood. Has money on hand for cashing checks employees Brightwood R.R. shops. Amount supposed to be $10,000.

"Before I was released, Dillinger questioned me about the possibility of robbing the Indiana National Bank, where I was formerly employed. I told them at that time that it could be robbed and that they could get about $2,000,000.00. We decided then that it could be robbed and Dillinger might attack this bank in the future."

(It is interesting to note that Dillinger hadn't given up on the bungled Haag collector job, that he was thinking of robbing a store in his old neighborhood at Brightwood, and that even when he was in prison he was at least toying with the notion of returning to the gun as a means of making a living.)

Huntington asked McGinnis to meet him at ten o'clock the next morning, then telephoned Lieutenant Howe and made a date to see him at nine. Howe read the information McGinnis had given the detective and said he thought it very accurate except for the statement that he didn't know the address of Crouch's girl. McGinnis's car had been seen near her apartment, Howe said, and he was sure the informer had called on her.

Before he next saw Huntington, McGinnis was visited by Dillinger, who came alone to see him about 10 A.M. on Monday, November 13. Dillinger displayed eight $1,000 Liberty Loan bonds apparently taken in the St. Mary's robbery and said he would give McGinnis a percentage of their sale price.

During the conversation, McGinnis verified that Dillinger, Makley, Copeland and Pierpont had pulled the Greencastle job. Dillinger left after arranging to meet him at 2 P.M. in a Loop parking lot. As soon as his caller had gone, McGinnis reported to Huntington, but with his hopes of a reward higher than ever, he refused to reveal the meeting place unless he had Huntington's promise not to arrest Dillinger.

Huntington was not in a position to make such a promise. He telephoned Lieutenant Howe, who said he would have to get permission from Commissioner Allman. Howe and Huntington then called on Allman. Told to use his own judgment, Howe said he felt that McGinnis deserved this much consideration.

Huntington and Howe then met McGinnis, who said the meeting place was a parking lot near a cafeteria at 222 North State Street.

The two detectives hurried there at once, and Howe loitered on the street while Huntington, whose face Dillinger would probably have recognized because of their talk in Dayton, went into the cafeteria and watched through an upstairs window. At 2 P.M. McGinnis appeared and stood on the corner, obviously nervous. A minute or so later Dillinger came, with another man. The three talked for several minutes, then moved off, walking right past Howe.

Huntington rejoined Howe after the others were out of sight, and both agreed that Dillinger was one of the two who had met McGinnis; neither knew the other man.

Later that day they met with McGinnis, in whom they now had increased confidence. He said that he had gone with Dillinger to a bar on Lawrence Avenue, where he had left some guns that Dillinger planned to pick up, but that the bartender, having spotted three detectives in a car across the street, had refused to surrender the key to a neighboring building where the guns were hidden. Howe said he had assigned men to watch the bar.

McGinnis also gave Huntington other information. He told him the license number of Dillinger's Terraplane, and said he and the outlaw had been driving on the West Side that afternoon when a Ford V-8 pulled alongside and a round-faced heavyset man about forty, wearing glasses, asked Dillinger whether he had disposed of "the stuff" and added that he would like to join the mob since he needed money.

Dillinger, McGinnis said, replied that this was all right with him, but that it would take full approval of the gang, and that he would discuss it with them. Later Dillinger suddenly asked McGinnis if he knew Huntington; he said Makley had told him that McGinnis and Huntington were related. McGinnis calmly replied that there was a remote relationship through marriage and that Huntington had inquired once or twice about the gang, but that he had told him nothing.

Dillinger told McGinnis also that Copeland, Burns and Van Meter were in town and that Detrick and Hamilton had gone to St. Louis. He said he had been looking over a possible bank job at Antioch, Illinois, but had given it up as "too tough." McGinnis promised to pick up the guns from the saloon on Lawrence Avenue and deliver them to Dillinger about 7 P.M. at the house on Irving Park Boulevard where McGinnis was staying.

A check of the auto license given for Dillinger's car by McGinnis showed that it was issued to a "Joseph Harris" on West Washington Boulevard in October, 1933, and later information disclosed the car was bought in South Bend, Indiana, August 17, for cash, from the Boswell Motor Company.

McGinnis then added that Dillinger was suffering from barber's itch (an inflammation of the hair follicles) and had an appointment for that very evening with Dr. Charles Eye in the latter's offices at 4175 Irving Park Boulevard, about a block from where McGinnis was living. Again McGinnis asked that Dillinger not be picked up, since, he said, he was sure he could turn in the whole gang if given a little time.

Huntington went back to his hotel, and Howe returned to his

headquarters, where he told Butler and Ryan about McGinnis's report. The Indiana detectives called Matt Leach and relayed the information to him. Leach promptly called Huntington. He was very much excited and said he wanted Dillinger taken or killed that night, since another chance as good might not offer itself.

EIGHT

"THEY LOOKED LIKE BANK EXAMINERS WHEN THEY STARTED WORKING, IF IT HADN'T BEEN FOR ALL THE GUNS THEY WERE CARRYING."
—JANE WILLIAMS

Several spirited conversations were held among Leach, Howe and Huntington during the next hour or so. Leach was given no promise, however, except that his men, Butler and Ryan, would be permitted to go with Huntington and Howe to watch Dillinger visit the physician's office.

Huntington agreed with Leach's argument that it should be possible to grab Dillinger if he showed up. But the insurance detective added that he was anxious to seize the whole gang and believed McGinnis, given more time, could arrange for this. Also, Huntington told Leach, if an attempt to take Dillinger failed, McGinnis would be the logical suspect when the gang tried to figure out how the police had been tipped off. So the final decision was that no effort would be made to capture Dillinger that night.

Howe, Huntington, Ryan and Butler parked within view of the entrance to Dr. Eye's office at 6:30 that evening. They watched as Dillinger arrived in an Essex Terraplane about 7:15. He was driving, and a man and a woman—probably Harry Pierpont and Mary Kinder —were in the back seat. Dillinger went into the office alone, came out about fifteen minutes later, and drove off without interference.

McGinnis met with Huntington again on Tuesday, November 14. The informer gave Huntington the registry number of a .38 special blue steel revolver he said Dillinger had given him, and which had been stolen from either the Peru or the Auburn police station. Mc-Ginnis said Dillinger had picked up the guns that had been hidden in the building on Lawrence Avenue, and the gang leader boasted of having two suitcases filled with weapons belonging to Pierpont and himself.

The stolen bonds were still proving a problem to the mob. Dillinger told McGinnis that Pierpont was having trouble trying to get rid of them in Milwaukee (although later evidence showed that the secretary of a prominent Milwaukee businessman had been negotiating for them) and that it might be necessary to take them to New York if McGinnis could not find an outlet. Dillinger, McGinnis added, was carrying a .38 automatic in the right-hand pocket of his overcoat.

Although McGinnis had an appointment to see Dillinger at 4 p.m. Tuesday at the office of the Chicago dealer in stolen bonds, the informer waited in vain for him to appear. At 12:30 on Wednesday, the fifteenth, McGinnis left this note at Huntington's hotel:

> Forrest: D. did not show up last night and I think they should try to tail him from the doctor's as he is supposed to show there this afternoon. When he comes to the loop he invariably parks his car at 222 North State Street.
>
> I have —— staying at home in case he shows there and if they never turned those [bonds] in Milwaukee, I should get a play by tomorrow morning. When I do you will have to be ready to go to bat.
>
> I will call you at 2:30.
>
> Mac.

McGinnis called Huntington later to say that Dillinger's appointment at Dr. Eye's office was for 7:30 that evening. The informer once more asked that Dillinger not be taken, but again suggested that it might be possible to "tail" him. Howe at first agreed to let Dillinger come and go unmolested. But later that afternoon Inspector Rooney of the Lima police department arrived at Howe's office. Rooney was anxious that something be done to avenge the slaying of Sheriff Sarber; he joined Leach and the other Indiana officers in a request that every effort be made to arrest Dillinger that night. Huntington still objected, but Howe eventually yielded and called in William Blaul, assistant chief of detectives.

Blaul promised to furnish three squads to assist in the capture. The plan was for them to follow Dillinger for a few blocks before closing in. It was hoped that by taking this precaution suspicion might be diverted from McGinnis, who had, of course, sent Dillinger to Dr. Eye.

Huntington's report of the trap follows:

We met the squads about three squares from the doctor's office and they remained there while officer Artery and I drove to the vicinity of Dr. Eye's office. We waited until 7:25 P.M. when Dillinger and his girl, Evelyn Frechette, drove up in the Essex Terraplane. He parked his car facing South on Keeler Avenue, alighted, crossed the street and entered the doctor's office upstairs. The girl remained in the car.

We drove back to where the squad cars were concealed and described the car and location to the squad leaders. An Indiana officer got in each squad car. Lieutenant Butler in one squad car, parked across Irving Boulevard in the rear of Dillinger's car and our car and two other squad cars parked a square South on Keeler Avenue. The Chicago officers kept saying they would lose their man if they did not get closer to his car. Five minutes before Dillinger came out of the doctor's office, fearing he might get away if he reached his car, I told them I would withdraw any reservation in favor of protecting the informant. They knew Chief Blaul's instructions and they could use their own judgment about getting him. We did not want to miss him under any circumstances!

The two squad cars pulled down immediately in front of Dillinger's car and parked less than seventy-five feet away from the Terraplane. Our car remained a block South on Keeler Avenue.

A few moments later we observed Dillinger leave the doctor's office, get in his car and start backing into Irving Boulevard! We started after him at once, passed the two police squad cars, and caught up with Dillinger's car about two squares East. We pulled alongside the left side of his speeding machine and Indiana State

Police officer Art Keller fired five loads of buckshot from a twelve-gauge riot gun into the left door of the Terraplane, as well as the window and front tire. But Dillinger kept going. Officer Rooney and Artery also fired their revolvers into Dillinger's car but without effect! These guns were fired at a range of less than ten feet, travelling at a speed of about sixty miles per hour.

After this Dillinger drew away from us and, at times, reached seventy-five miles per hour. We kept his car in sight about five miles when suddenly he turned down an alley with his lights out. Our squad car over-ran the alley and we lost him.

Only one Chicago police car kept in sight of our car, though they drove the same kind of machine as ours. Why the squad cars did not close in on Dillinger when he backed out I cannot explain though these officers said they did not observe Dillinger get into his car.

The newspapers stated that our car was shot full of holes by Dillinger and the girl and a man in the car with a machinegun. This is untrue as only the girl and Dillinger were in the car and they did not fire a shot! The holes through our windshield were caused by shots fired by the officers in our car. However, when Chief Blaul examined our car, the officers in it did not disillusion him about being shot at.

Evelyn Frechette's subsequent statement about the same incident confirmed Huntington's claim that no shots were fired from Dillinger's car. Miss Frechette said Dillinger had no suspicion of a trap when he came from the doctor's office, and merely made a routine turn—an accidental maneuver which apparently took the police by surprise.

The police officers nearest to Dillinger explained that they purposely avoided firing directly at him, for fear wounding or killing him would send his car swerving into the squad car at high speed.

With the failure of this attempt, Huntington promptly called McGinnis, who had been at a party and was surprised to learn of the shooting. Despite warnings from Huntington, however, McGinnis said he thought there would be less suspicion if he continued to see the mob. He promised to try to make further contacts.

The morning of the sixteenth, Chicago police found the speedy Terraplane standing in front of 7600 Greenview, on the far North Side. There were the marks of twenty-two bullets on the car, none of which had gone through. At the same time police were investigating an abandoned Buick, which turned out to be stolen, at the rear of 4310 Clarendon, less than a block from the apartment Copeland had been using. Investigation showed this to be a gang hideout. A resident told police he had heard noises in the alley the night before, and on approaching found four men and three women standing near the Buick. One of the men was trying vainly to start it.

The informant said one of the men pointed a pistol at him and ordered him to leave. He said he hid in some bushes nearby and saw the whole group pile into a maroon Plymouth coupé and drive away when they could not start the Buick. He thoughtfully took the Plymouth's license number and police checked it out to Pearl Elliott, who seems to have been trying to corner the license plate market that year.

But this was as close as the police came to the gang at this time. Seemingly they had fled town, although word drifted to McGinnis along the underworld grapevine that Pierpont and Russell Clark were out to "get" him for his part in selling out Dillinger. At the same time the ex-convict with whom McGinnis had been living told police *he* could turn up all members of the gang except Detrick, Shouse, and Joseph Fox—supposedly in East St. Louis—and said it was he who had told Dillinger that McGinnis had "fingered" him. This informant also said he could engineer the recovery of some quarter of a million dollars' worth of bonds stolen in various robberies. He was given a brief trial but failed to deliver.

Huntington, who had argued against trying to capture Dillinger at the physician's office, was angry when the trap was sprung with no other result than the probable exposure of his informant. His report for November 16 read, in part:

> The root of our trouble throughout this investigation has been interference with the work of our informant by an over-zealous and jealous state police department under fire generally by the press of Indiana for inefficiency; and, in this case, they would do anything for some favorable publicity to alleviate the "heat" on the present administration for playing politics with the penal institutions and the State Police force.

McGinnis, warned by a friend that the gang was hiding out somewhere near his place with a machine gun in hopes of rubbing him out, telephoned Huntington, who arranged with Chief of Detectives Blaul for three squads of detectives to accompany the informer to his rooms in the Revere Hotel, then to the railroad station. Huntington left with McGinnis for Indianapolis.

The next break came on the night of November 17, when a bystander saw an Auburn convertible pull into the curb at Harlem and North Avenues. A man and woman in the car were in a heated discussion. When the man finally ran out of arguments and pulled a gun, police were called.

Patrolmen Edward McBride and John Ryan of the Cragin Street station picked up the couple for questioning. The man, who offered no resistance, gave his name as John Santon. In addition to the pistol, he carried forty-four dollars and a title for the car.

The woman was fingerprinted, and "Santon" was taken to the detective bureau at Eleventh and State Streets. A check of his prints disclosed that the police had Copeland in custody. Lieutenant Richard Barry at once posted machine-gun and shotgun squads at front and rear.

"There won't be any jail delivery here," Barry said grimly.

The woman, questioned before being released, said she had been introduced to Copeland the previous night by a bellboy in the Olympic Hotel at 1015 North Clark Street, and that after Copeland gave her ten dollars and fell asleep, she extracted thirty-five dollars more from his wallet, which she found beside a gun beneath his pillow.

The 1933 Auburn—a twelve-cylinder job—proved to have been bought in Burlington, Wisconsin, with money from bonds sold in Milwaukee. Two of the $500 Liberty Loan bonds used to buy the car were identified as having been taken in the Greencastle robbery.

Early on the morning after he was arrested, Copeland was returned to Michigan City for violating his parole. He was questioned there by state police and the ubiquitous Huntington. The insurance detective tried to loosen Copeland's tongue by suggesting that information on other members of the gang, or on the whereabouts of the stolen bonds, might help ease Copeland out of the murder charge facing him in Lima, where his photograph had been identified by Sharp. Copeland said he would have to think this over, and Huntington promptly urged Greencastle officials to demand that the outlaw be sent there for trial.

Other identifications—these by two residents of Avon, Indiana—also linked Copeland to the Dillinger gang. He was picked as one of the four men who sought to have their damaged car repaired on November 8, a car which had been stolen from a Chicago doctor.

For exactly four weeks—an unusually long period of inactivity—the Terror Gang had held up no banks and raided no police stations. But on November 20, the same day Copeland was taken under heavy guard to the prison at Michigan City, the Dillinger bandits pounced again. This time it was on the American Bank and Trust Company in Racine, Wisconsin, and the holdup was one of the most spectacular of any staged by the mob. Even the getaway car, a 1934 blue Buick sedan with yellow wire wheels and Illinois license plates, was an almost contemptuous contrast to the anonymous black sedan usually associated with bank robberies.

Somehow the bandits had acquired an extensive knowledge of the bank, the town, and the surrounding countryside. It is probable that some member of the group—perhaps Homer Van Meter, who did not take part in the actual holdup—had visited the bank two or three times at approximately the hour planned for the holdup (2.30 P.M.) so that conditions would be as much as possible like the ones to be encountered during the robbery.

It is known that Pierpont, possibly accompanied by Mary Kinder, drove through Racine several times before the job was pulled. It is obvious, from later events, that at least two members of the gang had carefully plotted the escape route, complete with times and distances, and planted a spare can of gasoline so that no public stop would be necessary during flight.

The most provocative story, which is firmly believed in Racine, is that Pierpont hung around the Hotel Racine, a block away from the bank, for a few days just prior to the holdup, and on the afternoon of the robbery strolled into the bowling alley in the hotel basement and fell into conversation with some of the women bowlers, in the American Legion Auxiliary league, finally offering to keep score for them. He proved a dependable scorekeeper until shortly after two o'clock when, according to Mrs. Joseph Chadwick, one of the bowlers, he consulted his watch, excused himself, and quickly left the room. Forty-five minutes later, the alley man came hurrying in, bursting with excitement, and blurted, "That fellow keeping score for you just robbed the bank!"

This is the sort of flamboyant action it would be pleasant to believe in, but other testimony, by one of the gang, says Pierpont came to town in the Buick that afternoon like all the rest and had no time to keep score for anyone. Give us our druthers and we'll take the bowling alley yarn, but probability leans the other way.

Pieced together, the excited and necessarily fragmentary accounts of a dozen witnesses give what seems as accurate an account of the event as possible:

The fancy Buick, driven by Leslie Homer, forty-one-year-old native of Lebanon, Indiana, who had been paroled from Michigan City about a month before, stopped twice at downtown corners to let the four passengers out in pairs. As they walked toward the bank, on the northeast corner of Main and Fifth Streets, Homer drove to the rear of the building and parked in the lot.

The four armed pedestrians, weapons under their overcoats, met in front of the bank on Main Street. Makley and Dillinger entered first. While Dillinger went at once behind the cages, Makley walked up to the window where Harold Graham was at work. Clark and Pierpont came in a few seconds later. Clark remained just inside the front door and Pierpont followed Dillinger to where the money was.

By this time Homer had parked the car and entered the bank. He began at once to paste Red Cross posters over the windows on both sides of the front door, so that the view from the street would be obscured.

Graham, thirty-four-year-old assistant cashier and head teller, had been working on the books with some auditors. He had just been sent by Grover Weyland, bank president, to count his cash so that the office force wouldn't be delayed after hours any longer than necessary. He entered the cage and put up a sign reading, "Next window, please." Then he heard Makley say, "Hands up!"

Graham paid little heed to the command but kept scooping up the silver.

"I thought some darned fool wanted me to wait on him," Graham said later, "and because there was a lot of currency there it was not too unusual for someone to make a crack like that. I thought, 'Oh, you darned fool, go down to the next window and get waited on!' As I turned, he caught me with a shot that went through my arm and into my side just below the right elbow, cutting the top off my right hip. When I fell to the floor I thought, 'My God, it's a holdup!' So I reached up and hit the alarm button with my left hand. The fingers of my right hand were tingling, and I thought I'd hit my funnybone when I fell. The next thing I remember, I looked and saw the blood and knew I'd been shot. Through the grille of the sliding door I saw Dillinger and Pierpont dashing for the back of the bank.

"Then one of the others [probably Homer] came in and took the money. He gave me a kick and said, 'You will press the alarm, will you?' It wasn't a hard kick, not a savage kick, not a swift kick. He opened the drawers and threw the money into a bag, then went on to the next cage. It took him about a minute, but he missed fifty thousand dollars.

"In 1933 things were bad, and we'd get one-thousand-dollar bills to pay the difference in clearings between banks. We settled in cash. I had this stashed away in the back of one of the drawers—not the money drawer—behind some stuff. He pulled the drawer open, saw deposit tickets and so forth, and paid no attention."

The gang put things on a businesslike basis in a hurry. Barney Cowan, a local merchant, who was holding $185 as he waited to deposit it, was menaced by Makley's machine gun while one of the other bandits took the money from him. Eight or nine employees—including John Schmitz, twenty-two-year-old bookkeeper; George Ryan, the young interest teller; Harold Anderson, twenty, who ran an adding machine; Don Steele, twenty-seven-year-old assistant teller; Miss Jane Williams, a stenographer; Miss Helen Cespkes, a clerk; and Mrs. Ursula Patzke, another office worker—lay on the floor or crouched beneath one of the counters in the vault room. Some have vivid recollections of the holdup.

"I was disturbed by *something*," Miss Williams (now Mrs. Mc-Coy) says, "and ran to the window. But I never could remember exactly what I saw. I had heard the shot and, whatever I saw, I turned and tried to get down the back stairs. I was almost down when I was called back. Then I remember Harry Pierpont—he was the glamour boy of the outfit, a gentleman type. Pierpont went into the vault . . . he started reloading his machine gun. I can remember George Ryan saying, 'For God's sake, mister, point that gun the other way!' Pierpont laughed and said, 'As long as you're a good boy, you don't have to worry.' "

Don Steele, who had been made a teller the previous week, had gone to the rear of the bank when Graham took over at window four. He was sorting checks when he heard the first shot.

"I looked up and I can't remember whom I saw, but he had a revolver in his hand as big as a stovepipe," Steele says. "I thought of running down the back stairs. I took one step and quit. He told me to lie down on the floor. I started looking around and Dillinger told me to look at the floor, not them. I remember he had on a striped suit.

"Pierpont was tall and good-looking. He reminded me of a man I knew. Another fellow had a wool muffler around his throat. There was an old .32 in one of the cages and they tossed it out the window onto the lobby floor. I believe it was loaded."

When Makley shot Graham, L. C. Rowan, the assistant cashier, sitting in front near the teller's cage, immediately pressed an alarm button under his desk. The alarms registered in the police station three blocks away, and also started a bell outside the bank.

At approximately the same time, Dillinger nudged Steele with his foot as the latter lay on the floor, and said, "Hey, you, open the vault!" Steele said he did not have the combination, and that only officers of the bank could open it. Dillinger immediately went to the front and took Rowan, Grover Weyland, the bank president, and Loren Bowne, another officer, back to the vault.

As he walked around through the vault, Dillinger accidentally stepped on Anderson's little finger.

"I didn't even say 'ouch!'," Anderson says, adding, "we all used to talk about what we'd do in case of a holdup—do this, do that; but when the chips were down none of us did anything. All those things, whatever they were—none ever happened. When you look down the barrel end of a .45 it looks like a cannon."

The middle-aged Weyland, unanimous choice of all those present as the coolest man in the place during the excitement, was being prodded along by Dillinger because he wasn't walking quickly enough. He kept saying, "It takes two to open it up! It takes two to open it up!"

Mrs. McCoy has a bright picture of Weyland at that moment: "I can see him coming down the aisle, just as calmly and slowly as he dared, smoking a cigarette. He had a certain way of smoking a cigarette. They told him, 'Get into the vault and open it up, and you'd better not miss it. We don't like bank presidents. We'd as soon shoot you as look at you.'"

Weyland stopped at the vault and said the combination was in his inside coat pocket. He was told, "Be damned careful getting it out!" He opened the vault on the first try, with Bowne's assistance, even though as a rule he never opened the vault unless someone else was off duty.

"He was very cool," says Schmitz, "just like it was all in the day's work."

While Weyland and Bowne opened the vault, Rowan was left standing outside the door to the vault room. He felt very exposed.

"I knew the cops were coming," he says, "and I figured if anything happened the gang would use me for a shield. There was a stairway leading to the basement about fifteen feet away. Dillinger was occupied and the others were not watching me, so I went down. There were a couple of windows at sidewalk height, and I threw a clinker from the furnace at one of them but missed. Then I quit because I was afraid of attracting the attention of whatever bandit might be outside."

Rowan was not the only quick-witted occupant of the bank. There were several bank examiners present, and one of them stepped quietly into the men's room and locked the door when he heard the commotion. Schmitz, seeing his chance later, dashed for a closet in the directors' room, only to find two other examiners there before him, and a customer, Mrs. E. C. Wilson, sat patient and unnoticed in one of the safety deposit booths, waiting for things to stop banging.

Garrett Veenstra, Racine lumberman, catches the feeling of the holdup in his description of what he saw when he reached the bank as the police arrived:

"About that time of day the cops usually came up to help in transferring the money, so I was quite used to seeing them. But this time they came with their sirens wide open. I held the door for a moment before going in and said, 'Gee, you guys made a lot of noise coming up today.' So I went in ahead of them and to the teller's cage. Then it struck me. I put my deposit in the cage and the guy inside kind of looked at it, but made no effort to wait on me.

"He [Pierpont] was going through this stuff. It struck me how quiet it was—like a bank holiday. No machines going. Then I heard somebody say, 'Get the guy with the machine gun,' and the shooting started. I turned in a hurry and the cop went down. He hit the floor hard. There was a woman at the door at the north end of the bank and she went down [apparently from fright]. Then a big vase of flowers went down. I was as scared as could be. I had my hands up. I was near a big post in the middle of the bank and I never saw a post that looked so good in my life. I thought, 'If I could only get back of that post!' I moved my toes a little bit and my heels a little bit until I got there. There was a marble counter there and the whole thing was full of money. A fellow from the poolroom had put his money out and was sorting it. I could see Hansen [the policeman who had been shot] lying there, and people looking in from the south side of the bank. I thought they were dumb. I thought, 'If I could only get out there I'd be on my way.'"

Shortly before the holdup began, Patrolman Cyril Boyard and his partner, Rudy Speaker, were riding their beat on a motorcycle and sidecar. They answered a call-box light and were told that one of them was needed for a funeral escort. It was a raw and windy day.

"I had some seniority on him," Boyard says, "and I told him, 'Go ahead. It's your baby.'"

Speaker went to the funeral and Boyard returned to the station. He was there when the alarms sounded. No one was very excited since for about a month the alarms had been ringing so often that the telephone company was checking to determine why.

"They'd been coming in so frequently," Boyard says, "that we thought it was just a matter of routine. The others all had been false alarms. Officer Franklin Worsley had the keys to the squad car, a Willys parked in front of the station. Sergeant Wilbur Hansen grabbed a submachine gun [the department's only one] and I had my sidearm. We went down Lake to Fifth, and as we drove up Fifth we passed the parked bandit car, although of course we didn't know it.

"When we drove alongside the bank there was one of our squad cars there, and I said, 'The dicks finally beat us for a change.' [The two detectives from the parked squad car were actually in a nearby cigar store.] Worsley was driving. We stopped in front of the bank and I got out quicker than the others. Worsley was on the left, and Hansen was wearing a heavy overcoat and had to wriggle his way out of the back.

"As I stepped in the front door, Clark shoved a machine gun in my back. I looked around and he grabbed me by the Sam Browne belt and pulled me out of sight. He had a Thompson submachine gun with the stock off. Meanwhile Makley had been coming toward Clark and me. He had just come out through the swinging door in the middle of the bank when Hansen walked in with his machine gun hanging down at his side. Clark yelled, 'Get the cop with the machine gun!' Makley lifted his automatic pistol and fired twice. Wilbur pitched on his face and lay there unconscious."

Makley picked up Hansen's machine gun and returned to his position in the middle of the lobby.

Crowds were gathering outside, attracted by the police siren and the urgent jangling of the alarm. Leo Kruse, manager of the O'Connor and Goldberg Shoe Store four doors north of the bank, and Edward Kirt, his assistant, heard the commotion and came hurrying to the bank. They approached the door cautiously and saw Boyard standing inside. He shook his head in warning, so they went around the corner to Fifth Street. They were standing on a ledge, peering through the window into the bank, when Makley saw them. Without hesitation Fat Charley sent a burst from Hansen's machine gun over their heads.

The bullets went through the plate glass and across the street, where they smashed the windows of Joseph Mezines' photographic shop on the second floor, narrowly missing the proprietor before burying themselves in the walls.

The money gatherers—Dillinger, Pierpont and Homer—had harvested as much as they could find ($27,789 and some securities), and Dillinger decided it was time to leave. He and Pierpont looked out the back windows of the bookkeeping room but found it was too long a drop, and Dillinger said, with no apparent dismay, "We'll have to shoot our way out the front!"

Without hesitation he ordered Weyland and the three women to accompany them. The women were still under the marble counter, and Dillinger said, "All right, you, come on out of there!" Mrs. McCoy recalls saying, "Oh, do you mean me?" and the answer: "Who the hell do you think I'm talking to? Get up and get out of there!"

"I could see the fellows coming out of the cages, shoving loose stuff into their pockets," she goes on, "and I can still see an occasional bill dropping to the floor. There was a crowd out in front, but why on earth they stayed around I can't figure out."

Boyard was added to the bag of hostages as the group reached the door. Wally Nelson, a customer who had just walked in, and Lawrence Keyes, an off-duty policeman, who also had entered during the robbery, were marched right out again. Nelson had walked up from the Hotel Racine to cash some checks and found the bank windows broken and the crowd standing there.

"I couldn't figure out what was going on, so I went inside," Nelson says. "Makley stuck a gun on me and said, 'Come along with me!'"

Weyland, fighting a delaying action to the last, was struck for not hurrying.

"His glasses skidded across the lobby on the floor," says Mrs. McCoy. "My impression is he was slapped across the head, he was not hit with a gun."

Veenstra, who witnessed the gang's withdrawal from behind his coveted pillar, says:

"They came out of the back room, down the left side of the bank. I heard orders given: 'You come along, and you, too!' Then I heard a girl's squeaky voice: 'You mean me?'

"They took Weyland along and he didn't move quite fast enough. One hit him with his fist or something and Weyland stopped and turned. He said, 'If you didn't have that gun in your hand you wouldn't have that much guts!' I worried about that remark afterwards, while Weyland was gone."

The bandits literally had to push their way through the throng of spectators to make a path along the sidewalk to their car. During the forced march two of the women, Miss Williams and Miss Cespkes, slipped away into the crowd, and both Nelson and Keyes also escaped or were ignored as the car was being backed out of the lot.

While this was going on, someone came running into the Ace Grill half a block south and told the owner, Harry Cohen, that a holdup was in progress. Cohen grabbed a .38 he kept in the store, jammed it into his back pocket, and dashed out. Traffic was halted and people stood in Main Street, watching. Cohen saw a car parked in the middle of Fifth, headed downhill, and the uniformed Boyard beside it. Cohen thought the policeman had captured the gang and was about to take them to the station. He stepped off the curb toward

Boyard, and a man standing beside the policeman pointed a gun at Cohen and shouted, "Get back!" Cohen retreated to the corner and stood there.

At this juncture one of the machine gunners spotted the two detectives from the squad car. They had left the cigar store for a millinery store two or three doors away, and from there, crawling below window level, they had reached a little alley beside the Fifth Street entrance to the Venetian Theater. The bandit opened fire, spraying the building but—apparently—not trying to hit anyone. The slugs smashed a mirror in the millinery store, however, near where a clerk was standing. The detectives ducked for cover but did not return fire because of the onlookers.

When everyone had reached the car, Dillinger got behind the wheel, with Makley beside him. Pierpont, Clark and Homer sat in the back seat, and three of the hostages were told to stand on the running boards, where they served as shields. Mrs. Patzke was beside Dillinger with Weyland behind her. Boyard stood on the right side of the car. One of the gang held onto his belt to prevent him from jumping off.

Chief Grover Cleveland Lutter, a 245-pound former professional baseball player, arrived just before the bandits pulled away. He had walked from the station because all the cars were gone. Lutter ran upstairs and peered down on the scene from an office window, but did not shoot because of the hostages and the bystanders.

The fleeing car made a sharp right turn into Lake Street, passing within fifty feet of Lieutenant Arthur Muhlke, who was kneeling with a sawed-off shotgun in readiness, and Worsley, who was armed with a carbine. Muhlke started to lift the shotgun, but realized the futility of using it just as Weyland saw him and waved a frantic signal not to shoot. Worsley also held his fire.

Dillinger wheeled into Seventh, traveling at high speed and sounding the horn frequently. He followed Seventh to Wisconsin, then turned south as far as Eighth, went west to Marquette, north to Sixth, and west again to Lafayette. There he stopped for a traffic jam. He had run through two stoplights on the way, and Mrs. Patzke, clinging desperately to avoid being thrown off, felt her skirt brushed by a passing car during a near collision at one intersection.

A friend who recognized her as the car flashed by thought she was riding on the running board because of some grave emergency—probably rushing to an accident scene—and a motorcycle policeman who met the bandit car on the Sixth Street viaduct apparently had the same thought, since he went right by.

When traffic forced the halt at Sixth and Lafayette, Boyard was ordered off. He stepped down and started to turn to walk to the curb but was ordered to stand where he was. Boyard stood, expecting to be shot, but the car pulled away.

"It all looked like a movie," he says.

The other two got into the back seat when Boyard was dropped. Weyland rode on Homer's lap and Mrs. Patzke between Homer and Pierpont. Clark sat on the right-hand jump seat and the bags of money were in front of Weyland.

The police had not given instant chase, because Chief Lutter was afraid of a running gunfight in which the captives might be shot or thrown from the running boards. Three or four pursuit cars set out shortly, however, and after a pause to pick up Boyard, soon had the bandit car in view. The police cars were cut off by a North Shore train a moment later, and the trail was lost.

When it became evident that they were away clean, at least for the time being, there was a slackening of tension among the bandits. Mrs. Patzke remembers some of the conversation: a warning from Makley that the prisoners would be shot if there were a blockade set up, and someone's remark that the police were "pretty dumb."

Makley kept track of the odometer and the turns, and Homer read directions from a pad. Shortly after leaving Racine, they turned near Highway H, and from then on never hit paved roads.

Dillinger stopped the car two or three times to change license plates (a curious precaution in view of those yellow wire wheels), and at the same time money was transferred from bags to suitcases and given a rough count. There were quite a few new one-dollar bills, and one of the gang remarked angrily that someone at the bank had "pulled a fast trick." Dillinger suggested that Weyland had taken them to the wrong part of the vault. There was a discussion of Weyland's being a "gentleman farmer" and some mention of the possibility of hiding out on his farm. Makley suggested that Mrs. Patzke could do the cooking, and Dillinger half turned, keeping his eye on the road, to ask her, "Can you cook?"

"After a fashion," Mrs. Patzke replied cautiously, not sure whether Dillinger were serious or not.

During the ride they met several cars, which turned out to be coming back from a funeral. At one farm there was an auction, and the size of the crowd made the gang grow tense once more. They rolled the windows down and held their guns in readiness as they cruised past. Later they met two men on a hayrack, and Mrs. Patzke says, "I can still hear Dillinger saying, 'Hi, Joe,' as he waved his hand." The impulse is irresistible to wonder whether Dillinger's thoughts flashed back to Mooresville for a moment at this point.

Makley had been cursing during the early part of the trip, but quit when Pierpont told him, "Cut it out, Mac, we got a lady in the car."

It was late afternoon by this time. Mrs. Patzke, who had been hustled out with nothing over her dress, complained of the cold. Pierpont took off his coat and gave it to her. Weyland then asked whether he could get a handkerchief from his pocket to put over his head, explaining that his bald spot was cold. Pierpont handed the banker his hat.

About an hour after they left Racine, the car turned into Highway X, known locally as Lovers Lane, between Routes 83 and 58 near Saylesville. Half a mile or so off the main road the car turned again up a faintly discernible trail and stopped. As one of the gang pulled a can of gasoline from a hiding place and began replenishing the tank, Pierpont ordered Weyland and Mrs. Patzke from the car. The three walked a little way into the woods, Pierpont pausing politely when Mrs. Patzke said she had to tie her shoelaces. Then he told them to stand on opposite sides of a large tree, facing each other. He tied their hands together with a new pair of shoelaces from his pocket.

Pierpont retrieved his coat and left, warning them not to try to get loose from their bonds for twenty minutes. A moment later he returned, and Mrs. Patzke had a sudden fear he was going to shoot them. But he said, "Sorry, mister, I'll have to have my hat." Then he went away and they were alone. In the distance they could hear some farm machinery in operation, and through the trees they saw a child go by on the road. Assuming the child was on the way home from school, they thought it was about four o'clock.

Weyland managed to get an Eversharp pen from his pocket and used it to work one of the knots loose. When they were free he gave Mrs. Patzke a handkerchief to put around her head, and tied another over his own. They climbed a fence and began walking through the fields toward the sound of the machinery. After going over a little rise they came upon William J. Klussendorf, a farmer, who was cutting corn for his silo. He later told them his first thought on seeing them in the distance was that they were Holy Rollers, coming to beg.

"I was throwing off bales into the filler and the horses were getting fidgety," Klussendorf remembers. "They started prancing, and that set me looking around. I saw a man and a woman coming down the hill from the northwest. The man's coat pocket was torn off and I thought there had been an accident. His right hand was tied to the woman's hand. They had no overcoats and both were shivering.

"When they got up to the wagon the man asked whether we had a telephone. Then he started to tell us how they were kidnaped by bandits who robbed the Racine bank. He asked if I could drive them back to Racine and I said after I finished loading. They had been tied up in Brown's Woods, named after Bill Brown, the Saylesville blacksmith who owned the property."

Mrs. Klussendorf gave the couple some coffee, cake and canned raspberries, and Weyland telephoned his wife. Then the farmer drove them the 35 miles or so back to Racine.

The imperturbability of Weyland during the holdup was matched only by that of Walter Wagner, who was immediately behind the bank during the whole affair but could hardly be called a witness. Wagner, a former German soldier from Königsberg, in East Prussia, was on a stepladder at the Copper Lantern Restaurant, owned by Barney Richter. He was painting some windows when the shooting began. Wagner kept on painting. When it was all over, Richter asked why Wagner hadn't turned to see what was going on. He drew a priceless answer: "Mr. Richter, that was none of my business."

As soon as the gang left the bank, Don Steele went up to see how Graham, the assistant cashier, was.

"He was lying on the floor," Steele says. "When I saw the blood I asked if I could do anything for him. I can't remember if I suggested whiskey or he did, but I ran down the street to a place that was padlocked [this was during the closing phase of Prohibition] and in the back door. I paid three dollars for a pint of whiskey and went back to the bank, where I poured a pretty good Dixie cupfull. I asked Harold if he wanted it and he refused. Three or four of us killed that bottle. Then we balanced the books. I went out and had a few drinks and some oysters and walked home sober as a judge. I didn't begin to feel the effects until two or three days after the holdup. Then I trembled so I could hardly stand up."

That same night District Attorney John R. Brown and several members of the Racine police force went to Milwaukee to look at rogue's gallery photographs. Huntington was there with other photographs, and the Racine delegation identified Dillinger, Pierpont and Makley. Clark was named a few days later, but Homer seemed to have come and gone without anyone's getting a memorable look at him. The fifth member of the holdup crew was believed at first to be Joseph Burns.

Homer might have been excused for believing he was home free. What he didn't know was that the same day, before the holdup, Lieutenant Howe had received a letter from Chief of Police Mike Morrissey of Indianapolis saying that Homer was with Dillinger and Pierpont in Milwaukee. He had wired flowers to his girl in Indianapolis and telephoned her both from there and from Chicago.

It turned out to be a brief but expensive romance.

NINE

●●●●●●●● "THERE WASN'T A HEAVY DRINKER IN THE
CROWD. . . . THEY WAS ALL NICE CLEAN
BOYS." —MARY KINDER

After disposing of the two hostages, the gang headed for Milwaukee, keeping to minor roads. They split the money as soon as they reached town, each of the five receiving a little more than $5,000. The remaining $2,000, in brand-new one-dollar bills, was placed in a pot, to be given to a fence in exchange for bills of larger denomination, since it was feared the new money might be traced.

This pleasant chore completed, all but Homer went on to a second hideout. On arrival they found that little homebody, Mary Kinder, doing her laundry.

"They all come in kidding Harry," Mary remembers, "because he took his overcoat off to put around the girl. And they said to me, 'You didn't give a damn whether we got killed or not. You ain't even got the radio on.' I still had some stockings and lingerie hanging out. We traveled so much that when we got to a place I had to wash things out. They didn't say nothing about any shooting."

(This account of the gang's movements after the Racine holdup differs from that later given by Homer. He said they went directly to Chicago and divided the loot there. It is improbable, however, that they went to Chicago, then back to Milwaukee. Miss Kinder's account seems the more likely to be correct.)

The gang lay low in Milwaukee for twenty-four hours to give the roads time to cool off. Then they packed and went to their various Chicago apartments. Ed Shouse was no longer with the gang. He had left Chicago October 21, stealing Clark's new car, after an argument which—Shouse later charged—would have been certain to end fatally for him if he had waited. But the others were a close-knit and seemingly amicable corporation.

"Sometimes," Mary says, "we had separate apartments, but mostly two couples stayed together. John and Harry and I stayed with Billie [Evelyn Frechette] for a while, then we'd change. Russell Clark was the handsomest of the bunch, and the nicest fellow you'd ever want to meet. He used to say he could stick me in his hip pocket [Mary Kinder was 4 feet 11 and weighed 97 pounds]. Hamilton was the oldest. He was nice, and quiet as could be. The only snotty one was Shouse.

"We'd all go to dances, taverns, restaurants, and prizefights. Nobody hid around. We'd read different stuff, listen to the radio and everything. Nobody was boss. They'd sit down and talk things over, and when they got money they'd count it, then divide it between them. There wasn't no boss at all. Everyone tries to say Harry was so mean and Dillinger was boss, but there wasn't no boss or nothing like that.

"We lived four or five places in Chicago, paying in advance for a month. We'd stay in a place until we thought we had to move because we were seeing too many strangers or something. I just cooked day and night, frog legs, chicken and stuff. They'd eat anything I'd cook. Johnnie used to like Schlitz beer. There was a little delicatessen under us where you could get Schlitz, and he'd go down there."

Miss Kinder didn't know Van Meter until the gang came to Chicago, and saw little of Leslie Homer, who was a sort of probationary member of the mob. His benefits until the Racine holdup had been purely fringe ones. Just before that job, Homer had fallen in love and wanted to quit the gang and get married. It was because of the gang's desire to "heat him up" that Homer was taken along to Racine. They wished to involve him in a serious crime, in case he did quit, to lessen the chances of his talking.

On November 24, four days after the Racine expedition, Homer was arrested by Sergeant Thomas Harrison of the Chicago police department at LaSalle and Ohio Streets. He was in the company of Jack Liberty, a former convict whose dossier included robbery, car theft, violation of the Prohibition Act and the sale of obscene photographs. Homer carried a satchel in which were a bulletproof vest, a loaded pistol and two extra clips. He had in his possession, police said, only $511, all in crisp new one-dollar bills.

Since Homer was wanted for parole violation, Chief Morrissey requested that he be returned to Indianapolis. Morrissey also reiterated his belief that Homer was tied in with the Dillinger operation. Homer was questioned by Federal men and Chicago police, then—when little of importance was learned from him—sent to Indianapolis. There, however, he was far more cooperative (except when discussing the Racine holdup). In an apparently frank statement he gave details about the gang's *modus operandi* and such highly useful data as a list of apartment addresses and descriptions of motorcars owned by the gang.

Billie Sparks (Evelyn Frechette) and Mary Kinder rented the apartments, Homer said. Dillinger's last known address was in the 2000 block on Lawrence, where he had been living with Billie. Pierpont (who was using the name Harris) had been living at 150-54 Parkside in an apartment above that occupied by Pearl Elliott. John Hamilton lived in an apartment in the 5000 block on Winthrop, but was contemplating a move to the 1300 block on Argyle.

Dillinger, Homer said, was getting another Terraplane to replace the one shot up in the November 15 trap, and Pierpont had a 1933 Auburn. Makley owned a 1933 Essex Terraplane—seemingly a status symbol with the group—and Clark's Essex was believed to be in Fort Wayne or Terre Haute, where Shouse had driven it. Hamilton's car was a 1929 or 1930 green Auburn convertible.

Dillinger and Pierpont were traveling companions, Homer said, like Clark and Makley. He also told them that Van Meter had taken part in the Racine job—a bit of misinformation that may be excused on the grounds that Homer could hardly have been expected to admit that he himself had been the fifth man at Racine.

Homer said the gang used a black cowhide bag, 27 inches long and 8 inches wide, to carry its machine guns in, and that they had 50 cartridge drums, 20 cartridge clips, and some riot guns, wrapped in blankets for concealment. Each man carried a .38-caliber super-Colt automatic on his person.

The informer said the gang members were very cautious about giving apartment locations to anyone outside their immediate circle, and that the usual code signal for callers was four short rings. Even when the code signal was given, Homer said, it was the custom of whatever gang members were present to draw pistols and have their machine guns ready for use.

Homer told police the mob had three or four "contacts" in Chicago, and gave the names of two who were trying to peddle the Greencastle bonds. He said Pierpont had written his (Homer's) mother on October 12 to have Homer meet him at the Kokomo hideout. Homer did so, and Pierpont gave him two suitcases to deliver to Cincinnati, and $450 for expenses. Homer met Pierpont in Cincinnati (this was just after the Lima jail delivery) and took him to an apartment where Homer was introduced to Dillinger, Clark, Mary Kinder and Billie Sparks.

Homer remained overnight, and in the morning Clark gave him $500 for himself and $450 in an envelope addressed to a relative. Dillinger gave him $130 in silver and a letter addressed to his brother Hubert, and Homer went to Louisville to mail both letters.

Three days after the Greencastle holdup, Homer told his questioners, he received an envelope with two claim checks in it for something to be picked up at the Pennsylvania Railroad station in Terre Haute. Homer went there and picked up two suitcases—probably containing some of the loot from the Greencastle bank—which he transported to Chicago. He met Pierpont at the Rogers Park Hotel and Pierpont took him to an apartment in the 800 block on Montrose Avenue, handed him $130 and told him to stay the night.

Pierpont returned the following day and gave Homer $1,500 in silver and new dollar bills, which Homer took to Indianapolis and traded for larger bills. Three days later he met Pierpont in an apartment in the 4300 block on Clarendon and was paid $300 for the trip. He remained in Pierpont's apartment for several days, ran some more errands, then returned to Indianapolis.

A few days later he was summoned to Chicago again and went to the Clarendon Avenue place. Pierpont gave him a package and some letters for Pierpont's mother, but this was the day Dillinger was chased from Dr. Eye's office, and the gang spent several hours —until 4 A.M. on the sixteenth—moving to new apartments after Dillinger gave the warning. Homer helped by leaving some of their luggage at the Illinois Central Railroad station before checking into a Loop hotel for the night.

The next morning he picked up a pistol and bulletproof vest from one of the suitcases and went to Indianapolis. He reached there November 17 and was back in Chicago the twentieth (in time— although he did not say so—to help rob the Racine bank). Skipping lightly over the Racine episode, Homer said he next met Dillinger on November 23 in the Winthrop Avenue apartment and was asked to take a suitcase and some money to Indiana. Homer said he told Dillinger he was "hot" in Indianapolis and did not wish to go there.

Dillinger seemed annoyed at this and went off to discuss something with Pierpont. He returned to ask Homer to meet him at 8 P.M. next day at the northeast corner of Montrose and Western, and to bring the two suitcases with him. Homer, however, fearing he was about to be "put on the spot," watched the meeting place from across the street. He said he saw Dillinger, Pierpont and Makley cruise by, and thought they had become suspicious of him. So he threw one of the suitcases into the river and bought a second-hand car to leave town in. He was about to drive away with Jack Liberty when the police picked him up.

Ironically enough, it was the new dollar bills the gang had been worrying about which tied Homer in with the Racine holdup.

Detective Lyle George and Oscar Edwards, the assistant district attorney at Racine, had read about Homer in the Chicago papers. The interest of both was caught by mention of the new one-dollar bills, since a large number of such bills had been taken from the Racine bank. They had driven at once to Chicago, but reached police headquarters after Homer had been sent to Indiana.

They found Homer in the Indianapolis police station and were permitted to talk with him. He denied any knowledge of the Dillinger mob or the Racine raid, but failed to explain the new bills to anyone's satisfaction—including, it is to be presumed, his own. "He was a pretty smooth operator," Edwards says. "We went back to the hotel late that night. We got hold of a quart of whiskey and we sat there with it on a table, adding up in one column all the facts that seemed to convict him and on the other side all the facts that seemed to be in his favor. At the end of the quart and the adding and subtracting, we decided he was guilty.

"We came back to Racine. Now we had a picture of Homer. We went to the bank, and two of the people there—Mrs. Patzke and one of the men, though not Weyland—seemed to recognize him. They said he *looked* like one of the gang. But when they saw him they could not make positive identification. So Brown [the state's attorney] and George went to Indianapolis with two other witnesses, one of them from the shoe store. Through some mistake, Brown and George and the witnesses walked into a room where only Homer and a cop were sitting—there was supposed to be a showup, of course.

" 'Why sure,' one of the witnesses said. 'There's one right there!'

"Homer wilted. 'There's no use kidding you,' he said. 'I was with the gang.' "

Homer waived extradition, saying he wanted to go back to Racine.

"I think he was afraid of being involved in some other holdup in Indiana," Edwards says, "and was satisfied, if he had to be caught, to be caught in Wisconsin."

After his return to Racine, Homer talked freely once more and gave a detailed account of how the gang operated. He said their method was to work out of apartment houses in thickly populated areas where they would be most likely to escape notice.

The only part of his statement that varied greatly from information later supplied by Mary Kinder was his declaration that Pierpont and Dillinger were the gang's leaders, did most of the planning, and gave the orders. According to Homer, they were in possession of any secret information within the gang and seemed to trust each other, if no one else.

Homer said that very careful preparations were made for each of the holdups. One or two men would look over a bank for several days before it was decided to rob it. Sketches were made of the interior, showing the cages and how many employees to expect.

Escape routes were charted in great detail and everything was set down by both time and distance—the latter measured to tenths of a mile.

Homer said the gang would make their getaway in as unobtrusive a manner as possible, driving slowly when there was no pursuit (as at St. Mary's) and never exceeding the speed limit unless they knew they were being chased (as at Racine).

He also spoke of himself. "I have been in trouble before," he said. "I have spent sixteen out of the last seventeen years in prison. I am under parole. I came out of prison with very little money. I was approached by one of these men to simply run a few errands, for which I was well paid. I was guilty of aiding and abetting the escape of criminals. As time went, and certain things occurred, I wished to withdraw from the connection, and I found myself in the position of the man who couldn't let go. In other words, I got in the position where I knew too much."

Homer said he had completed three years of high school . . . "but I have acquired some self-education since then. I worked for myself at one time, doing remarkably well. Mother is living with me. My father is living, I don't know where. He deserted my mother and me when I was sixteen."

Homer's record showed that he had been imprisoned for burglary in 1917 and released in 1928. He was rearrested the same year for armed robbery and given five to twenty-one years. He had been paroled October 10, 1933, and four days later Pierpont had written him, inviting him to join the gang.

While he was about it, Homer even handed out some generous advice to the Racine authorities. After saying that the gang had tossed away the two .38s taken from Hansen and Boyard as useless, he added, "Guns of that type won't put a dent in a bulletproof vest, and that machine gun of yours would make just a small dent in one. If you want to give your coppers an even break with present-day gangsters, you want to equip them with the new super-.38 caliber. A gun of that type will shoot a hole right through any bulletproof vest ever made."

Homer verified that the mob was planning to kill McGinnis, if they could find him, for betraying Dillinger at Dr. Eye's office. He added he was afraid they were planning to rub him out, too.

"It was either a case of being exterminated by them, or the law,"

Homer said unhappily, "and the law wasn't as deadly as they were. I knew too much and they wouldn't let me go."

One reason Homer talked freely may have been the humanely intelligent treatment he got while being brought back from Indianapolis, a 300-mile journey, by car. When they reached the outskirts of Racine, Homer apparently felt the walls begin closing in, because he suddenly asked if he could have a final bottle of beer. (Prohibition had just ended, and Homer may well have been tempted to ask for something stronger.) It was then about midnight, but a stop was made and he got the beer.

During the twenty-four hours he was in the custody of the Racine authorities, Homer was given the prize-package treatment, since there was a fear, shared undoubtedly by Homer, that there might be a "rescue" attempt. Indiana troopers had convoyed the Racine delegation to the Chicago Loop, and when Homer was brought before Court Commissioner Eugene Haley in Racine at 9:15 on the morning of December 7, four police cars escorted him from the jail.

He was arraigned in a courthouse guarded by police and deputies, as men with rifles stood in the corridors. He was held for trial, and a short while later was taken before Municipal Judge E. R. Burgess and entered a quick guilty plea. Homer was sentenced to twenty-eight years in the state prison at Waupun. A small cavalcade of cars left for Waupun shortly after the sentence was passed. Homer was again shackled to George, as he had been since leaving Indianapolis, except when behind bars. Homer entered Waupun at 3 P.M. and—despite an abortive escape attempt some years later—didn't come out until he was paroled in 1943.

Before leaving for Waupun, Homer wrote a long letter to his mother in Lebanon, apologizing to the deputies for delaying them, and just before departing he got off a mild quip: "This is a nice town you have here. Only it's NRA—no robberies allowed."

Homer's apprehension made his associates lie low for a while. But his several statements gave Chicago police a line on the green convertible used by the Dillinger gang, and about the time Homer was being driven to Waupun, Sergeant Dan Healy of the detective bureau had traced this car to an auto repair shop at 1135 Catalpa Avenue, where Carl A. Blomberg, the shop owner, told Healy he had repaired its faulty muffler. Healy told Blomberg to notify police if the car showed up again.

Official attention was diverted from the Dillinger gang December 13, when a daring smash-and-grab robbery at the Unity Trust and Savings Bank on Chicago's West Side netted more than $50,000 in cash for a group of several men who overpowered the elderly caretaker and broke open a number of deposit boxes. The whole operation took about three hours. This was not the work of the Dillinger mob, apparently, even though Hamilton was mentioned as a possible suspect. But it did cause a flareup of police activity. The following day this flareup became an explosion: on December 14, rather than return to complete his term at Michigan City, John Hamilton, the rope skipper, the quiet one, shot and killed Police Sergeant William T. Shanley, father of four and an usher at St. Gertrude's Church.

Hamilton had returned to Blomberg's shop to have a fender on the green car straightened, and the garageman said he didn't have tools to do work of that sort. He referred Hamilton to an auto repair shop on Broadway, then phoned the police. Sergeant Shanley and Patrolmen Martin Mullen and Frank Hopkins were cruising when they received a radio message from Chief of Detectives William Schoemaker telling them to hunt for the convertible in a given block on Broadway.

A search located the car in a repair shop at 5320 Broadway. The man and woman who left it had promised to return in a few hours. Shanley radioed this information to Schoemaker, who told him to arrange a stakeout but to be careful. The squad car parked at Catalpa and Broadway, about a block and a half distant, and Shanley and Hopkins walked to the shop, leaving Mullen in the car.

They waited until almost 4 P.M., the hour when the night shift came on duty. Then Shanley told Hopkins to go and tell Mullen to take the police car back to the detective bureau and send out a new squad. Hopkins left, and a moment or so later Hamilton and the woman entered. Sam Tower, the garage mechanic, gave this description of what happened then:

"They walked over to the car. Sergeant Shanley walked up to them and asked, 'Is this your car?' Hamilton told him, 'No, it belongs to my wife.' The woman took out a vehicle receipt and handed it to the officer. Shanley told Hamilton, 'Keep your hands out of your pockets!' and began to pat his [Hamilton's] hip pocket for a gun. As he did so, Hamilton pulled a gun from a shoulder holster and shot Shanley twice.

"Sergeant Shanley yelled, 'I'm shot. Call the police.' Then he fell down, with the license receipt still in his hand. Hamilton grabbed the woman by the hand and ran out the front door, dragging her behind him."

Hopkins was just returning from his talk with Mullen.

"I was about two hundred feet from the garage," he said, "when I saw a man and woman run out the door. I knew something was wrong and started towards them. The man left the woman and ran through a vacant lot and she ran ahead on the sidewalk until she met me. I grabbed her and she started to struggle and curse me. I took her back to the garage and Bill Shanley was lying there in a pool of blood."

The forty-three-year-old Shanley, winner of a *Chicago Tribune* hero award for entering a darkened store alone to catch two safe-crackers, died fifteen minutes later in Edgewater Hospital. He was the thirteenth Chicago policeman killed in line of duty during 1933. He left his widow nothing but the furniture, his paycheck (due the following Monday), and a small insurance policy from the Policemen's Benevolent Association.

The woman caught by Hopkins, who gave her name as Mrs. Elaine Dent Sullivan Burton DeKant, was questioned by Schoemaker and his assistant, William V. Blaul. That evening Blaul took Mrs. DeKant and six squads of detectives to raid an apartment in the Logan Apartment Hotel, 2530 North Sacramento Avenue. The apartment was empty, but inquiry showed it had been rented November 19 (the day before the Racine holdup) by Hamilton, using the name Orval Lewis.

He had been living there with three women, this quiet man. One of them was Mrs. DeKant, although she had given police officers her address as 3607 North Kedvale. It is quite possible two other male members of the gang were living in the raided apartment, unknown to the landlord. One gun was found there.

Police thought it was Pierpont who had killed Shanley until witnesses said the killer had parts of two fingers missing on his right hand—thus, if you will pardon us, putting the finger on Three Finger Jack, whose real name Mrs. DeKant probably had not known.

The plump redheaded prisoner told police she had met Hamilton, who told her his name was John Smith, at the Stevens Hotel restaurant, where she was a waitress.

"He used to come in for coffee every morning," she said, "and when I was fired from the hotel he promised to take care of me and I went to live with him. He said he was the son of a wealthy family and had just come into his inheritance. Once he showed me seventy thousand dollars in thousand-dollar notes. I took him to my mother's house for Thanksgiving dinner, and my folks thought he was a great catch and encouraged me to marry him."

Mrs. DeKant was arraigned on a charge of being an accessory to the murder of Sergeant Shanley, at which time she denied having known that Hamilton was a gunman. She added with understandable bitterness, "If I ever get out and he tries to get in touch with me, I'll put the button on him [tell the police]. What a surprise it was to me that he should turn out this way. Why, I never heard him say 'damn.' And was he clean! He'd take two baths a day. I'm accustomed to meeting gentlemen, and I thought he was one."

This put-upon lady was later released, when the authorities became convinced she had not known that Hamilton was a criminal.

The slaying of Shanley, coming on the heels of the Unity Trust robbery, touched off a series of police raids throughout the city, which continued for weeks and netted a number of ex-convicts, some guilty of nothing more than knowing Dillinger, others of recent crimes. But they failed to turn up Dillinger or Hamilton or Harry Pierpont or Russell Clark, and for an excellent reason. When the heat had come on, they had gone south. Not knowing this, however, the Chicago police pressed the search relentlessly. On December 16, State's Attorney Thomas Courtney met with Chicago police officials and announced that a nationwide hunt was being planned to wipe out what he described, inaccurately, as a tie-up of four gangs: Dillinger's, Roger Touhy's, John (Handsome Jack) Klutas's, and the Harvey Bailey–Verne Miller combine from Oklahoma.

Courtney said the gangsters specifically sought included Klutas, whose downstate Illinois gang was suspected of half a dozen kidnappings; Basil Hugh (The Owl) Banghart, then believed to be with Miller; and Charles (Ice Wagon) Connors, said to be a contact man for the Touhy mob. Oddly, there was no specific mention of any of the Dillinger gang, including John Dillinger himself.

Two days later Supervising Captain John Stege was named to head ten police squads consisting of fifty of the finest marksmen in the Chicago police department whose specific full-time job was to capture the Dillinger and Touhy gangs or drive them out of town for good. Its purpose was explained thus by Captain Stege: "It's our belief that the Dillinger and Touhy mobs have joined hands. [This seems never to have been true.] We hope, although their trails are cold, to be able either to drive them out of town or bury them. We'd prefer the latter. That's the reason we picked marksmen for the special-duty squads."

Stege said the first business of the new squad would be to study photos of the Michigan City escapees still at large, and their second would be to study photos of the Touhy gang. He added that nearly 300 ex-convicts from the Michigan City prison were living in Chicago. All police were given the numbers of twenty-two license plates, supposedly stolen and used by the Dillinger or Touhy gangs. Police were warned that if one of these cars were spotted, they should request aid before halting it.

About this time Captain Leach was tipped off that Shouse had returned to the Middle West from California and would be in Paris, Illinois, December 20, with bank robbery on his mind. Leach promptly laid plans for an ambush. On the twentieth the Indiana State Police, led by Leach, surrounded the Paris Hotel and waited. Presently a car pulled up, containing two men and two women, and Shouse stepped out. The police called to him to surrender; instead, he leaped back into the car and began shooting.

Trooper Eugene Teague, twenty-four years old, had pleaded to be allowed to come on the raid, even though he was not yet fully recovered from injuries incurred when his motorbike blew a tire. He now fired into the rear of the car and the gunman quit. Shouse yelled in surrender and Teague leaped eagerly forward to grab him. But Lieutenant Chester Butler failed to hear Shouse, and as Teague jumped from behind the car, Butler's riot gun cut his comrade down.

Butler later tried to take the blame for this tragedy, which was obviously an accident, but Leach refused to ascribe it to anything but Teague's overeagerness.

Shouse, questioned at state police headquarters the next day, called Dillinger and his men "daring and desperate" and said they had sworn never to be taken alive. Shouse, who seems to have had a flair for colorful and conceivably inaccurate detail, added that the members of the gang—whom he listed as Dillinger, Pierpont, Hamilton, Makley, Russell Clark and Burns—held daily rehearsals for their expected battle-to-the-death with the police, a thoroughly improbable tale.

"They are kill-crazy," said Shouse solemnly, "and that is why I left them."

The two girls, who had driven in from California with Shouse, were freed because they did not know who he was. He had been "swell" to them. The second man escaped and a third was found later inside the hotel and captured.

Another notable success was chalked up on December 23, when Hilton Crouch, one of Dillinger's aides in the Massachusetts Avenue Bank holdup almost four months before, was seized at his apartment at 420 Surf Street. He was armed with a .45, but did not try to draw, since he was covered at the time by five policemen, commanded by Sergeant Edward Bazarek.

Crouch, who was using the name of Price, was caught after a police squad had stopped a car with a known license number earlier in the afternoon, and questioned the driver, owner of a North Side tavern. This man said the car had belonged to his partner, from whom he had just bought it. The police, also learning that "Price" had a sweetheart, picked her up for questioning. Then they went to the Surf Street apartment and waited until Price-Crouch showed up.

After being rushed to the headquarters of the newly formed "Shoot to Kill" squad, Crouch admitted his part in the Massachusetts Avenue Bank holdup and said his share of the loot had been $8,300. He said Dillinger and a third man had been with him. Three months later he was sentenced to do twenty years for the holdup.

By this time Huntington was beginning to feel that he had lost the trail. But a telephone call from a Wisconsin official, who was investigating the Racine robbery, informed the insurance detective that Leslie Homer had asked to see Huntington and several other persons, including Chief Morrissey of Indianapolis, about a plan to capture the Dillinger gang.

Several officers went to Waupun at once to talk with Homer, only to discover that his "plan" consisted of being released from prison, getting in touch with the mob once more, then turning them in.

Somehow this failed to appeal to anyone but Homer, and everyone left except Huntington and Morrissey, who were curious about a leak Homer had mentioned in Indiana State Police circles. This turned out to involve Captain Leach, but only to the extent of careless talk.

Homer said he had been sent to Indianapolis by Dillinger to confer with a lawyer, who had then consulted with Leach. The police captain, Homer insisted, had told the lawyer much of what the state police knew of the Dillinger gang's operations. The lawyer in turn told Homer. Homer made it a triple play by relaying the information to Dillinger, and Pearl and Dewey Elliott, who had not previously known they were suspected of aiding the mob. The Elliotts left town hurriedly.

Homer, once more in a highly talkative mood, also gave several addresses to his visitors, and at one of them police seized a former convict for questioning about the sale of some of the Greencastle bonds. The suspect gave police a tip to which they paid little heed. He told them Dillinger and his men were in either Texas or Florida. The tip was a solid one.

Dillinger and Evelyn Frechette had driven to Florida shortly after the Shanley killing, as had Pierpont and Mary Kinder, and Clark and Opal Long. By December 21, Van Meter and Makley also had joined the party at Daytona Beach.

Dillinger and Billie shared the beach house with Clark and Miss Long. Van Meter and Makley lived nearby. Pierpont and Mary Kinder had checked in at a Daytona hotel. Two days after their arrival, Harry and his girl friend came down from their room to find uniformed police swarming through the lobby. Pierpont hesitated, then the two walked slowly through the crowd, learning a moment later that a fellow guest had leaped from one of the upper windows.

It was a relaxed and happy life, for the most part. There was swimming (Mary Kinder was afraid of the surf, which kept knocking her down) and they even went to Miami to view the air races. On Christmas Day gifts were exchanged—Johnnie gave Billie a diamond ring—but a short while afterwards they quarreled violently; Billie and Mary had bought some champagne and grown tipsy, which infuriated their men. Johnnie hit Billie and ordered her to go back to Wisconsin. Pierpont, just as angry, apparently forgave his Mary; she was neither hit nor banished.

New Year's Eve the gang celebrated by shooting at the ocean with their tommy-guns, and about New Year's Day Dillinger missed his French-Indian sweetheart so much that he set out to bring her back. Whether or not they returned is not known.

There is also sharp disagreement as to where Dillinger was on January 15. The weight of evidence indicates that he was with John Hamilton in East Chicago, Indiana, pulling the holdup in which Policeman William O'Malley was killed, and that it was Dillinger who fired the fatal shots. But Dillinger himself always insisted to his family that he was not there. Mary Kinder has repeatedly said (even long after Dillinger was buried) that he and the others heard the news of the holdup over the radio, and Mrs. Hancock, Dillinger's sister, stoutly insists she was once told by an FBI man that her brother had never killed anyone.

Before this East Chicago holdup took place, however, another of the ten who escaped was recaptured. Walter Detrick and Jack Klutas were cornered in Bellwood, a suburb of Chicago, and when they resisted arrest Klutas was slain by police bullets and Detrick arrested. That was on January 6, and boosted to .400 the batting average of the law in its contest with the prisoners still at large.

At this time Dillinger had only six months in which to travel many miles, to see many people, to do many things. And until January 15 he still had a chance to rewrite the script and give himself a happier ending. But that date was the point of no return.

John Dillinger had been captured in Dayton, Ohio, the day before this photo was taken. Meanwhile, a plot he had earlier launched to break his confederates out of the Michigan City, Indiana, jail was successfully underway. They, in turn, would free him.

Dillinger, at about 16 years old, in a photo that hung for years in Audrey Hancock's living room, where his funeral was later held.

A never-before published photograph taken in 1924 of Beryle Hovious (girl on left), Dillinger's only wife. She divorced him while he was in prison in Michigan City.

Dillinger on route from Tucson, Arizonia, where he had been captured, to the Crown Point, Indiana, jail.

Photo courtesy of the John Dillinger Historical Museum, Nashvillle, Indiana.

Dillinger in 1933 in a pose that said much about the man and the image he wanted to project.

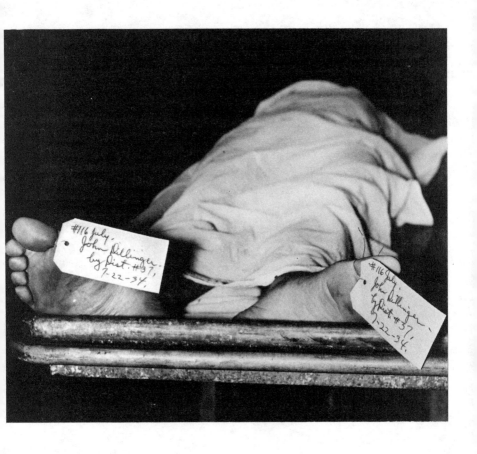

John Dillinger in the Cook County Morgue, July 22, 1934.

TEN

●●●●●●●●●● "YOU MAY AS WELL HAVE THIS. MY LUCK
IS RUNNING OUT ANYWAY."
—DILLINGER, GIVING RABBIT'S FOOT
TO INDIANAPOLIS NEWSMAN

The exiled Evelyn Frechette spent December 31 on the Indian
Reservation in Neopit, Wisconsin. This was not the liveliest place
in which to welcome the new year, but she had no reason to com-
plain of boredom for long.

Some time after January 1 she was summoned to meet John
Dillinger in Chicago. She may have returned to Florida with him,
although she probably did not. Dillinger, as has been noted, insisted that he was in Florida on January 15. This must be doubted
since too many other persons, with better reputations, said he was
the machine gunner who cut down William Patrick O'Malley, a
forty-three-year-old East Chicago, Indiana, policeman, during the
holdup of the First National Bank on that date.

Bearing in mind Dillinger's disclaimer, then, but outweighing it
with what others said they saw, this seems a fair account of what
happened on that disputed day:

Shortly before 3 P.M.—and the time would indicate experience on the part of the holdup men, since the nearer to closing time a bank is "hit," the more profitable the haul should be—two men walked into the First National Bank in East Chicago. They were John Dillinger, carrying what looked like a trombone case but wasn't, and John Hamilton. A third man, never identified, remained in a car parked near the bank entrance.

The pair paused in the vestibule, where Dillinger removed a submachine gun from its nest. Then they stepped into the bank, and Dillinger yelled with noisy menace, "This is a stickup! Put up your hands, everybody!" The phrase "This is a stickup" was identical with that used by Dillinger in earlier holdups. One of the two also told all women and children to stand apart so they would be out of the line of possible fire.

Edward L. Steck, vice-president, whose desk was near the front door, and about a dozen employees, were at work. Some fifteen or twenty customers were at the various desks and windows.

"We all obeyed the command with alacrity," Steck said. "But another of our vice-presidents, Walter Spencer, touched off the alarm that notified the police station, a block and a half away, of the robbery. [*Spencer, who was on the phone to the Union National Bank at Indiana Harbor when the gunmen entered, broke the conversation off by saying: "We're held up!"*] When we were all lined up, the machine gunner called out to his companion, 'Go in and get it!' The second man ... stepped behind the counter and scooped up all the money in the cages. While he was at work Patrolman Hobart Wilgus, the first to arrive from the station, walked in with his pistol drawn, but the gunner-bandit got the drop on him and forced him to drop the pistol and line up with the rest of us. [*O'Malley and two other policemen backed out as Wilgus was captured and waited for the bandits to emerge. Four other policemen also arrived.*]

"That machine gunner, who the police say is Dillinger, is a terrible man. While the second man was getting the money he [Dillinger] glanced out the doorway and saw other policemen congregating. Instead of appearing frightened, he called out, 'There's been an alarm and the police are outside. But don't hurry. Get all that dough. We'll kill these coppers and get away. Take your time.' "

When the money [$20,736] was gathered up, the two bandits walked calmly into the street, using Spencer and Wilgus as a shield. Policeman O'Malley was near the door but couldn't shoot at first for fear of hitting the banker. Then O'Malley saw an opening and fired four times at Dillinger, the shots apparently hitting the latter's bullet-proof vest. Dillinger pushed Spencer out of the way and got off a quick burst, which seemed to knock O'Malley's legs out from under him, then shot the policeman again as he fell, mortally wounded.

Using Spencer as a cover once more, the two bandits dashed for their car. They let Spencer go and he dropped back, giving the seven policemen on the street a clear target. During the ensuing fusillade Hamilton staggered and dropped his gun. He was helped to the car by Dillinger.

The getaway vehicle, a small blue Plymouth sedan with Ohio plates, swung quickly out into the street as the policemen and two passing game wardens concentrated a heavy fire on the fleeing car. One door of the bandit car swung open as it shot away from the curb, and was almost torn off when it struck the side of another machine, an incident which should have brought back memories to Dillinger.

The gang car headed south toward Hammond or Indianapolis as the police kept firing without apparent effect. Pursuit also was futile. The police later expressed the belief that the car was equipped with bulletproof glass and that both Dillinger and Hamilton were wearing bulletproof vests.

Captain Matt Leach was informed at once of the holdup, and from his Indianapolis headquarters ordered a detail of state police from the Tremont barracks to take up the chase. But the next report on the blue Plymouth came from Chicago. The bullet-riddled car, with bloodstains on the cushions, was found abandoned the following day, January 16, at Byron Street and California Avenue. It was identified by East Chicago police.

It is hard to give an accurate account of the gang's activities immediately before and after the holdup. But Charles Makley seems to have left Florida for Tucson some time early in January with the idea of calling on a girl he knew. Russell Clark and Opal Long departed at about the same time, and reached Tucson on the ninth or tenth of January. Harry Pierpont and Mary Kinder, who left on the same day as Clark and Opal Long, drove more slowly and did not reach Tucson until about the sixteenth.

The elder Dillinger saw his son on January 17. John said he had just returned from Florida and had not been in East Chicago. He left Chicago with Miss Frechette, it is probable, a day or so later. They spent the first night in a St. Louis motel and reached Tucson about the twenty-first, where they again checked into a tourist spot.

Clark and Makley, meanwhile, without Dillinger and Pierpont to keep an eye on them, had gone on the town in Tucson. Makley picked up a girl singer he is said to have known before, and with Clark and Miss Long went on a tour of the city's nightclubs. During their various stops the two men spent too freely and talked too much. Several things seem to have drawn the attention of the Tucson police to the gang at about the same time.

Early on the morning of January 22 the Congress Hotel in Tucson caught fire. Clark and Makley, who were registered there with Miss Long, paid two firemen fifty dollars—a sum large enough to make the incident memorable—to bring their luggage down. A day later one of the firemen noticed photos of the two men while leafing through a detective story magazine. He notified the police. Apparently about this time, also, the police were told by someone who had chatted with Clark and Makley during one of their nightclub visits that they had been talking in a manner to arouse suspicion.

And last, but hardly least, there are grounds for believing that the Federal Bureau of Investigation, while not officially working on the case, had been taking an interest in the Dillinger mob and knew it was in Tucson. According to a confidential memorandum still in the files of a Middle Western police department, the government agents previously had learned that members of the gang had been staying in a cottage near Venice, Ohio, owned by the former wife of an ex-convict. This place had been raided, and although no leads were uncovered at the time, the woman owner of the cottage had then gone from Hamilton, Ohio, to Phoenix, where her mail was "covered" by the FBI, and it was discovered that she was in communication with the gang at Tucson. It seems logical that this information was forwarded to the Tucson police.

Regardless of how it came about, on January 25 the Tucson police became interested in a house on North Second Avenue where it was known that two of the wanted men were living. Sergeant

Chester Sherman, in charge of the robbery detail, arrived there in the early afternoon with Detective Dallas Ford, Patrolman Frank Eyman and Mark Robbins, an identification expert. A tan-colored Studebaker was standing in front of the house. The police squad watched from behind a nearby hedge and after a wait of ten minutes or so, the front door of the house opened.

"A gentleman and a lady came out of the house," Sherman said, "and the man walked around to the right-hand door with the lady and helped her into the car, and he walked back to the left front door and got in the car, turned around in the block and went the opposite direction, and I followed him."

The man—it was Makley—drove to the Grabbe Electric and Radio Store downtown and was pricing a radio capable of picking up police calls when Sherman, who was in plain clothes, came quietly into the shop. He asked one of the clerks to walk back and see whether the top of Makley's left index finger were missing. It was, and with identification virtually certain, Sherman went out to where Ford, Eyman and Robbins were sitting in the car. They came in and covered Sherman while he made the arrest. Makley was not armed.

Trying to brazen it out, Makley gave the name of J. C. Davies and asked Sherman to take him back to the house on North Second, ostensibly so that he could get some papers to prove his story of having just come in from Jacksonville, Florida, after selling his garage. Actually, he was hoping to get back to Clark for help. Sherman politely refused to take him anywhere but to the station, where Makley was held. His woman companion was quickly released when it became evident she had known nothing of his criminal activities.

Sherman, having learned that the other man in the house was known as Long, then returned to the North Second Avenue address with Eyman, Ford, and Kenneth Mullaney. They stopped the police car in an alley half a block away. Mullaney and Eyman, who were in uniform, went to the back of the house. Sherman, carrying an envelope in his hand as though searching for an address, came down the sidewalk while Ford kept within easy distance of him on the opposite side of the street.

Sherman stopped in front of several houses, as if checking numbers, then came to 927. He glanced at the house, then at the envelope, and started up the walk. As he approached, he looked through the window and saw a man get off the davenport in the front room, snatch a beer bottle from a table, and hurry toward the rear of the house. Sherman mounted the steps and calmly rang the bell.

"A woman came to the door," Sherman said. "She asked me what I wanted, and I had this letter in my hand. I said I had a letter to Mr. Long from Mr. Davies. She said, 'I will take it,' and she started to pull it out of my hand and I pulled it back. I said, 'No, Mr. Davies told me to give this letter to Mr. Long in person.'"

As Sherman talked to Opal Long, Clark came out of the bedroom and stood near the front door.

"I was standing astraddle the door sill," Sherman went on. "I had my left foot in front of the inner door, and the screen door was against my back. Mr. Clark was standing not in the doorway but just to my right inside the door. I asked him if he was Mr. Long. He said yes. When he said yes I shifted my pencil that I had in my right hand to my left, and pulled my gun. I just got it out of the holster, didn't have it leveled at him, when he grabbed it in such a manner that I couldn't get the hammer forward or backward. We wrestled right there in the doorway for a few seconds and he pulled me into the house.

"As soon as I was in the house, the lady that was there closed the front door [banging it on the hand of Dallas Ford, who was running to Sherman's aid, and breaking Ford's finger]. We wrestled around the living room for quite a little while, it seemed, and he worked me into the bedroom which was just to the left of the front door running off the living room. We were still wrestling over the gun and we were standing right alongside the bed. The bed was to my left and his right.

"We wrestled down onto the bed and while we were there someone hit Mr. Clark on the head with a gun. When Mr. Clark was hit he wasn't hit hard enough to knock him out. He turned and looked over his left shoulder and saw Dallas Ford standing there. When he saw Ford he let go of my gun and had only one hand on it. I got the gun and hit him on the head with the barrel of my gun and that was about all."

Neither man had said anything during the struggle. Clark,

bleeding freely, and Miss Long, who during the wrestling match had been "pecking" (the word is Sherman's) at the policeman, were taken to the station to join Makley. Three machine guns, several Colt automatics, several hundred rounds of ammunition, some home-made clips for .351 automatic rifles, and three bulletproof vests were found in the house. There was no partridge in a pear tree, but there were two wardrobe trunks, closets filled with women's cloth-ing, and drawers full of men's apparel. There was no gun on Clark, or beneath his pillow, but one was found under the the the mattress at the foot of the bed. Clark later said he had left the gun under the pillow, "but somebody had switched it." And he told Sherman, "If I had known who you were, you would never have gotten on the front porch. You looked too small and too young to be a copper."

Not long after Clark and Opal Long were taken away, Pierpont and Mary Kinder came calling, but left hurriedly when they noted blood and such other storm warnings as overturned furniture and kicked-up rugs. A neighbor, however, copied the license number of their car and called the police. Pierpont and Miss Kinder were found by Eyman and two other officers—Jay Smith and Earl Nolan—on South Sixth as they were on their way out of town in a 1934 Buick.

The police car pulled alongside and Pierpont was waved over, in as casual a manner as possible. Eyman then climbed out of the police car and told Pierpont, in easy and friendly fashion, that a check was being made on all cars with Florida licenses and he would have to go to the station.

The outlaw, playing the game by the same rules, agreed with seeming unconcern to go, and invited Eyman to ride along to show him the way. Eyman got in the back seat and the other two officers followed. Eyman became nervous when he saw Pierpont adjust the rearview mirror to keep him in sight, however, and the policeman quietly took out his gun and held it in his lap. All went well until Pierpont saw some of the luggage from Clark's house as he walked into the office of Chief C. A. Wollard. Then Pierpont went for his gun.

Wollard, Eyman and Jay Smith all grabbed the gunman's arm at the same time, and he was quickly disarmed and handcuffed. A search disclosed two other guns on his person, one of which turned out to be the .38 taken from Sheriff Sarber's office in Lima the day the sheriff was killed; and there was a submachine gun in his luggage.

Pierpont denied his identity until fingerprints gave him the lie. He was rueful after finally admitting his name.

"These cops out here ain't like the kind they have in Indiana," he was quoted as saying. "They pull too fast for us."

Mary was equally morose, and later told newsmen that if the gang had listened to her they never would have come to Tucson. Mary explained that a woman who did not identify herself—a fortune-teller—had visited at the Kinder home in Indianapolis some time before, and during a conversation with Mary's mother told her to warn her daughter to "stay away from Tucson." Mary said she had argued against the trip, and even after their arrival had tried to persuade the others to leave.

A few hours after Clark's arrest, a man and woman in a new Terraplane bearing Wisconsin license plates stopped in front of the North Second Avenue address. The man got out, leaving the woman in the car, and started up the walk. As he did so, Officer James Herron, who was watching from across the street, started toward the car. Two other policemen, Mullaney and Milo Walker, were inside the house.

The stranger, apparently sensing a trap, or perhaps seeing signs of the battle that had preceded Clark's capture, reached the porch, then turned and started back. Herron, close to him by now, asked, "What do you want?"

"I am at the wrong house," the man calmly replied.

"Oh no you're not," Herron said, covering the other with a revolver as Walker and Mullaney stepped into view.

The prisoner was searched and an automatic removed from a shoulder holster. He gave his name as Frank Sullivan and said he was a businessman from Green Bay, Wisconsin, in town on a vacation. His woman companion identified herself as Anne Martin. Both were taken to police headquarters, along with the woman's Boston bull terrier.

"Sullivan" was soon identified as Dillinger, and a further search of his person and the Terraplane disclosed more than $8,000, part of it in a money belt around his waist. Some of the cache was in five-dollar bills, and Carlton J. Enders, a special agent of the FBI, said a number of them had been stolen from the bank at East Chicago.

The news stories also credited Dillinger with one of the most improbable remarks of his career. "My God," he supposedly cried, "how did you know I was in town? I'll be the laughingstock of the country. How could a hick-town police force ever suspect us?"

The language could hardly be called Dillingeresque, and the expressed attitude was not typical. Dillinger, when caught, tended to become friendly and cooperative, at least on the surface. A far more probable tale is one ascribed to Sheriff John Belton that as crowds filed through the Pima County Jail to gawk at the outlaws, Dillinger urged those who passed his cell to vote for Belton in the next election.

The prisoners were given a preliminary hearing January 26 before Justice of the Peace C. V. Budlong in the Pima County Courthouse, as sightseers overflowed into the corridors and out onto the lawn. Budlong finally ordered the courtroom cleared of all except those with seats. After a brief hearing the four men were held in bonds of $100,000 each on charges of being fugitives from justice. The three women—Opal Long, Bernice Thompson (Mary Kinder) and Anne Martin (Evelyn Frechette)—were held on bonds of $5,000 each on charges of obstructing justice. Miss Kinder's bond was raised to $100,000 a day or so later when she was accused of having helped in the escape from Michigan City.

While nothing could be learned from questioning the men during the hearing, the list of material recovered by the police spoke rather eloquently: It included five "baby" machine guns, $36,000 in cash, and $12,500 worth of jewels.

Dillinger was the surliest of all in court. He refused to answer when his name was called, saying, "I ain't Dillinger." He was yanked to his feet by a courtroom attendant. Clark and Makley sat mute, and Pierpont, usually quiet, stepped into Makley's role as the jester. He joked throughout the hearing until ordered to be silent, and when his name was called, stood, laughing, and said, "That must be me." When the clerk called the name of Anne Martin, Pierpont laughed again and said, "There ain't no such animal."

Dillinger added a romantic touch to the proceedings, at least from the viewpoint of sentimental spectators in the crowd, when he paused while being led out of the courtroom to smile at "Miss Martin." Then he leaned down and kissed her.

Whether or not this tender scene was responsible, an unnamed reporter was moved to write a short while later, "Dillinger has none of the look of the conventional killer. Given a little more time and a wider circle of acquaintances, one can see that he might presently become the central figure in a nationwide campaign, largely female, to prevent his frying in the electric chair."

Attorney John Van Buskirk of Los Angeles, hired to represent the seven, fought without success to have the bonds lowered, and said he would battle extradition. He said he would file writs of habeas corpus and added the men were being "framed," a charge Dillinger reiterated at length.

According to press accounts, Dillinger said after the hearing that he would "go the limit" to escape extradition, and he screamed angrily at guards in the Pima County Jail, "You're framing me for crimes I never even read about. You can't keep me in any two-by-four jail like this. I'll get out and kill you all."

Dillinger, reportedly, also expressed scorn for police in general and said he had committed none of the crimes of which he was accused but had done many other jobs the police had failed to associate him with.

"I'm an expert in my business," he was quoted as saying. "I can play tag with the police any time. They just dodge around on old trails like hounds that don't know what's going on. And the dumbest ones in the world are the Chicago kind. Right now none of those smart-alec coppers have got a bit of evidence that I killed anybody or robbed any bank."

This is how he was quoted, but the statements sound apocryphal since he had already confessed holding up the Bluffton bank and had been identified at Racine and Indianapolis.

Van Buskirk told Chief Wollard that the entire gang had been in Florida for seven weeks before coming to Tucson and had nothing to do with any crimes committed after Dillinger was sprung from Lima.

As soon as newspapers throughout the nation carried the story that the gang had headed into what appeared to be its last roundup, authorities from Indiana, Ohio, and Wisconsin began competing for the prisoners. The Indiana delegation was the first to arrive, and came from both Indianapolis and Crown Point—the county seat of Lake County, in which East Chicago is located. The group included Leach, Prosecutor Robert Estill of Lake County, Sheriff Lillian Holley and her nephew Undersheriff Carroll Holley, Chief of Police Nicholas Makar of East Chicago, and several others.

Dillinger, pointed out by one of the group as the killer of O'Malley, "growled and nervously paced his cell." But he did shake hands, although reluctantly, with Leach, who reached through the bars for this strange display of camaraderie between hunter and hunted. Leach, noting that Dillinger had grown a mustache, asked about it and drew the obvious answer—that it had been cultivated as a disguise.

Dillinger quickly made it plain that he had no intention of returning to his native state voluntarily. "I'll fight extradition to Indiana to the last ditch," he said. "I'm in no hurry to return to Indiana. I haven't a thing to do when I get there."

Pierpont, who had been relaxed and friendly since his arrest, "raged and swore" when Leach approached his cell. "I should have killed you when I had the chance, you dirty———. You put my mother in jail in Terre Haute, you———. If I ever get out of this, the first thing I'm going to do is kill you, you rat!"

Whether Pierpont was quoted accurately or not, there seems no doubt that he was in a rage so violent that Sheriff Belton had trouble quieting the other prisoners in the cellblock, stirred up by the clamor. Pierpont's reference to his mother's arrest stemmed from the fact that she and her other son had been held for questioning after they were involved in an auto accident in November— although Leach had no part in this and said it hampered his own investigation. Nor is the reference to killing Leach "when I had the chance" obscure. Dillinger had told his family, during a visit to the Mooresville farm, that on one occasion he and Pierpont were walking through downtown Indianapolis and found themselves behind Leach on Capitol Avenue. Dillinger said he had great difficulty restraining Pierpont from shooting the police captain immediately.

When Pierpont grew sulky and refused to talk, a young Texan, locked up on a minor charge, posed as the gangster and collected money from the crowd in a tin cup as Makley urged him on and aided the deception. His take was enough to pay his fine and his lawyer, and he was freed the next day.

Aside from the reaction aroused by Leach's visit, however, the prisoners could have been called model ones. Miss Frechette played with a jigsaw puzzle in her cell while Miss Kinder read some movie magazines she had asked for and been given. And when Governor B. B. Mouer visited the jail and asked Miss Frechette how she liked being behind bars—a tactless remark Mouer probably would have left unuttered if she had been a registered voter—Evelyn primly replied, "I suppose one gets used to it eventually."

The Governor also visited the men, and while Dillinger said nothing, Pierpont, curiously merry, told the chief executive he was sorry to see the Governor in jail. Makley was quoted as telling the Governor he thought he would be free soon since "I've broken out of better jails than this."

Newsmen were permitted to interview the group, and Makley denied having been present when Sarber was shot. He said he was in Jacksonville, Florida, when the East Chicago holdup took place. During the questioning, he also was asked about the Bremer kidnaping. (Edward G. Bremer, a wealthy St. Paul banker, had been kidnaped in January and freed after twenty-two days and the payment of $200,000 ransom.) Makley was indignant at the suggestion that he could have been connected with it. He said, "What, kidnaping? That's too low a business for a good gunman. I would never stoop to that. Bank robbery's my trade!"

Pierpont spoke briefly of the gang's stay in Chicago, and said they had paid $1,000 a week for "protection" while there. Dillinger chatted at some length with Tubby Toms of the Indianapolis *News,* who had accompanied the Indiana authorities. The outlaw asked about his father, and when told the elder Dillinger was happy to hear his son was still alive, replied, "That's fine of Father. He's a great scout. I'm sorry that I have caused him so much worry, but—well—that's how life goes. We can't all be angels."

He then gave Toms his rabbit's-foot luck piece, with the wry remark: "You may as well have this. My luck is running out anyway."

Later Dillinger spoke with another newsman, saying of his father,

"He's a good scout, and I wish for his sake I had taken up some other line of business."

The Wisconsin delegation—Chief Lutter, Prosecutor Brown and Detective Lyle George—checked in on Sunday morning, January 28. Wisconsin said it wanted all four men, and Lutter said there was positive identification of each for the Racine holdup. Extradition papers were en route from both Indiana and Wisconsin, although Governor Mouer, reportedly, had promised Indiana first choice.

Prosecutor Ernest Botkin of Lima remained in Ohio, but announced that he had communicated with Indiana authorities and been assured that their only interest was in Dillinger and they would be glad to turn over Pierpont, Clark and Makley to their neighboring state, where all had been identified in the murder of Sarber. Governor McNutt said he did not know whether this arrangement would be satisfactory, but added, "There will be no trouble between George White [the Ohio Governor] and me."

Estill of Indiana expressed confidence that Dillinger would be convicted of the slaying in East Chicago, saying, "We have a perfect case against Dillinger and Hamilton, for half a dozen detectives witnessed the shooting of Policeman O'Malley." Hamilton at this time was presumably still in the Middle West, recuperating from the wounds he received in the East Chicago holdup.

Tucson officials, while awaiting the outcome of the legal maneuvering before turning the mob over to one or another of the out-of-town factions, treated the prisoners well. Sheriff Belton permitted some of the money found in the possession of the gang to be used to buy food from outside the jail. Furthermore, plans were made to permit Miss Kinder to marry Pierpont. Belton offered to pay for the license, and Mrs. Elizabeth Oney of the jail staff went to the cells of both prisoners to obtain the information needed for a license application. However, the project failed to come off—perhaps because there was some doubt about whether Miss Kinder had actually been divorced.

Although there was considerable question which state would wind up getting possession of Dillinger and his associates, it quickly became evident where the prisoners themselves preferred to go.

Lutter still has one of Attorney Van Buskirk's business cards, on which the attorney wrote, for Dillinger's benefit, "These men are from Wisconsin. John L. Van Buskirk. Chief Lutter, George, OK."

After looking at the card, Dillinger talked freely to the visitors from Racine.

"We done a lot of kidding with him and his other pals," Chief Lutter says. "We talked two or three hours. One thing he gave me credit for was not shooting during the Racine holdup. I said, 'I know better than that. You had a copper and two bankers and there were too many people on the street.' He said, 'It's a good thing you didn't shoot. You'd not only have killed us but the copper and the bankers.'"

After this conversation, Lutter says, Dillinger told him, "I want to go back with you fellows. You look more sociable."

All four of the men prisoners then signed extradition waivers, early Monday morning, agreeing to return to Wisconsin for trial. But word of this got out. Brown had conferred with Prosecutor Estill and agreed to give Dillinger to Indiana and Pierpont to Ohio. But Prosecutor Houston of Tucson refused to turn the gang over to Wisconsin, which had no capital punishment, saying, "I wouldn't hand the gang over to that state's officers under any consideration." Leach, hearing of the waivers, flew to Phoenix to see Governor Mouer. Mouer quickly signed papers authorizing extradition to Indiana.

These were rushed back to Tucson, and Dillinger was forcibly removed from his cell Monday evening when he refused to come out voluntarily. The state of mind of the usually self-possessed outlaw was quite different from the calmness he had shown when he thought his destination was Wisconsin. He braced his feet against the bars and struggled against the combined efforts of five men before being hauled from his cell.

"Where's my mouthpiece?" he demanded, as he was being taken away. "He told me this was illegal! They can't take me East without a hearing!"

An hour after the manacled Dillinger was hustled out of the jail —to be flown by charter plane to Douglas, Arizona, to make connections with an American Airways flight—attorney Van Buskirk appeared before Superior Court Judge Frederick W. Fickett, who signed an order, returnable January 30, for the authorities to produce Dillinger and his companions in court and show cause why they should not be released. But Dillinger was gone. This maneuver did, however, slightly delay the departure of Mary Kinder and the three other men, whose extradition to Indiana had also been authorized by Governor Mouer.

The only consolation for Wisconsin was that Chief Lutter, after an argument, recovered the machine gun stolen during the Racine holdup. It was autographed by Dillinger himself, and proudly taken back to Racine.

News that the gang was to go to Indiana also gave Brown a chance to make a highly pertinent remark. "Indiana, a state which turned these mobsters loose on the Middle West, has them in custody again," he commented bitterly. "It is hoped that the negligence of the officers of that state will never be repeated."

The Crown Point party took off from Douglas at 11:14 P.M. Monday with every evidence that they appreciated the importance of their charge. Before takeoff, Dillinger had been forced to change clothes, presumably in an effort to make identification more difficult in case of a possible rescue attempt. He was shackled to Carroll Holley, and Chief Makar was one of the guards. The plane landed at Dallas, where the passengers switched to another plane. Other stops were made at Fort Worth, Little Rock and Memphis, where there was another change of planes, with large crowds and a turnout of local police each time the plane touched down. The last stop before Chicago was St. Louis, where Dillinger asked what had happened to the rest of the gang, and was told they had left Tucson aboard the Golden State Limited at 7:55 A.M. Tuesday.

In St. Louis, also, Sol Davis, photographer for *The Chicago Times,* bought all four vacant seats on the plane (thus cutting out opposition cameramen) and flew to Chicago with Dillinger. Davis found the gunman "very quiet and congenial" and says Dillinger had no objection to being photographed after the plane, a Ford trimotor, took off from Lambert Field. One of the shots by Davis shows the handcuffed Dillinger peering listlessly out the window. Eventually Dillinger grew weary of Davis's questions and said, "Go away and let me sleep."

Stewardess Marge Brennan draped a blanket around Dillinger's shoulders when he complained of the cold, and she also put a pillow beneath his head when he wanted to sleep. Miss Brennan later told newsmen she felt sorry for Dillinger "who looked like a little puppy with his tail between his legs."

Dillinger seemed nervous at times and twice said he wished the trip were over. He also complained of a headache, and Davis gave him some aspirin and a drink of water.

"As for Dillinger himself," Davis said, "here is my impression of him: He is the type of guy you wouldn't want to be left alone with unless he was your friend. He has a crooked mouth and an unhealthy smile. I served a long stretch in the army, and I met plenty of tough guys, but I don't think I ever met a tougher one than Dillinger."

Tough or not, it looked like the end of the road for the man from Mooresville.

ELEVEN

●●●●●●●●●● "A JAIL IS JUST LIKE A NUT WITH A
WORM IN IT. THE WORM CAN ALWAYS
GET OUT."   —JOHN DILLINGER

A special welcoming delegation of thirty-two Chicago policemen—
wearing bulletproof vests and carrying rifles, machine guns, pistols,
and shotguns—was waiting when the plane carrying John Dillinger
rolled to a stop at the Midway Airport, Cicero Avenue and 63d
Street, on Chicago's West Side, about six o'clock the evening of
January 30.

In addition to the Chicago force, twenty-nine troopers from Indiana were ready to escort the outlaw on the thirty-mile drive from
the airport to Crown Point, where he was to be held for the murder
of Patrolman O'Malley.

Sixty other Chicago policemen were also on hand, but their only
duty was to see that nothing happened to Dillinger or anyone else.
They were there to maintain order.

The plane taxied to a halt and Dillinger, handcuffed to Carroll
Holley, was half led and half carried down the steps as a host of
photographers set off flash powder. The outlaw blinked in the

glare, answered a few questions tossed by reporters, and was hurried immediately into a waiting auto. The thirteen-car cavalcade then pulled out for the trip to Indiana.

Lieutenant Frank Reynolds, in charge of the Chicago police detail making the trip, had been told by Captain Stege, "If any effort is made to raid the caravan and release Dillinger, or if he makes a break at escape, kill him at once!"

While this command must have kept Reynolds, at least, on edge, the trip was without incident.

The protective force was increased at the Indiana state line by police from East Chicago, Hammond and Gary, and the motorcade reached the Lake County Jail in Crown Point at 7:40. The Crown Point *Register* gave this description of the arrival:

> John Dillinger came to town Tuesday evening. He came with an escort of police, deputy sheriffs, special detectives armed with machineguns, rifles, revolvers, sawed-off shotguns, bulletproof armor and bulletproof vests such as was never seen before at one time in the middlewest. He was met by a volunteer reception committee of some four or five hundred citizens gathered from all parts to catch a glimpse of the noted bank robber and killer.

Sheriff Lillian Holley—thirty-eight years old, 5 feet 5, and 110 pounds—was in charge of the Crown Point jail. Her husband, Dr. Roy F. Holley, a Gary dentist, had been killed during a gun battle with a madman he was trying to arrest seventeen days after beginning his second term as sheriff of the second-largest county in the state. Mrs. Holley had been named by the county commissioners to succeed him. Although a thoroughly feminine figure—Mrs. Holley belonged to a bridge club and Ladies' Aid and missionary societies —she looked and acted the part of a competent sheriff. She wore a pistol and had no hesitation about performing the duties of the job she had held for a year.

A little while after reaching Crown Point—a quiet and pleasant town which he soon was to make immortal in criminal annals—Dillinger obligingly posed for a photograph which was printed around the world, became the subject of heated comment, and permanently dimmed Estill's then bright political prospects. The prosecutor, weary from the trip to Tucson and back, and obviously not thinking beyond the moment, yielded to a combination of the charm Dillinger could turn on when he wished and the authoritative air all good news photographers possess.

Estill was the victim of what thousands upon thousands of persons before and since that evening have yielded to—a crisp order, voiced in this case by Rocky Nelson of Chicago, that the subjects posing for a picture move closer together. Estill obligingly obeyed, then responded automatically again when Nelson added, "Now put your arm around Dillinger."

This, at least, is the explanation given by Harold Revoir of the *Chicago Tribune* photographic staff, who was among the cameramen present when the controversial "fraternizing" photo was taken. Revoir says he felt sorry for Estill ever after, since the scene never would have materialized except for the persuasive voice of Nelson uttering the photographer's immemorial plea.

Frank J. Loesch, president of the Chicago Crime Commission, reacted in typical fashion when the photograph appeared the next day. "I was shocked at seeing newspaper photographs of a prosecutor who is about to prosecute a vicious murderer posing with his arm around the murderer's neck," Loesch said, "both of them smiling and exhibiting friendship. For a state's attorney to put himself in such a familiar attitude with a criminal is to instill in the mind of the criminal the hope of escape or of avoiding the death penalty. Perhaps it isn't unethical, but it is certain that such familiarity breeds contempt for law enforcement in the minds of criminals."

A story in the *Chicago Tribune* the next morning said that Dillinger, after posing with Estill and Sheriff Holley, agreed to a press interview "with an air that demonstrated him to be as mild-mannered a man as ever shot up a bank." During this interview Dillinger said flattering things about the Chicago police and the "nice fellows" who brought him back from Tucson. He added, "I like Mr. Estill, and Mrs. Holley seems like a fine lady."

Asked about the shooting of Patrolman O'Malley, however, Dillinger quickly entered the denial he continued to express the brief remainder of his life—even in private conversation with his family.

"They can't hold me for that," he said, ignoring the fact that they *were* holding him. "When that job was pulled I was in Florida. I never had anything to do with that East Chicago stickup."

During the interview Dillinger also described himself as "an unfortunate boy" at the time he and Singleton held up Morgan, the

Mooresville grocer, mentioned his time behind bars, and went on, "In the prison I met a lot of good fellows. I wanted to help them out. There's no denying that I helped fix up the break at Michigan City when the ten men got away. Why not? I stick to my friends, and they stick to me. . . ."

Dillinger did his best, also, to take the pressure off John Hamilton, who was still being hunted. After blandly admitting what was already known—that Hamilton had killed Sergeant William Shanley in Chicago—Dillinger added with a thoughtful disregard for the truth, "Poor old John. Well, he's dead. They shot him four times and he's under the sod. Maybe I'll tell you where sometime. I wasn't with him when he got shot, but one of the boys told me about it. Hamilton's got some kids. Before he died he sent me some money to take to them. It was in one of the sacks that the Tucson police took away from me. I guess it was about sixty-eight hundred dollars."

Some of the more skeptical newsmen felt that if Hamilton was indeed dead, this statement was intended less as a tender tribute to his memory than as an explanation of how money from the East Chicago robbery came into Dillinger's possession if, as he maintained, he was not among those present. Captain Stege had yet another theory. He thought Dillinger was trying to talk the authorities into relaxing their hunt for Three Finger Jack so that the latter would have a better chance of rescuing Dillinger.

During this same interview Dillinger showed that Huntington's concern for the health of his informant, McGinnis, was well founded. "We stuck around Chicago," Dillinger said, "living a few days in one place and a few days in another. Stege and Reynolds and the rest of the police were sure hot on our trail [this was in direct contrast to the statement attributed to him in Tucson]. Just about a day behind, I guess. They almost got me once, out on Irving Park Boulevard. That was because a stool pigeon turned me up to the police. His name is Art McGinnis. I fed him and clothed him when he was broke but he squealed on me. The police found me in a doctor's office where Art had sent them. They shot at me *and I shot at them* [in view of other testimony it is doubtful that Dillinger actually said the italicized phrase] but my car was too fast and I got away.

"Those," he added with a revealing touch of nostalgia, "were exciting times. We moved from house to house, rented one, stayed a few days, and moved on when the neighborhood got too hot. But we used to go to downtown theaters whenever we wanted to. [*The Three Little Pigs* was one of Dillinger's favorite movies.] Once a detective at the Chicago theater asked us to explain why we had a certain twenty-dollar bill. It wasn't counterfeit but it was hot, from a robbed bank. So we ducked out on the detective."

One of the questioners asked how long it took Dillinger and his men to rob a bank. The reply was carelessly boastful. "Oh, about a minute and forty seconds flat."

The talkative leader blamed Makley and Clark for the mob's downfall, saying they had paid so much to have some luggage carried down when fire broke out in their Tucson hotel that the firemen who aided them became suspicious.

"If the saps had made it only a couple of bucks," Dillinger said morosely, "we'd still be safe—and happy."

As the outlaw was being questioned, deputy sheriffs with machine guns were on guard outside the jail, and other armed lawmen were stationed in the corridors. At the same time, the Chicago policemen who had served as part of the armed escort were in the jail dining room with Captain Stege, where dinner and half a barrel of beer had been provided by the hospitable Hoosier authorities.

When the interview ended, Dillinger was taken to a cell on the third floor of the old portion of the jail. Whoever wrote the story of Dillinger's arrival in the *Register* qualified as a Cassandra, first class, by setting down this statement, which later events validated in every detail: "The measures taken by Sheriff Holley to guard her noted prisoner make it almost impossible to stage an attempt to rescue him and none will be tried."

The jail was floodlit, the *Register* went on, "and in a protected corner a special police officer sits night and day with a machine gun trained on Dillinger's cell, ready to repel any attempt to liberate him."

This was a safeguard which was permitted to lapse, however, and what the sheriff and the *Register* both overlooked was the possibility of a do-it-yourself delivery. They were thinking in terms of Lima. Dillinger had other thoughts.

The precautions against a possible rescue attempt were spurred by a report from Greencastle that three carloads of armed men were on the way to Crown Point to free Dillinger. (This war party vanished, however, like the dream it probably was.) Captain Stege also made the use of extra guards—which finally reached the point where they cost $150 a day—seem reasonable when he said he had learned that members of the gang had sworn an oath to aid each other even at the risk of death. This sounded like something Leslie Homer or Ed Shouse might have "revealed," but Lieutenant Reynolds said Dillinger had told him that such an oath had been taken, and that each member of the gang also had sworn—in the event of the slaying or capture of any member—to take revenge by killing a close relative of the policeman responsible.

Back in Tucson, Opal Long and Anne Martin—still not identified as Evelyn Frechette—had been released. They arranged for bus fare out of town by claiming the deposit made with the Tucson water company. Miss "Martin" claimed her dog when she left the jail.

The rest of the prisoners—Pierpont, Clark, Makley and Mary Kinder—reached the LaSalle Street Station in Chicago on February 1. Leach had gained favor with Pierpont by permitting the gangster and his sweetheart to share a seat during much of the train journey. The four prisoners were in a special car, guarded by Leach and his troopers as well as by a railroad detective who boarded the train in New Mexico. Marie Grott, a fingerprint expert for the Indiana State Police, was along to serve as an escort for Miss Kinder, and reporter Toms was also present, and allowed to talk with the prisoners.

Toms got little that was newsworthy, however, except a statement from Pierpont that Hamilton had been fatally wounded at East Chicago and his body thrown into the Calumet River. Pierpont, too, probably by prearrangement with Dillinger, was trying to draw attention away from one of the only two important members of the gang still at large.

Captain Stege and a large group of Chicago police officers met the train, and once more there was a speedy motor trip to Indiana, this time direct to the penitentiary at Michigan City. The cavalcade moved out about 10 A.M. and took the main roads. At the outskirts of Michigan City 50 more policemen joined, bringing the total to 115, a mute but flattering comment on the respect in which the missing Hamilton and Homer Van Meter were held.

A clue to the cause of the September 26 jail break was provided by remarks made as the prisoners were being hustled through the prison gates.

"Do me a favor," said Makley to Reynolds. "Shoot me through the head so I won't have to go back in there."

Pierpont was similarly candid. "Every day for years," he said with obvious sincerity, "something has happened to make me hate the law."

Even Clark, his battered head still wrapped in bandages, joined the chorus with the statement that he hoped "to die soon." And all three criticized the administration of the prison, saying they would not have broken out had the treatment been better.

Such attitudes, of course, did nothing to enhance the regard in which prison officials held them, and each of the returning inmates was placed without outer clothing in solitary confinement on bread and water while it was being decided where they would be sent.

Before this, however, they were questioned by Captain Leach, Lieutenant Reynolds and Warden Kunkel. Among the questions asked was one about reports that the gang had paid a thousand dollars weekly for "protection" while they were in Chicago during November and December. Whatever their answer, it was not revealed in the public prints.

Another visitor to Michigan City was Huntington, who on other occasions had found Makley willing to make a deal. Huntington came February 7, and found Makley so angry because of the ambush attempt against Dillinger at Dr. Eye's office that he flatly refused to consider any sort of trade. He told Huntington that he had not been in on the Greencastle job, but that he didn't really care whether he went to Ohio to face a murder charge or remained in Indiana. He added that he and Pierpont had had Huntington under observation in Indianapolis one night after Dillinger's escape from Lima, and that his only regret was that they hadn't killed the detective.

Huntington next made a fruitless journey to Crown Point, where Dillinger said only that all the Greencastle bonds except those with coupons had been burned, a statement Huntington knew to be untrue. Dillinger then walked away from his questioners.

Three days later Pierpont, Clark and Makley signed waivers which would permit their removal to Ohio, and Huntington hastened to confer with Putnam County authorities in an attempt to keep at least Makley, Clark and Copeland in Indiana for trial for the Greencastle holdup. Huntington warned that if they were sent to Ohio it was possible that the money seized in Tucson would be returned to them, which would permit them to finance a long legal fight during which some of their comrades might once more crack the Lima jail.

Warrants for the three, plus Ed Shouse and Copeland, were sent to Michigan City. But only Copeland was handed to the Putnam County authorities. The rest went to Ohio.

Despite the almost clean sweep at Tucson, which virtually wiped out the Dillinger gang, the rumors of an imminent attempt to free Dillinger persisted. As a result, in spite of the insurance provided by the extra guards, Sheriff Holley, a conscientious official, sat up until the small hours virtually every morning, even as she was insisting that there was no chance whatever that Dillinger could be snatched from her grasp.

The first thing Dillinger did the morning after reaching Crown Point was to ask that a telephone message be sent to Attorney Louis Piquett of Chicago, a man Dillinger seems not to have known except by reputation. It is probable that Dillinger had read of Piquett when the latter was defending Leo Brothers, who was tried for the shooting of Jake Lingle, *Chicago Tribune* reporter.

Jail officials left word for Piquett, who returned the call, then came down to confer with Dillinger. The fifty-three-year-old Piquett had been a lead miner in Platteville, Wisconsin, and later a Chicago bartender. But he studied law at night and was admitted to a different kind of bar in 1916 when he was twenty-six. Piquett was prosecuting attorney from 1920 through 1924, then went into private practice. His courtroom eloquence quickly earned him a reputation as a spellbinder.

After conferring with Dillinger and—those close to Piquett say—checking various sources in Florida, Piquett announced that Dillinger's defense would be a simple one: an ironclad alibi proving that he was in Florida on January 14 and could not have held up the East Chicago bank on the fifteenth. Piquett's pronouncement of his client's innocence was made despite the identification of Dillinger on January 31 by a score of witnesses to the shooting.

Dillinger's father, told of the Tucson arrests, said, "I'm glad he's alive. I've been haunted by the thought of having to bury my boy in frozen ground."

He said he couldn't go at once to Crown Point, because he had no clean shirts. But he showed up February 1, after having gone to Indianapolis en route to hire Attorney Joseph Ryan to represent his son. During his father's visit, the outlaw seemed ill at ease. The older man said John apologized for the notoriety he was bringing his father—and borrowed ten dollars.

The gangster was arraigned February 5 before Judge William J. Murray after proper precautions had been taken, including the posting of fifty guards. Before the hearing all two hundred spectators were cleared from the courtroom, searched, then readmitted. Dillinger was brought in handcuffed to Carroll Holley, who wore a bulletproof vest. The prisoner seemed sullen as he and Holley stood, still manacled, before the bench.

Some onlookers thought Dillinger scowled, tightened his lips, and looked tough when the flashlights went off, signaling that photographs were being taken, then relaxed into dejection again when the cameras stopped clicking.

After the preliminary hearing, the arraignment was postponed to February 9, when an additional hearing was scheduled on the writ of habeas corpus sought by Piquett and Ryan. The petition for the writ declared that Dillinger was "a law-abiding resident of Arizona who had committed no crimes in that state."

The February 9 hearing was a stormy one. Dillinger again was manacled when brought into the courtroom, although the cuffs were ordered removed when his attorneys protested. Trial was finally set for March 12 despite violent protests by defense attorneys, who asked for a four-month delay to permit finding and transporting witnesses from Florida and preparation of the case. The state declared that ten days was sufficient. (When Estill suggested that ten days was long enough for the defense to prepare its case, Piquett came to his feet shouting, "That would be legal murder! There's a law against lynching in this state!" Estill, however, had the last word. "There's a law against murder, too.") The bickering was halted by Murray's gavel. Murray finally allowed a month.

Judge Murray refused Attorney Piquett's plea that Sheriff Holley be ordered to give Dillinger one visiting day weekly, and Dillinger stood mute when the murder indictment was read. An automatic plea of not guilty then was entered, and Dillinger was taken back to his cell.

Judge T. Joseph Sullivan, sitting in the same courtroom, overruled a petition for the writ of habeas corpus, ruling that the extradition of Dillinger from Arizona had been legal. It seemed as though there were nothing left for Dillinger to do but sit quietly in his cell whittling, as he had begun to do, to pass the time until his trial began.

Two of the arresting officers from Tucson, in town to testify, said at the hearing that in their opinion a "regiment" of gangsters couldn't break into the jail and free Dillinger.

But even though it seemed impossible that Dillinger could be freed from his Crown Point cell, Prosecutor Estill, uneasy at the thought of losing the outlaw as Lima had lost him, asked Judge Murray on February 10 to order the prisoner transferred to the more modern penitentiary at Michigan City. The jurist said he felt that Dillinger was adequately guarded and that "a hundred men" couldn't take him out of the jail. Murray also explained that the law did not permit him to transfer a prisoner unless there were a threat of mob violence, which in this case did not exist.

One reason for the expressed confidence that Dillinger could not escape may have been that the guards outside the jail remained impressively alert. The *Register* reported that a car with Illinois license plates had been seen circling the jail, and that when it stopped for the traffic light on Main Street, two of the special guards stepped up and asked the driver his name, address and business. A check of these showed that he was, as he claimed, only a sightseer. A day or so later a news photographer paused behind the jail long enough to take a quick picture. He was halted a block away and politely asked to return to the sheriff's office. There his identity was established by a telephone call to Chicago, but Warden Baker confiscated the exposed film, promising to return it when the trial was over.

Though trivial, these incidents indicated how closely the jail was guarded against any attempt to break in. To no one but Dillinger, apparently, did it occur that the break could come from the inside, and that it could be a solo one.

There was a court hearing in Lima, too, where on February 17 Pierpont, Clark and Makley entered not guilty pleas to charges of murdering Sheriff Sarber. On the same day Hilton Crouch pleaded guilty to taking part in the Massachusetts Avenue Bank robbery and was sent to prison for twenty years. Mary Kinder had better luck. The state was unable to prove its case and she was freed by Judge

Frank P. Baker, with a stern warning. Miss Kinder told newsmen she still loved Pierpont, but was afraid to visit him for fear of arrest.

By this time Dillinger had been transferred to a cell with three other prisoners. He was permitted to play cards and have magazines and books, but no newspapers. Someone sent him a Bible, and he was allowed to receive mail, which the sheriff read first; he heard from his father and sister, to whom he also wrote. His outgoing mail was censored.

Dillinger acted like any ordinary prisoner, making no trouble and no demands, and ate the regular jail food. Among his visitors was Police Chief Jerome Fraker of Valparaiso, a huge 6-foot-5-inch man of dark complexion. During their conversation Dillinger told him that the preceding fall while Fraker was directing traffic around a dead horse on the highway, one of the passing cars held Dillinger and others of his gang.

"You big Indian," Dillinger said, laughing, "you don't know how lucky you were, or how many guns were trained on you."

Sheriff Holley had tried to bar visitors completely, including Piquett, but Judge Murray ordered that the attorney be admitted and allowed to talk to Dillinger in private. All his other visitors were forced to speak through the bars of his cell, and these talks were listened to by one of the guards. Piquett was refused permission to bring a witness into the jail who supposedly could identify Dillinger as having been in Florida January 14, but who actually was a state police informant who had ingratiated himself with Piquett.

"If your man can identify Dillinger now," Carroll Holley told Piquett, "he can identify him when the trial is called. He cannot visit him now without an order from the court."

The order was forthcoming since Judge Murray knew the man's identity. All visitors were searched and brought into the jail by way of the elevated bridge from the adjoining courthouse.

Piquett visited Dillinger four or five times during February, bringing Evelyn Frechette along on February 26, when she chatted with the prisoner for half an hour. Sheriff Holley personally searched Miss Frechette, however, before permitting her to see Dillinger. On this day, too, Piquett gave some details of the elaborate alibi he was building in his effort to free Dillinger from the murder charge. The attorney said that "five or six" Florida residents would testify that Dillinger had been living in Daytona Beach as late as January 14, along with Miss Frechette, Miss Kinder, Pierpont, Clark and Makley. Piquett also told Estill that he had found three residents of Hobart, Indiana, who were prepared to swear that Dillinger was not the machine gunner who had killed O'Malley.

Impressive as this array of alibi witnesses may sound, Dillinger apparently was not convinced that their testimony would be sufficient to outweigh the even larger number prepared to swear that he was the machine gunner. So on March 3, a Saturday morning, he strolled out of the supposedly breakproof jail and left town.

The escape was made through the persuasive power of what may have been a genuine pistol, somehow smuggled in to him, or, as Dillinger gleefully announced just before leaving the premises, with a wooden gun, fashioned from a washboard during his seemingly aimless whittling sessions, colored with shoe blacking, and tricked out with pieces from a safety razor to look like the genuine article.

Dillinger made his move about 9:15 A.M., as Don Sarber and a delegation from Lima were nearing Crown Point with plans to take a deposition from Dillinger about the Lima delivery and the fatal shooting of Sarber senior. Dillinger and fourteen other prisoners were in the exercise bullpen on the second floor in the rear of the building. Sam Cahoon, a sixty-four-year-old repairman and turnkey, who earned fifty dollars a month working in the same jail in which he had served several terms for intoxication in other years, walked into the bullpen with two jail porters, as he had done many times before, carrying soap for the Saturday night baths, and other supplies.

As he stepped into the passageway, Dillinger thrust what appeared to be an automatic pistol into his side and said, "Get inside quick or I'll kill you."

The outlaw told Cahoon to summon Warden Baker, but the turnkey bravely refused. Dillinger forced Cahoon and the porters into one of the cells. He inquired how many doors there were between him and the outdoors, and then walked a few steps toward the center of the building. Peering cautiously down the corridor, he saw Ernest Blunk, the fingerprint expert, walk by the end of it. At Dillinger's insistence Cahoon went to the foot of the stairs leading to the old jail and called Blunk, as Dillinger watched from hiding.

Blunk came and found himself peering down the barrel of what looked to him "like a .45." Dillinger then forced Blunk to call

Warden Baker, who came on the run. He was ambushed by Dillinger from the rear and ushered into the cell with the others.

Dillinger then asked Herbert Youngblood, an accused murderer, and Harry Jelinek, awaiting trial for robbery, if they would care to come along. Youngblood said he would. Blunk summoned Deputies Kenneth Houk, eighty-four-year-old Matt Brown, and Marshall Keithley, one by one. Each time Blunk went to call another guard, Dillinger followed to the middle of the corridor and stood out of sight with his gun pointing at Blunk's back.

All who answered Blunk's summons came unarmed, because jail rules quite properly forbade the guards to bring weapons into the cell area. Houk, a special deputy, had been posted in a small room near one of the building entrances when Blunk called. Houk walked into the corridor leading to the quarters where Dillinger was supposedly locked up, and as he stepped through the door saw Dillinger standing on his left.

"What are you doing here, John?" Houk demanded, reaching for the blackjack in his hip pocket.

Dillinger shook his head warningly. "Don't do it," he snapped. "I don't want to kill you, but I'm getting out of here no matter what happens."

Houk then noticed, he says, that Dillinger was holding a .38 automatic, and whatever thought the deputy had of making a fight for it vanished completely when he suddenly realized that another prisoner, Herbert Youngblood, was standing at the right of the doorway with a sturdy mop handle in his hand.

There should have been no chance, up to this point, for Dillinger to have obtained a weapon from any of the guards, who were weaponless. But Houk insists Dillinger was armed with a real gun.

"When I hear people say he got out with a wooden gun," Houk says, "I get so mad I could spit. You look down the barrel of one and you know the difference between a wooden gun and a good one. There's a difference between metal and wood covered with shoe blacking."

Whether the gun was real or imitation (and the argument still survives in Crown Point), Houk joined the others. Soon five of the guards or deputies, the warden, and thirteen prisoners were locked in adjoining cells. Dillinger and Youngblood then forced Blunk to lead them downstairs.

"He later told me he was carrying a dummy wooden gun that he had carved out of a washboard with a safety razor and painted with black shoe polish," Blunk explained when it was all over. "I didn't know it was a dummy then and it was the best imitation of a gun I ever saw.

"As far as I know, Dillinger never obtained a real gun until he made his first trip to the outer room. He made me go ahead of him, down the old jail corridor and into the receiving room. Here he made me have the turnkey open the doors. He forced the turnkey to go into the office room outside and stand facing the wall with his hands up. Then Warden Hiles, a National Guardsman, came in.

"Dillinger took his .45 automatic. This was the first real gun he got, as far as I can recall. Then he went into the office and grabbed two machine guns lying on the sill of the window." (One of these, incidentally, had been borrowed to help guard Dillinger.)

Dillinger herded his two new captives upstairs and locked them in, took up a collection from the guards, which netted fifteen dollars, and just before leaving rapped on the bars with one of the guns he was carrying, laughed, and reportedly said, "I did it all with my little toy pistol."

With Blunk again leading the way, Dillinger and Youngblood left the building by way of the kitchen, where the outlaw put on a hat and raincoat belonging to Cahoon, which he spotted hanging on the wall. Dillinger refused Blunk's request that he be allowed to get a hat and coat, saying, "If things work out, you'll be in a warm climate so soon you won't need an overcoat."

The trio walked through the yard to the combination garage and laundry in the rear, beneath the new addition. When they entered the garage, they found Mrs. Mary Linton, Baker's mother-in-law, who had just returned from a trip with one of the bailiffs. The gunmen tried to start two of the cars, but couldn't find the keys. So Dillinger ordered Mrs. Linton and some other jail employees into the laundry room.

At this juncture, Mrs. Baker walked in looking for her mother and saw Dillinger.

"My God," Mrs. Baker said, "you're John Dillinger!"

"Right," Dillinger said crisply. "You do as I tell you."

His voice was harsh and Mrs. Baker became hysterical. Dillinger put her into the laundry room with the others. Then, leaving Youngblood on guard, he coolly returned to the main building and went back upstairs to see whether Cahoon or Baker had keys to the cars. Neither did, and Dillinger asked Blunk where the nearest public garage was. Blunk told him it was just north of the courthouse, two doors from the jail.

The three then walked behind the jail and into the back door of the Main Street Garage. Edwin Saager, a mechanic, was working with his head under the hood of a car, and Robert Volk, a young post office employee who had just come in to park a mail truck, was standing with one foot on the bumper chatting with Saager. Volk had a gun belt, with a .45 in the holster, slung across his shoulder.

Neither paid any attention to the three men who walked in the back door until Dillinger asked Saager which was the fastest car in the place. Saager, who thought Dillinger was a special deputy, indicated one of the sheriff's cars, a black V-8 with a red headlight and siren, which was standing on the south side of the door, facing out.

"Let's get going," Dillinger said brusquely.

Despite the machine gun, neither Saager nor Volk realized at first that they were in the middle of a jail break.

"The man was carrying a machine gun," Volk says, "but I thought nothing of it. There were a lot of guns around in those days. Then he hit Saager on the leg with the gun. Saager said, 'I can't go. I'm working on a car.' Then I looked up and saw the Negro [Young-blood] with the tommy gun, although he never raised it. Blunk, standing behind them, said, 'Yeah, come along with us.' He looked kind of white around the gills. Dillinger told Blunk to drive and Saager to sit in the back seat. Blunk started the motor. Dillinger got in with his tommy gun by the window and I ducked behind a car. Saager got into the car and it started away and I thought, 'That's Dillinger!' And I froze. I don't think he ever seen my gun, or maybe he played it cool."

The car pulled out of the garage, narrowly missing a passing motorist, and headed north on Main Street. Blunk, perhaps deliberately, ran through one red light, and as they passed the First National and Commercial Banks, Dillinger, who seemed amazingly relaxed, said he would be tempted to stop and hold them up if he knew the whereabouts of a couple of key deputies—ones he seemed to respect.

"Dillinger began asking about highways," Blunk said later. "He wanted to turn west on State Route 8, but I was past it, so we turned on the macadam road just north of the Pennsylvania Railroad tracks on the edge of town. Dillinger was as cool as could be. He hummed and whistled 'The Last Roundup.' As we were driving away from Crown Point he showed me a dummy gun and said, 'You wouldn't think a guy could make a break with a peashooter like this, would you?' Then he laughed. I looked at it, but I couldn't see much but the machine gun. Every time we hit a bump the barrel of the machine gun bumped me in the side."

As soon as the stolen car vanished up the street, Volk ran to the telephone and called the Gary police to report the escape. He then darted next door to the prosecutor's office, where numerous special guards were posted to await a possible attack on the jail. He told someone, "Dillinger escaped!"

"You're nuts," was the skeptical reply. "You want us to lock you up?"

The frustrated Volk then hastened to the jail and pressed the door button. Nothing happened. Then someone opened a window in Sheriff Holley's quarters and called down, "We're locked out!"

At this point Floyd Vance, deputy prosecutor, walked up and Volk told him, "Dillinger escaped."

"Is that right?" Vance said. He and Volk then tried to get into the jail.

Inside the jail Sheriff Holley was told of the escape by John Hudak, a trusty, and quickly notified the state police. She called the escape "too ridiculous for words."

"Dillinger took one chance in a million," she later told newsmen, "and all the breaks were with him and against me. Ordinarily I would have walked out of this room into the jail just about at that time. In the six weeks he's been here, though, I have been on the job until 3 A.M., and haven't tried to sleep until 4 A.M. At 5 A.M. I had gotten to sleep. I was dressing when a trusty ran into my room with a shotgun and said, 'Dillinger's out!' I thought he had gone mad. Then I saw he hadn't. He said, 'Have you got a gun there? I can't shoot with this thing.' I handed him my pistol and said, 'Kill him.' But they had gone. . . . How this could have happened I don't quite see."

Asked whether she had been correctly quoted in another paper as having said that she now realized the job was too big for a woman, she retorted, "Oh, hell's fire, of course not."

Houk later said of Dillinger's manner, "I never heard him cuss or be abusive in any way, shape or fashion. The morning he came out he was tough, but not the tough 'killer' type. He would have killed if his life had been at stake, but as far as being a deliberate killer, I can't believe John Dillinger was that way. I'm skeptical as to whether they ever would have found him guilty of that East Chicago charge. I asked him about it a couple of times and he said, 'I wasn't there, but I got some of the money.' I don't believe the man *was* there."

Carroll Holley had a similar impression of the outlaw. "He'd give up if cornered, and you'd better give up if he had you cornered. But there were twenty in the jail I'd less rather have dealt with than Dillinger."

The escape car was leaving the vicinity of Crown Point at a steady and purposely inconspicuous pace. Dillinger told Blunk, "Take your time. Take your time. Thirty miles an hour is enough. There's no hurry."

Blunk later said he tried at one point to sideswipe a passing car but was warned by Dillinger that he would be shot if he tried it again.

Dillinger ordered Blunk to turn at virtually every corner, and to stick to gravel roads. The only town they passed through was St. John, and Dillinger seemed worried only when they approached the town, which was on Route 41. It was a natural spot for a roadblock. At one point he asked if there was anything on the vehicle to identify it as a police car. Saager said only the red light, and Dillinger ordered Blunk to stop until the give-away light was torn off. Saager said Dillinger also asked how he and Blunk would "like to go to Ohio to get those other guys out." Neither man answered, apparently considering the question rhetorical.

At Lilley Corners, a few miles east of Peotone, Illinois, the car skidded and went into the ditch. This clearly was an accident, and Dillinger remained calm. He simply asked if there were chains, and when Saager said yes, told him to put them on.

"It was the first time in my life I ever put chains on without jacking the car up," Saager said, "but I did her. There was water in the ditch. Youngblood stayed in the car but Dillinger got out in the muddy road with the machine gun. It took half an hour to put two chains on the rear wheels, then we walked right out as Youngblood helped to push." Dillinger seemed unworried by the delay, saying, "What's time to me?"

"We went on the Peotone road about two miles," Saager continued, "and Dillinger said, 'There ain't no telephone along here. It's a good place to let you guys out.' So we got out and he shook hands with us and he handed me four dollars for 'carfare.'

" 'I'd give you more,' he said, 'but I only got fifteen dollars. But I'll remember you at Christmas.' Then Dillinger slipped behind the wheel and told Youngblood to lie down in the back, and they took off south."

Blunk and Saager had not walked very far when they were picked up by a passing farmer, who took them to Peotone. There they spread the alarm. They also borrowed a police car, and, accompanied by the farmer, went back to try to find Dillinger. For a while they followed the marks of the chains, then lost them and gave up.

"We went back to town, called Sheriff Holley, and spent a little of the money for a cup of coffee," Saager said. "I don't know what we would have done if we'd caught up with them anyway.

"I never saw him again," Saager went on. "They got him before Christmas. I was hoping they wouldn't. I thought he'd come through. He seemed like an honest fellow."

TWELVE

●●●●●●●●●●●● **"FROM WHAT I HEAR, I'M SURPRISED
DILLINGER DIDN'T SERVE TEA TO THE
GUARDS BEFORE HE WENT AWAY."
—PROSECUTOR ROBERT ESTILL**

John Dillinger's flamboyant departure from the Crown Point jail
became immediate headline news across the world, and jarred loose
an avalanche of spoken and written comment.

Some of the criticism was politically inspired. The Indiana and
Lake County governments were Democratic, a fact the Republicans
pointed out loudly and happily; but most of the attacks were honest
and justified. Other comments were in a humorous vein, some
malicious, some merely jocular. And, of course, word of the escape
brought comfort to those who knew Dillinger and loved him, or
who expected something from him.

The elder Dillinger heard the news in Mooresville with a sort of
uneasy relief. "It makes a fellow feel a little better," he said, "but of
course they may catch him. . . . Guess I'll start listening to the radio
again now. When he was out before, that's about all I did when I
wasn't working."

Mary Kinder was at home with her sister, Mrs. Behrens, when she learned about it from a reporter who called for an interview. Mrs. Behrens shouted an uninhibited "Hurrah!" But Mary, admonishing her sister, showed only a discreet delight. She was obviously gratified that no one could tie her in with the incident, as they had tried to do after the Michigan City escape.

"Whew, I'm glad I'm home!" she said.

She later held a press conference in the office of Attorney Jessie Levy to let the world know just how fortunate she had been.

"A state cop was at the same dance that I attended last night," she told reporters. "I kind of bawled him out and accused him of having been sent to keep an eye on me. He told me he wasn't, but I knew better, and it made me angry then. But, gee, I'm glad he was there, now. If he hadn't been there a lot of persons would have said I helped engineer Johnnie's escape from Crown Point."

In Washington, J. Edgar Hoover, chief of the Federal Bureau of Investigation, called the incident "a damnable outrage" and added, "Someone is guilty either of nonfeasance or malfeasance. Either negligence or corruption must be at the bottom of this. That is true of nearly all jail breaks. Escape from a good jail is impossible if the jail authorities are both diligent and honest."

Colonel Henry Barrett Chamberlin, operating director of the Chicago Crime Commission, reported that he was "speechless." But he managed a few words anyway: "It's just one of those impossible—why, I'm speechless! The idea of a man with a record like his getting away! There should have been a competent, trustworthy, proven guard assigned to watch Dillinger day and night. I can't understand it!"

Acting Chief Justice Donald S. McKinlay of the Criminal Court in Chicago spoke with judicial sternness: "There is too much sentimentalism in the country in regard to criminals, and it has permeated jails and penitentiaries. This may have something to do with the successful escapes that are all too common. [*Thirty convicts had escaped from Indiana prisons since the preceding May.*] The graft and corruption existing in many quarters probably also enters into the picture."

A holier-than-thou attitude, curious in view of Chicago's gaudy crime picture, was adopted by Mayor Edward J. Kelly. "I'm sick about it," he said. "It couldn't have happened here."

The Crown Point guards were singled out by H. C. W. Laubenheimer, United States marshal in Chicago, who declared, "This thing is absolutely incredible. There's something wrong with those guards. Even at the risk of their lives they should have prevented his escape. Apparently they didn't take the chance that every officer of the law is expected to take as part of his job."

Clarence Marley, the Mooresville justice of the peace who had ordered Dillinger held for trial in the Morgan holdup ten years before, posted a notice on the city hall bulletin board, which read:

JOHNNY ISN'T WITH THEM ANY MORE.

One news account spoke of the "half-comic exploit of Dillinger in taking complete possession of the fortress-like prison" and described his escape as "typically Dillinger like. It was marked by desperate courage, unhurried precision, and an occasional laugh for punctuation."

The Crown Point *Register,* in an editorial a few days after the event, said, "It takes a hard-boiled Republican to suggest that Lake County Democrats adopt a hand-carved wooden pistol as a party emblem in place of the time honored donkey. That is rubbing things in a little too much." A week later the *Register* reported with obvious glee that a letter mailed in California to "Harry Meyers, Wooden Gun, Indiana" had been delivered without delay.

There were also published suggestions that the name of Crown Point be changed to "Clown Point" or "Dillinger," and at a Republican dinner in Indianapolis wooden pistols were given as favors.

Sermons were preached about Crown Point, and *The Literary Digest* took occasion to suggest that such an escapade need not be wasted: "As an object lesson of scandalous futility or corruption or the two in combination," said the *Digest* editorially, "nothing more stinging than the Dillinger escape could have been invented by the greatest satiric genius bent on lashing the nation into sweeping reforms in the handling of its crime situation."

That portion of the public which writes letters to the papers was largely pro-Dillinger or at least anti-authority. One writer said:

These politicians can sit in a nice little office every day, and make comments about a fellow who does get caught doing something in the open when they sit around plotting to keep the people from finding out what they really are.

A certain Mr. Hoover called Dillinger a rat. What does he mean by that? At least Dillinger is a gentleman. Could we say the same about you? We would like to see you serve some time. Perhaps your attitude on life would be different.

Governor McNutt, why not give Dillinger a gold medal and a pardon? He deserves both. Hurray, for you, John. May you never be caught!

A similar letter, signed "A Group of Citizens," began:

We say hurray! Hurray for John Dillinger. Myself and everyone I have come into contact with would love to shake his hand. He is really a man Indiana should be proud to know. He has brains, and if Governor McNutt and all the politicians who are so against him would give him a chance for freedom and give him a chance to live without being afraid of the law every time he turns around, he probably would make a good citizen.

A few more sensible writers, of course, criticized the gangster, deplored his criminal activities, and blamed the press for its share in creating the "legend" of Dillinger. But these were in the minority.

Investigations of the jail break were ordered by Sheriff Holley, Governor McNutt, Prosecutor Estill, Judge Murray, County Commissioner Charles Baran, and the East Chicago chapter of the Fraternal Order of Police. The Lake County Protective Association also talked of a probe, and the *Register* said wryly, "About all that is now needed to make the list complete is for Congress and the League of Women Voters to launch an inquiry."

The *Register*, however, in a less playful moment, did offer a sound analysis of how Dillinger could have succeeded in his escape attempt, assuming it *was* made with a wooden gun. Publicity increased his chance for freedom, said the paper, "because it served to build up an unwholesome fear of him and made his toy pistol a dangerous weapon. What would have been just a prank in the hands of an ordinary prisoner helped to bring an instant compliance to Dillinger's commands."

It seems unbelievable that Dillinger and Youngblood could have reached Chicago without being apprehended, but it must be remembered that in those less organized times there was no widespread radio system through which the police could direct the swift weaving of a car-tight network of roadblocks. In fact, the Indiana State Police post at Tremont, 25 miles from Crown Point, was notified of the escape by state police headquarters in Indianapolis—which reportedly learned from the local newspapers that Dillinger was loose! Also, there was some confusion among those searching for the stolen car and the two fugitives, since Crown Point officials gave out a wrong license number because of a mixup at the garage. Even so, a Chicago detective, Lorimer Hyde, said he spotted and lost the hunted car twice during the afternoon. And there is no doubt that Dillinger was in town on March 3.

Attorney Piquett received a telephone call about 9:45 A.M., while Evelyn Frechette was in his office, telling him of the escape. Miss Frechette, who during a visit to Dillinger at Crown Point had told him that she planned to rent a room at 901 West Madison Street, had not yet done so. She promptly went out and rented the room.

Piquett talked with Dillinger for a minute or two about four o'clock that afternoon, in a car on Belmont Avenue, as Youngblood crouched in the rear seat. The lawyer also met his much-sought-after client again about 8 P.M., after Dillinger had separated from Youngblood and—Piquett said—picked up Miss Frechette and another woman. This meeting was on Halsted Street half a block from the Town Hall police station.

"I told him," Piquett later insisted, "that it was impossible for him to defeat the law. I told him it was my duty to advise him to surrender, and let me take him to Town Hall station. He said he would do it later."

Piquett also said that Dillinger displayed a wooden gun and said he had used it during the jail break.

Ira McDowell, acting commissioner of Chicago police, had issued an out-of-bounds warning to the Hoosier desperado shortly after the escape, saying, "If Dillinger sticks his head inside Chicago he will be shot at first sight. Those are my orders."

Dillinger either failed to hear this threat or was unimpressed, or perhaps he figured the same fate awaited him anywhere he went, since Assistant U.S. Attorney General Joseph Keenan, director of the criminal branch of the Justice Department, had repeated McDowell's word in slightly more veiled form: "I don't know when or where we will get Dillinger, but we will get him—and I hope we get him under such circumstances that the government will not have to stand the expense of a trial!"

The day after Dillinger's escape the search for him was widened to include Missouri, Ohio, New York, Oklahoma, and Arizona, even though it was known that the stolen car carried fuel enough for only 100 miles, and there had been no reports that the fugitives had stopped for gas. Dillinger also was "seen" in New Stark, Ohio, not far from Lima.

It was reported that Pierpont, Clark and Makley, who had been lounging in their cells in pajamas, changed into street clothes "and seemed far more cheerful" after hearing a broadcast account of Dillinger's feat. The Lima jail was fortified hurriedly with sandbag barricades—manned by National Guardsmen—which were thrown up outside the entrance to the sheriff's residence in case an attempt should be made to rush the front door.

But the hunt narrowed again after the getaway car was found Monday afternoon, March 5, in front of 1057 Ardmore, on Chicago's North Side. The police posted a discreet guard, but no one was seen to leave the building, nor did anyone come back for the car.

It seems probable that by the time the car was discovered, Dillinger and Miss Frechette were long gone on their way to St. Paul, which was a favorite sanctuary for the hunted because of the strange immunity from arrest possessed by out-of-town criminals who behaved themselves while there.

(An "inside source" insisted that Dillinger left Chicago Saturday night, after obtaining a change of clothes and $1,500, and that he was traveling with another man and two women. The man probably was Hamilton. Miss Frechette herself later declared that she waited for Dillinger the night of March 3 on a corner near the Madison Street address but that he failed to show up until March 4. They had driven to St. Paul, she said, where he had immediately left her to do an errand. When he returned, he had money, and they rented an apartment in Minneapolis.)

In St. Paul, Dillinger made fast connections with such accomplished professionals as Lester Gillis, better known as Baby Face Nelson, and Tommy Carroll, Eddie Green, and Van Meter. The new organization wasted little time; three days after Dillinger's escape from Crown Point, they declared a dividend.

At 9:50 on the morning of March 6—the same day the selection of a jury was begun in Lima to try Harry Pierpont for murder—six men struck the Security National Bank in Sioux Falls, South Dakota. Their getaway car was a new Packard, stolen two days before from a St. Paul dealer. Two of the gang remained outside and four entered the bank, three of them carrying submachine guns. The alarm was sounded at once, which enraged one of the invaders, who yelled menacingly, "I'd like to know who the hell set that alarm off!"

The ringing of the alarm may have annoyed the mob, but it did nothing to impair the efficiency with which they conducted the robbery. The cash drawers and vault were looted quickly by one man, while a second guarded the rear of the bank and a third was stationed at the front door. The fourth—described as about 5 feet four and young-looking—stood on a marble-topped counter near the Ninth Street window. When he saw motorcycle policeman Hale Keith running on the sidewalk next to the bank, the bandit with the youthful face poured through the glass a burst of machine-gun fire that sent Keith sprawling with four bullet wounds.

The diminutive gunner, probably Baby Face Nelson, was delighted. "I got one! I got one!" he shouted gleefully.

A handful of customers in the bank when the bandits entered, or who had come in while the raid was in progress, were lined up in the middle of the lobby, along with the employees. Fred Anderson, a teller, was ordered to unlock the door leading to the teller's quarters, which he did after one of the gang kicked him to hurry him up. Dillinger then walked coolly in and out of the cages, collecting the money.

While the stickup was in progress, Gus J. Moen, a former bank president from Canton, came down from an upper floor and walked through the bank on his way out. One of the bandits ordered him to halt, but Moen didn't hear the command. As the door swung behind him, an inside gunner fired high, showering the unsuspecting Moen with broken glass. Outside, menaced by another of the gang, he dropped his briefcase and lined up with some other captives.

A number of police officers were on the scene, but none managed to interfere with the holdup. Patrolman Homer Powers, on duty at the corner of Ninth and Main, was immobilized at once by one of the lookouts, as were Chief M. W. Parsons and Detective F. C. White, who had been sent to the bank without knowing that a robbery was in progress. Parsons was forced to surrender his revolver, and Patrolman Peter Duffy, in the bank when the gang arrived, was struck and knocked down.

A fingerprint expert, Roy Donahue, arrived next and was added to the bag, which also included a couple of citizens who got too close to the action. Sheriff Melvin L. Sells showed up with a riot gun and a submachine gun. He was afraid to shoot for fear of hitting someone in the growing throng of bystanders, who numbered a thousand before the holdup ended. Sells hurried into the Lincoln Hotel, near the bank, intending to find a vantage point at a second-story window and snipe from there. But the bandits left while he was still in the lobby.

The four inside bandits came out with $46,000 and a group of hostages, and fired a burst or two into the air to serve notice that they were ready for trouble. Five of the hostages—Leo Olson (the teller), Emma Knabach, Mary Lucas, Mrs. Alice Blegen and Mrs. Mildred Bostwick—were forced to walk a block south, then stand on the running board of the Packard, which the gangsters decided to take after arguing briefly about its steaming radiator.

As the gang car passed Barnett's Laundry, Patrolman Harley Chrisman, who had run into Maxwell's Hardware Store and picked up a rifle during the excitement, fired a single bullet into the front of the Packard, but failed to halt it. The bandits began tossing roofing nails out of the car before they left town, and stopped near Radio Station WNAX on Minnesota Avenue to drop Olson off with a curt "Goodbye, Shorty, we don't need you any more." The women were told to get into the car at this point, presumably because they had been complaining of the cold.

Shortly thereafter the Packard began to show signs of trouble, and at the same time a couple of pursuing cars, carrying Sells, Chrisman, Deputy U.S. Marshal Art Anderson, and Deputy Sheriff Lawrence Green, began to gain. Shots were exchanged. Suddenly the Packard stopped and everyone got out. The women were ordered to stand near the gangsters, who fired some machine-gun bursts in the direction of the pursuers. The latter gave up the chase. The Packard was then abandoned slantwise across the road, and a Dodge sedan taken at gunpoint from a passing farmer. The gang drove off in this, leaving the women behind.

The Packard was spotted four miles south of Sioux Falls by a pair of light planes sent aloft to find the fugitives, but the Dodge crossed into Iowa without any further pursuit, then reportedly headed north into Minnesota near Luverne, apparently running for the friendly confines of St. Paul.

While Sioux Falls buzzed with talk about the holdup, there was new excitement in Crown Point, where Blunk and Cahoon were arrested and charged with having aided the Dillinger escape, an accusation which failed to hold up in court a short while later.

This dual action caught the roving eye of Will Rogers, and his syndicated column for March 8 said, "See where they caught two of the guards that got out of jail with Dillinger. They had him surrounded in Chicago, but he robbed a bank in Sioux Falls that day. So they was right on his trail. Just three states behind."

The Federal Bureau of Investigation was now officially looking for Dillinger. Although it had been aiding local authorities as much as possible even before this, on March 7 G-man Melvin Purvis obtained a warrant charging Dillinger and Youngblood with violation of the Dyer Act for transporting the car taken from the Main Street Garage across the Indiana-Illinois line.

Whether Dillinger was in St. Paul or Chicago immediately after the Sioux Falls holdup seems up for grabs. On March 7 a gas station attendant at 73d and Stony Island, on Chicago's South Side, reported that a man he recognized as Dillinger, and several others, had driven into the station in a gray sedan, and that Dillinger—if it was he—got out, dragging a foot as though hurt, and asked to wash up.

When he removed his coat to do so, the man revealed two shoulder holsters and a cartridge belt, or so the attendant, E. H. Deacon, later told police. Deacon promptly tried to hide his money changer, but the gunman reassured him by saying, "Never mind, I don't want your dough. Don't you know me?" Deacon said he did not, and the other replied, "Well, you'd better not!"

The stranger finished washing and left the station, turning to add, "You can tell your friends I gave those Indiana cops a good fooling." Deacon watched the gunman walk to his car, where he turned once more to warn, "Don't follow me, you___, or I'll shoot the hell out of you."

At police headquarters Deacon chose a picture of Dillinger without hesitation. The following day officials gave added credence to his story when several callers reported having seen Dillinger driving speedily past the Southmoor Hotel, at 67th and Stony.

Further evidence that Dillinger may indeed have returned to Chicago from Sioux Falls came the night of March 9 when he was identified as one of several gunmen—again in a gray sedan—who stole a 12-cylinder Lincoln from in front of 2440 Lake Shore Drive, on the near North Side, and forced the chauffeur to ride along to Clark and Orchard, a few blocks distant, where he was put out after being told to hand over his chauffeur's cap. Later that same night Chief of Police Robert Christian of Schiller Park, in the west suburbs, exchanged shots with occupants of two speeding sedans, one of which was believed to be the stolen Lincoln. Christian prudently gave up the chase when his own car was slashed by machine-gun bullets.

Whether Chief Christian was dueling with Dillinger or not, the Lincoln—obviously—was removed from town at once. On March 10 the stolen car was placed in a garage in Rochester, Minnesota, by two men and a woman who paid a month's rent (three dollars) in advance and said they would provide their own lock for the door. (The car was taken out only once between then and late April, when it was found by the sheriff.)

Seven days after the Sioux Falls robbery, on March 13, the Dillinger gang struck again. But this time, while their score was bigger ($52,000), they fared far worse in the shooting affray which accompanied the holdup. Both John Dillinger and Hamilton were wounded. The gang invaded the Mason City, Iowa, bank, but guard Tom Walters, sitting in his newly installed bulletproof enclosure overlooking the bank floor, was unable to fire at them for fear of hitting some of the fifty or so customers and employees. The gang fled after a speedy and efficient job of looting, apparently unaffected by the tear gas Walters released.

As they piled into their car, with Carroll at the wheel, they took along Emmet V. Ryan, the teller, and Mrs. J. J. Leu. They were fired on from a window over the bank, and Dillinger, hit in the shoulder, sprayed the sniping area with machine-gun fire before the car departed. After freeing their hostages at the edge of town, the mob headed for St. Paul.

There Dillinger and Hamilton were taken by Pat Riley, a minor member of the mob, to Dr. N. G. Mortensen, city health officer, who gave them superficial treatment for the shoulder wounds as Homer Van Meter stood by, a machine gun poorly hidden beneath his overcoat.

(Mortensen was suspended later, after admitting that he had failed to report the incident when the two wounded men failed to return. But a move to force his resignation was hampered when Governor Olson, in a letter, called attention to a statute forbidding doctors from disclosing patients' business, and said possible "assassination" awaited anyone who tried to do so under circumstances similar to those which faced Mortensen.)

Dillinger's shoulder may have been hurt, but his ego must have been given a tremendous boost by the preparations made at Lima to repel whatever attempt he might make to free Pierpont, Clark and Makley. Pierpont was the first to go to trial, and if Dillinger had been a rival foreign power with an army of his own, the defenses would hardly have been more formidable. Brigadier General Harold M. Bush, a combat veteran, was in charge of the Ohio National Guard units sent in to thwart the expected attack.

The jail was ringed by barbed wire, with machine guns placed at strategic intervals behind sandbag barricades, and other machine-gun posts—some of them dummy ones—on the roofs of nearby buildings. Grim-faced Guardsmen with steel helmets, gas masks and bayonets manned these positions, and at night searchlights restlessly probed the darkness in quest of the fearsome Dillinger. Two eight-foot board fences protected the entrances to the sheriff's residence, and there were machine guns mounted at the ends of the jail corridors, ready to rake the passageways. Captain Matt Leach had obligingly passed along a tip he had received: that Dillinger and seven men in National Guard uniforms planned a visit to the jail to rescue the three defendants. General Bush remained calm but ready.

The actual trial of Pierpont opened March 8 before Judge Emmit E. Everett in the Court of Common Pleas, in a curiously blended atmosphere of carnival and panic.

No one was permitted into the courtroom—kept locked during the trial—without a special pass signed by both Judge Everett and General Bush. Jurors, both actual and prospective, were searched before being allowed in, and during the trial itself there were armed guards in the courtroom even though Pierpont was shackled hand and foot. Don Sarber, son of the slain man and his successor as sheriff, was in court with a loaded machine gun during part of the proceedings.

Attorney Jessie Levy represented Pierpont, and while examining prospective jurors, asked with obvious sarcasm if they would be influenced by the fact that the trial was held "in a veritable fortress." This brought from Prosecutor Ernest Botkin the retort that because of Dillinger's escape, "the career and character of John Dillinger warranted the precaution, based on the possibility that he might at any time during the trial attempt to repay the plaintiff-in-error for the favor of October 12, 1933" (the date on which Dillinger was removed from the Lima jail).

The prosecutor asked the death penalty against Pierpont because "It was necessary, to accomplish their purpose in a few minutes, that they act viciously, cruelly, murderously, as they did, to secure the possession of the keys so that John Dillinger could be liberated. Death was a part of the plan for this crime."

Pierpont was identified by Sarber's widow, and by Deputy Sharp, as the man who fired the gun that killed Sarber. Against this, the testimony of Pierpont's mother, Mrs. Lena Pierpont, carried little weight: She said that when Sarber was shot, her son was "at my house eating supper."

Mrs. Pierpont told of the police raid at midnight the day of Sarber's death, and said none of the men remained at the farm by then except Harry, who with "his wife" (Mary Kinder) was in a secret room over the kitchen. Asked whether one of the men at the farm resembled Makley, Mrs. Pierpont gave a judicious reply: "To a certain extent in one way, and in another way he didn't."

Pierpont himself testified that Dillinger had given him Sarber's gun —found on Pierpont in Tucson—in Daytona Beach on Christmas Day. He also told the court that he had been denied a parole in August, 1933, while serving time for a bank holdup in Kokomo, even though he had recommendations from the judges, the prosecutor and eleven of the jurors (the twelfth was dead). He called Shouse, who testified against him, "insane." But the case against Pierpont was clear, and on March 11 he was found guilty of murder in the first degree with no recommendation, which meant a mandatory death sentence.

After the trial Pierpont walked back to his cell past Makley, who asked through the bars, "Well, what was it?"

"Well," Pierpont replied, "what would it be?"

Makley's trial was next, but before it began, Attorney Levy petitioned for a change of venue, citing "prejudicial" newspaper accounts, the "shoot to kill" orders in the event of a delivery attempt, and the presence of National Guardsmen "in uniform and armed with loaded rifles and pistols, machine guns, mob sticks and riot clubs, stationed at doors and entrances in hallways and on the stairways and at the elevator in the courthouse where defendant's trial is being held." She also mentioned that the codefendant had been given a death penalty for the first time in the county in fifty years. The motion was denied, and Makley's trial began March 12, after orders were given for all highway, railroad, streetcar, bus and airline routes into town to be patrolled.

On this day also, two squads of National Guardsmen were assigned to guard the executive mansion to frustrate a rumored plot by Dillinger to kidnap Governor George White and his daughter Mary, and hold them until Pierpont, Makley and Clark were released.

As Makley left for the courtroom, Pierpont called out, "Good luck, Charley."

There was little doubt about the outcome from the beginning, even though Shouse refused to testify against Makley. Fat Charley was quite happy to talk about anything except the shooting of Sarber. He freely admitted his past misdeeds, donned silver-rimmed glasses to consult some legal papers, and apologized for his inability to resolve a dispute over how to spell his name.

"It's been so long since I used my right name," he said, "that I wouldn't know. You look up the record."

While the jury was being chosen, one of the panel, a white-haired former college professor, was excused after saying, "No man who attacks a sheriff deserves mercy."

Makley was unperturbed by the remark. "Those are my sentiments exactly," he said blandly. "I am for the old guy."

A half brother, Fred, who testified that Makley was eating dinner in St. Mary's at the time of the murder, was the only defense witness. After deliberating for three and a half hours over a possible recommendation of mercy, the jury found Makley guilty, as they did in Pierpont's case, of murder in the first degree with no recommendation.

Makley was returned to the cellblock, and as he went to his quarters, Pierpont called to him, "What did they give you?" Makley kept walking. "I got everything," he said.

One of the oddities incidental to the trial was an order from Bush on March 14 that all basements in the area be inspected to be sure Dillinger wasn't busily tunneling into the jail.

Makley was convicted March 17. Attorney Piquett showed up in Lima the same day and was picked up for questioning after having declared that Allen County had sent two innocent men to the chair. Piquett said he had been hired by Clark's mother to help represent Clark; he was not held. Another visitor to Lima was Matt Leach of the Indiana State Police, who refused to say what he was doing in town. The assumption was that he was pursuing his favorite hobby: looking for Dillinger.

Clark's trial came next, and was notable principally for two things: Attorney Levy's curious request for a directed verdict, and the large amount of behind-the-scenes information supplied by Shouse, who returned to testify against his former friend.

Attorney Levy asked Judge Everett for a directed verdict of not guilty on the grounds that Clark "doesn't believe in capital punishment."

"That is utterly silly for you to say," said the court, seemingly startled, "because he is on trial for murder, that he don't believe in capital punishment."

"Well," Miss Levy answered, "it may be utterly silly, but nevertheless there are certain guarantees under the Constitution that this defendant is entitled to, and he does not believe in it, and he makes this motion and he deserves that the court rule on it."

The ruling was adverse.

A brother-in-law of Clark's, Andrew Stracham, testified that Clark was tired, haggard and hungry when he first showed up in Detroit after the Michigan City escape, and that he took a bath and slept for a long time. Clark would go out of the house for thirty-five or forty minutes, Stracham said, but wouldn't let anyone accompany him for fear they would be picked up. Stracham admitted sympathy for Clark because in 1927 "he was sent up for twenty years before the family was notified or had time to get a lawyer."

Clark's sister, Mrs. Beulah Stracham, testified that Clark was at her home until October 15, and that between six and seven o'clock on the twelfth he was (surprise!) eating dinner. This alibi was verified by another sister and Stracham, who said they remembered the date because it was the birthday of Clark's brother Edward, who had been expected to come up from Indiana for the occasion but failed to do so.

Clark's mother, Mrs. May Clark, told the court that Clark was one of seven children, and that he had worked on a farm until he was eighteen. He then became a coal miner, and later worked in Terre Haute in a glass factory, a commercial distillery and a tie plant. He had been married at twenty. She also admitted knowing that Clark was being hunted.

"And yet you didn't notify the police?" she was asked.

"No, sir. I wouldn't notify the police. He is mine."

Mrs. Stracham said her brother had left on October 15. She gave a bleak picture of his departure, with no farewells.

"He went away without talking to his mother?"

"Yes, sir."

"And you didn't even look to see which way he went?"

"No, sir."

Shouse, the most important single witness for the prosecution, was asked when the first discussions were held with Pierpont and Makley about springing Dillinger.

"Why, it was a matter of discussion all the time from the time we made the break," he said. "He was instrumental in freeing us from the Michigan City prison."

Shouse also was severely cross-examined on his relations with both Pierpont and Clark.

"What was the trouble between you and Pierpont?" he was asked.

"He didn't think I was tough enough to be with them."

There followed an exchange in which defense counsel tried to prove that Shouse's advances to his comrades' women brought his ouster from the gang. Shouse denied this.

"According to gangster rules I wasn't tough enough for them and they were scared of me. They were going to get rid of me. Pierpont mostly was the instigator of it. I don't believe the defendant was much for it. I believe if it had been left to him he would have told me to get out. He was the one who gave me the first hint of it."

"You took his car?"

"I did. It is the only car that I had to get away at that time; self-preservation will make you do plenty of things."

Mrs. Carter, who with her husband had chatted at length with Shouse outside the jail the evening Sarber was slain, came to the stand and was asked whether she recognized Shouse.

She said she did not. "He was dressed so much different. When I saw him out there he had on a swell overcoat and a nice light hat and he was nicely shaved and he was a swell-looking fellow."

"I think you almost said he looked like a Moose," Attorney Levy commented.

"Well," Mrs. Carter replied, "he looked like a nice fellow. Mooses is nice fellows. They have to be."

Pierpont and Makley were sentenced March 24 to die in the electric chair on Friday, July 13. Clark was given life.

Newspaper accounts of the sentencing described Pierpont as "brazen and defiant," Makley as "rotund and slow-moving" and Clark, who slept twenty hours daily in his cell and twice dozed off during the trial, as "sleepy-eyed."

On March 27 in a sleet storm the three were removed from Lima to the state prison in Columbus—in a caravan guarded by forty-five armed men. When they reached the prison, two truckloads of National Guardsmen trained machine guns on a crowd of spectators.

Makley, obviously holding no grudge for Dillinger's failure to pluck him from the shadow of the chair, said, "I'd rather take the hot squat than see Johnnie caught."

THIRTEEN

● ● ● ● ● ● ● ● ● ● ● ● ● ●   "I MADE HIM COCONUT CREAM
PIE, FRIED CHICKEN, EVERYTHING
THAT GOES WITH IT."
—MRS. AUDREY HANCOCK

While Dillinger was being hunted throughout the Middle West, Crown Point authorities were trying frantically to clean up the mess he had left behind him.

On March 8, five days after the escape, Judge Murray discharged the special grand jury investigating the incident, with the explanation that it could not function properly "because the foreman, Clyde Rothermel, owns the garage from which Dillinger stole the sheriff's automobile, and is the employer of Edward Saager, whom Dillinger kidnaped with him for a few hours. We need a prosecutor here of high renown and with no political ambitions. . . . This will be a good thing for your [Estill's] interests also, in view of the fact that you are a candidate for re-election."

Murray, who had defended Sheriff Holley and called Warden Baker "a responsible and reliable person," complained that "this investigation has been prolonged for no good reason" and reportedly was bitterly at odds with Estill since refusing to approve the prosecutor's suggestion that Dillinger be transferred to Michigan City for safekeeping.

Saturday, March 10, Judge Murray appointed former Circuit Judge Martin J. Smith, Murray's predecessor, as special prosecutor and called for a new grand jury to convene on Monday. The naming of Smith, a Republican who was said to be without political aspirations, was agreed on by Estill and Edward Barce, assistant attorney general of Indiana.

Judge Murray also suspended Blunk for the duration of the investigation. The fingerprint expert was at liberty on his own recognizance, and Cahoon was freed after a group of local businessmen had raised his $2,000 bond.

The start of the investigation was delayed Monday, however, when two of the six jurors failed to appear. A story that day by Willard Edwards of the *Chicago Tribune*, who may have typed it with tongue in cheek, also declared that plans to re-enact the escape were abandoned for fear someone else might get away with a wooden gun, and that a "cold negative" was given newsreel men who wished to film the proposed re-enactment with someone taking the part of Dillinger singing, "Git along, little dogey, git along"—"as he romped away with the sheriff's car."

The jury finally began work Wednesday, with instructions from Judge Murray to conduct a full inquiry.

"The national prominence of the escaped prisoner has resulted in much publicity," Judge Murray told the jurors, "and inferences have been made that graft and collusion were responsible for the break. It also has been inferred that politics, neglect and cowardice were elements in the escape. Owing to the fact that Ernest Blunk was my appointee, I urge you to make a most vigorous investigation into his part in the affair. I have been criticized for having myself refused to transfer Dillinger to the Michigan City prison. I want you to determine if the Crown Point jail is a proper place to harbor hardened criminals, and if it is not, recommend such improvements as may be necessary. Name everyone involved in your report, whether they are criminally liable or not."

The next day Blunk, who hadn't had many dull moments since Dillinger left, was seized by Indiana State Police detectives and questioned for two days in Indianapolis before being released.

"I think I'm going to be the goat in this case," Blunk said sadly.

His arrest came a week after Attorney General Lutz had sent four more men to Crown Point to aid the investigation, saying that each hour more information was being found to show that the delivery "did not just happen but was planned."

While the grand jury was settling down to its work, which ran on into early April, the other escapee made a final appearance in the Dillinger story. Thirteen days after breaking out, Herbert Young-blood was slain in a gun duel in Port Huron, Michigan, in which undersheriff Charles Cavanaugh also was fatally wounded.

Youngblood had come to Port Huron March 14, well supplied with cash and not at all hesitant to admit to casual saloon ac-quaintances that he was a "bad man." Early on the morning of the sixteenth, he became more and more voluble while loitering in a grocery store, and boasted of having been Dillinger's companion in the Crown Point fiasco.

Someone promptly telephoned Sheriff William Van Antwerp, who showed up with Cavanaugh and Deputy Howard Lohr. Cava-naugh grabbed one gun from Youngblood, who leaped back and drew another, then tried to shoot his way into the night. His bullets hit all three officers and a bystander, but Eugene Fields, son of the grocery store owner, snatched up a gun dropped by one of the wounded officers and put two bullets into Youngblood. The "bad man," who had fulfilled the warning of Gary, Indiana, police that he was dangerous and would shoot "at the drop of a hat," died four hours later, shortly before Cavanaugh succumbed.

Before he drifted out of reach, Youngblood sent police off on a false trail by telling bedside questioners that Dillinger and three other men had come to Port Huron with him. Five hundred peace officers promptly fanned out in a frantic search of the "thumb" area, stopping all cars within a fifty-mile radius of Port Huron and even checking out a report that Dillinger and two other men had crossed the St. Clair River by rowboat and had been met on the Canadian side by a fourth man with a car. Several officers from Indiana, in-cluding Captain Leach, who identified Youngblood's body, came rushing north to help with the hunt.

They were looking in the wrong place. Dillinger, after being treated by Dr. Mortensen, seems to have remained in the Twin Cities area, even though he dropped out of sight—at least public sight—for a couple of weeks. On March 20 he and Miss Frechette moved out of Minneapolis into the Lincoln Court Apartments at 93 South Lexington Avenue, St. Paul, where they lived as Mr. and Mrs. Carl T. Hellman. Eddie Green's wife Beth had rented the place for them for $60 a month. It was only a block from where Edward G. Bremer, the wealthy banker, had been kidnaped a couple of months earlier.

During their stay the "Hellmans" were visited by Hamilton, Van Meter, Opal Long and Pat Cherrington, and Miss Frechette bought groceries, cooked meals, and even pressed Dillinger's clothes. For ten days or so the most-wanted criminal in the country was leading what looked on the surface like a normal life. There were frequent trips to a nearby movie (a habit he should have kicked) and Dillinger himself subscribed, through a newsboy, to a St. Paul newspaper.

The nights must have been chilly, since the Hellmans requested (and got) additional bedding, and the new tenants presented a picture of tender domesticity. The occupant of an apartment across the court reported having seen Mrs. Hellman doing the dishes one night and ironing another.

But the Hellmans were so careful not to attract attention that they attracted it. When the caretaker brought up some items missing after the last occupants had moved out, he was refused admission. Again, wanting to mend a broken bathroom fixture, he was told that Hellman was taking a bath and would make the repairs himself. It also struck the caretaker as odd that the shades usually remained drawn until about 10:30 each morning and often were pulled at dusk, and he wondered particularly why it was the Hellmans' invariable custom to leave the building by the rear door. So on March 30 he telephoned the local FBI office to say that he thought the occupants of Apartment 303 would bear looking into.

Government agents watched the apartment that night and saw nothing out of the way, but decided that a routine check would be in order. Shortly after 10:30 the morning of the thirty-first, R. C. Coulter and R. L. Nolls, Federal agents, and Detective Henry Cummings of the St. Paul police force, came calling. Coulter and Cummings knocked on the door of Apartment 303, while Nolls remained on the street, keeping an eye on a Ford coupé parked on Lincoln Avenue. The car was known to belong to the Hellmans or someone else who seemed to be using the apartment.

The knock was answered by a sleepy-eyed Miss Frechette, who later told it this way:

"Mr. Dillinger and I were in bed that morning. There was a knock at the door and I answered it. Two men were standing there, and they said, 'We want to talk with Carl.' I had forgotten that John's name was supposed to be Carl Hellman, and I was confused for a moment. Then I remembered, and said he was not at home. I asked the men who they were, and they said, 'We are police. Can we come in and talk with you?' I said I was sorry but I was not dressed and told them to wait a minute.

"I went into the bedroom, and John asked me who the men were. I was nervous and excited, and he kept saying, 'Hurry up and get dressed' and 'Never mind, never mind.' As I was packing a bag, John was getting dressed. About this time I heard some shots, and I looked out the window but saw nothing. While I was still in the bedroom getting dressed, John started shooting through the door and I shouted to him, 'My God! Don't shoot! Try and get out without shooting!' I was so excited I didn't know what I was doing, and he kept yelling, 'Come on, let's go!'"

Meanwhile, shortly after Miss Frechette shut the door, Coulter started for the rear stairway to be sure no one could slip out that way, and bumped into a man he had not seen enter. He asked his business and the stranger said he was a soap salesman. Coulter asked to see his samples, and the other man said they were in his car. The "salesman" started down the stairs, with Coulter following, but by the time the Federal agent reached the ground floor, he found the suspect standing in a basement doorway, leveling a revolver at him.

The gunman—later identified as Homer Van Meter or (though this is improbable) Green—opened fire. The agent shot back. Van Meter darted out the rear door and escaped with a ruse that would have delighted Father Brown, G. K. Chesterton's fictional detective. He leaped to the seat of a passing ash wagon and borrowed the driver's cap, then rode slowly out of danger. He left the wagon at Fourth and Pleasant, still wearing the cap.

This fusillade was the one Miss Frechette heard, and a moment later, after Dillinger had cleared the way with his machine-gun burst, he and Evelyn ran out of the apartment and down the now unguarded rear stairs, as Detective Cummings fired at them from cover with his service revolver. Miss Frechette raced into a garage behind 1123 Goodrich Avenue and drove out a new black-and-yellow Hudson, bought three days before, as Dillinger, bleeding from a wound in the fleshy part of the left leg above the knee, coolly stood with his tommy gun ready.

The Hudson drew alongside and Dillinger got behind the wheel as Miss Frechette scrambled into the rear seat. Dillinger then sped away without pursuit. Bloodstains in the snow behind the apartment building gave some satisfaction to the baffled raiding party.

A new Thompson submachine gun with the stock removed, some maps of Minnesota, Michigan, and other places, and newspapers opened to accounts of Dillinger's escapades were found in the Ford coupé, the tires of which Nolls had punctured with bullet holes when the shooting began.

The FBI also made positive identification of the "Hellmans" as Dillinger and Evelyn Frechette through fingerprints found in the apartment and on the Ford. The couple's flight had been so precipitate that they left behind two automatic rifles, one .38-caliber Colt automatic with 20-shot magazine clips, a couple of bulletproof vests, a photograph of Dillinger in sailor uniform, and—with professional carelessness—a slip of paper bearing Eddie Green's telephone number!

One of the things which most intrigued the government men was a set of bank robbery "guides" found in the apartment. These consisted of explicitly detailed directions for traveling by back roads, and one set referred to the countryside near an Iowa bank which presumably was on the gang's worksheet. One guide offered information like this excerpt: "000—Rt. on N. 3d-X St. X St. -X St. -.02. X Stop St. symbol (triangle) on R-X St. -04 RT on E. 7th St. -X-slo -05. LT on H6-.09 x RR mefg co-1.3 Spanish Moon cafe."

A Federal agent subsequently followed several hundred miles of such directions and found they took him to St. Paul without passing through a single town.

A dozen or so of these "guides" were discovered, which led an agent to comment, "Whenever a bank is robbed, let us say in the vicinity of the Twin Cities, policemen immediately are ordered to watch all the major highways leading into St. Paul and Minneapolis. They might as well stay in the station, for bank robbers never use the main roads. They invariably travel on byroads, crossing the main roads only when they must do so."

While the Federal men were searching the vacated apartment, the wounded Dillinger and Miss Frechette drove directly to an apartment at 3300 Fremont Avenue, where the Greens lived under the name of Stephens. Miss Frechette went in to tell Green Dillinger was hurt, and Green took him to the vicinity of Dr. Clayton E. May's office. Green approached Dr. May alone, about 11 A.M., and told him he had a friend who had been hurt "in an explosion."

Dr. May testified later that he asked if the injured man were wanted by the authorities and Green said he was not. In any event, Green and the physician went to the corner of 33d and Dupont Avenue South, where Dillinger was huddled in the back seat of a parked car, machine gun within easy reach, with Mrs. Green beside him. Green told Dillinger that Dr. May would take him to a hospital, and drew an angry reply: "The hell with that. Take me to the private place you said you were going to take me."

Dillinger was then driven to the apartment of Mrs. Augusta Salt, Dr. May's nurse, at 1835 Park Avenue in Minneapolis, where Dr. May dressed the leg. Dillinger told him to come back that night and bring a shot to prevent lockjaw.

Dr. May asked his patient's name and drew a blank: "The hell with that. Go ahead and take care of me. That's what you are supposed to do. If you don't, the same thing will happen to you that happened to a doc in Kansas."

Dr. May said Dillinger then pulled out a revolver and added, "I'll blow your brains out if you do anything about this."

The Greens moved out of their apartment to a new location, and returned to Mrs. Salt's that evening with Dr. May, who had been promised a $500 fee (never received). Dillinger told them they had better keep Dr. May in their apartment that night, which Green said he would do. Evelyn Frechette arrived soon afterward.

Some time during Dillinger's stay, Mrs. Salt discovered a pistol under his pillow (Miss Frechette later testified he never slept without one there) and was told, "Don't be afraid of that. It won't hurt you if you do what I tell you to do."

By this time the Federal agents had located Green's hideout apartment, searched it, and discovered the stock to the machine gun found in the Ford, as well as a number of clips and much ammunition. Agents were posted there in case the Greens returned, and on April 3—Tuesday—two women showed up who were known associates of the late Frank Nash, killed in the Union Station "massacre" at Kansas City the previous June. They told the agents they had been sent by "Mr. Stephens" to get some luggage; "Stephens" had said he would pick it up at their place later that afternoon. The women were permitted to take the luggage, but some agents went with them.

Late that day Green and his wife drove up in front of the home of one of the women, and as he was leaving with the suitcases was shot in the back by the waiting agents, who said he had reached in his pocket for a gun when told to halt. His wife, who leaped from the car and ran to him, was caught.

Before he died eight days later, Green had given much information, including the names of the two doctors who treated Dillinger and Hamilton and the makeup of the gang which robbed the Sioux Falls and Mason City banks.

The revelation that Dillinger had been hiding and sheltered in St. Paul brought civic indignation of the sort reflected in the following editorial from the St. Paul *Pioneer Press*, which was headed WHO PROTECTED DILLINGER?:

Why did John Dillinger come to St. Paul to hide out?

Every decent citizen of St. Paul is concerned with the answer to that question. Every decent citizen of St. Paul should demand from Mayor Mahoney the reason why Dillinger, like Barker, Karpis, Bailey and others too numerous to mention have chosen St. Paul as their hideaway while the police and federal agents of the country were scouring the nation for them.

There can be only one reason why scores of big time crooks make St. Paul their hangout.

That reason is "connections"—some person or persons to smooth the way, to find them living quarters, to make necessary protective arrangements, perhaps to put the finger on possible victims of kidnapings or to show where good hauls can be made at the point of a gun.

What and where are these "connections" that invite "heavy" ex-criminals into Mayor Mahoney's town and protect them when they are here?

By all means let this investigation take precedence over all others. Let a grand jury if it please look into that question. Let Mayor Mahoney, who said two years ago he came as an avenging spirit against gangsters, tell why St. Paul has become a disgrace and a shame before the whole country, because gangsters have been given refuge here, have been sheltered here, and here have found a congenial and safe base for operations.

Who are these "connections" and how do they operate, how are they able to exist, how can Mayor Mahoney be the scourge of gangsters and still not know about such things, how can he plead ignorance, how deny the facts? Who brought Dillinger to St. Paul? Let us have an answer to that question.

Whatever the answer, Dillinger himself didn't wait to have it made public. Word of the shooting of Green reached him quickly, and on April 4, he and Evelyn left for Mooresville and a brief vacation on the farm. It is believed they reached Indiana on the fifth.

On April 6, the black-and-yellow Hudson was found in Mankato, Minnesota, where Tommy Carroll had taken it to be repainted. The same day, according to FBI information, Dillinger and his half brother Hubert drove from Mooresville to Leipsic, Ohio, to make contact with relatives of Harry Pierpont. Hubert was driving—perhaps because of John's leg wound—and fell asleep early the following morning during the return trip on U.S. Highway 31 near Noblesville. The Terraplane veered into an approaching Model-T touring car driven by Joseph Manning of Peru, Indiana, who was with his wife and sister-in-law; the crash ripped off the left rear wheel of Manning's car.

The Terraplane left the road, hurtled through a ditch, ripped down a strip of fence, and went a hundred yards into a stump-filled field before stopping. The brothers leaped out and came back to the road, where John asked Manning if anyone were hurt. Told no one was, the brothers split up, Hubert heading toward Indianapolis, about 20 miles south, and John—again according to the FBI report—taking refuge, with a machine gun, in a nearby haystack.

Hubert returned a few hours later and retrieved his brother, and that same day Evelyn Frechette, accompanied by an unidentified man, bought a new car from the Hatfield Ford Agency in Indianapolis, after she failed to find a used car that satisfied her. The buyer gave her name as Mrs. Fred Penfield and an address which checked to Fred Hancock, one of Dillinger's nephews. Hancock knew nothing at all about the transaction. Mrs. "Penfield" refused a green car that was on the floor and ready, saying she wanted a black one, and paid $730 from a purse bulging with ten-dollar bills.

"I must have the car this afternoon," she added. "I'm leaving town."

There was a family reunion at the Dillinger farm on Sunday, April 8, and while the police and FBI agents didn't know where Dillinger was, many of his neighbors did. There was no particular attempt at secrecy.

Said Mrs. Hancock, "I cooked dinner down there. My half brother come and told us somebody at Pop's wanted to see us. I knew pretty well who it was and went right away. He just like to squeeze me to pieces. I made him coconut cream pie, fried chicken, everything that goes with it. All our family was there. There must have been a dozen of us.

"The FBI played all around the place [this seems highly unlikely, but Mrs. Hancock is convinced it is so] and a plane came down and nearly knocked a piece off the house while we were walking across the lawn. John was as relaxed as anyone could be. He never seemed concerned except when the airplane pulled over. When a car came into the driveway, he grabbed a gun off the bed and said, 'You get in back of the house. I'll take care of this.' But it backed out and went away.

"He walked with my two girls, walked to the woods with a .45 sticking down in his belt. And he laughed and told my husband all about Crown Point. He made a sketch and told us every move he made, then burned the paper up. He told us he took a razor blade and whittled the top part of the gun, then blacked it and drilled a hole in the end and put in a piece out of the safety razor so it looked like a pistol."

Emmett Hancock, John's brother-in-law, added, "He was pretty tight-mouthed. I started to quiz him, and he said, 'Big boy, let me tell you something. If you don't know anything you can't tell anything, can you?' I said, 'No,' and he went on, 'Let that be a lesson to you.'"

Mary Hancock, Dillinger's favorite niece, had similar memories of this incredible picnic. "I remember him coming up the driveway with Evelyn," she said. "I think it was before dinner we walked to the woods. The rest were strolling around, and my grandfather went on about his chores—you go ahead and do things like that regardless. We ate in the yard right outside the back door, because that made it easy for us to be on guard.

"We felt that the FBI knew he and Evelyn were there, but perhaps felt there was a terrible element of danger with all of us involved. I really believe they sincerely wanted to do their duty. I like to think they didn't want to come in. It would be a terrible thing to shoot him down in front of our eyes. I think their G-man training made them other than merciless human beings.

"We walked hand in hand for a long time, a couple of miles along the lane. Not a soul but he and I. He said, 'You believe what's in the papers if you want to, but take it from me, I haven't killed anyone and I never will.' He said, 'Take about half a grain of salt, believe half of what's left, and you've got it made.'"

Before Dillinger left, someone drove Mrs. Hancock to Mooresville, where she bought adhesive tape and Mercurochrome with which to doctor his injured leg. Dillinger also posed for a photograph beside the farmhouse, holding a machine gun in one hand and a wooden gun in the other. His niece is very firm in declaring that it was the same gun with which he escaped: "He laughed about it," she said, "and told us all about it. That was one thing he did make light of. He wouldn't have been apt to go to all the trouble of making a wooden gun for our benefit."

(Mrs. Hancock said that Evelyn Frechette made an overnight visit to Maywood shortly after the Crown Point affair, bringing the wooden gun from Dillinger as a souvenir. The gun disappeared a few years ago after having been shown to a casual caller at the house.)

"They didn't leave till about four Sunday afternoon," she said. "Evelyn was driving and John was in back under a blanket. At the county line they stopped, and John got out and put on colored glasses. One of the FBI cars passed while they were stopped there, an agent told the elder girl later. With John and Evelyn were my daughters, Mary and Alberta, and my son, Norman. Mary and Alberta went to Maywood and Norman went to Chicago with them, almost.

"He was going up to see about some work. They stopped and changed license plates somewhere between here and Chicago, and when they got pretty near, John gave Norman some money and said, 'You'd better get out here. You might meet something you wouldn't want to be in.'

"That was the last time I saw him. The night he was killed we were lying in comfort on the front lawn at Maywood when a man from the Associated Press come and told us.

"John was awful good to me," she added wistfully. "He sent me scarves and things, one blue one with a silk fringe around it, I forget where from. Two or three scarves and pillow tops he sent to Hubert for me. But the last time or two he came he never brought anything."

Mary related, "When we left, we drove back to Maywood up the Plainfield Road. It seems to me he wore colored glasses, and I expect he was covered with a blanket."

She paused, interrupting her train of thought, and said musingly, "He never saw us that he didn't give us a great big bear hug." Then she continued, "Later I'm sure the FBI men were quite upset with me because I wouldn't tell them anything. They asked if I wanted them to get my young sister and put her through an ordeal. It may be they weren't positive he was in the car."

This idea that the FBI men were at least in the area during the weekend of Dillinger's visit is widely held, not only by the family but by friends and neighbors. One nearby resident said, "The FBI was around constantly. They had headquarters in Mooresville. My husband and his brother were questioned on why they didn't turn in any evidence about John, but we were friends of the Dillinger family and we didn't want to do that. They'd never harmed us in any way."

Although it seems not to have occurred on this particular visit, another former neighbor declared, "When the word was out that John was home, all the state cops would come. But they were so afraid of him they used to put their sirens on at West Newton [five or six miles away] and John Dillinger had time to dig a hole and bury himself. We'd hear 'em coming and say, 'John's home.' We figured they wanted John to know they were coming."

There even was a joke around Mooresville in those days that the newly widened Plainfield Road, on which the Dillinger farm stood, had been improved "so John could get here faster."

It is idle to speculate, at this distance, how it was possible for Public Enemy Number 1 to picnic with his family on a sunny Sunday afternoon without attracting the attention of the county, state or Federal police. By Sunday night, however, it was obvious to the police that Dillinger—his chestnut hair now dyed a reddish hue—had come and gone. The wrecked car near Noblesville, even though it had been stripped of license plates, was linked to Dillinger after a machine gun and a card bearing the name of a St. Paul concern were found in it. But this was the last time the prodigal returned home. The three months of life which remained for him were too crowded, too uneasy, too tense, and everything was closing in.

An hour or so after Dillinger and Evelyn Frechette pulled onto the Fairfield Road for the last time and drove away from the small white farmhouse on the bluff, about half a dozen G-men moved into a farm home a short distance down the road, occupied by the Lawrence Hensley family. From that time on the Dillinger place was under constant surveillance.

(The government men, taking care not to appear as a group, took turns dressing like farmhands and working in the fields or ostensibly mending the fences while they waited for Dillinger to return. The neighbors thought they were relatives of the Hensleys, and since no more than two at a time put in an appearance, only the Hensleys knew how many there were. Frances Dillinger used to drop in on Monday to read the comic section of the Indianapolis paper, and this caused great inconvenience to the government men, who had to hide in a stifling-hot bedroom until she had gone. One of the watchers, a Southerner who liked food, helped Mrs. Hensley with the cooking.)

Federal authorities also said Dillinger had been seen in an automobile in downtown Indianapolis during the day—the same Sunday —probably as he and Evelyn Frechette were leaving the area.

So two raids were staged in quick succession, on the Kinder home in Indianapolis and on that of Hubert Dillinger in Maywood. There were eighteen men in the party, armed with machine guns, rifles, shotguns, revolvers, tear gas and grenades. The group comprised four Federal men, four detectives and ten uniformed policemen, and at each house the police cars switched on spotlights to illuminate the area.

As the posse prowled the Kinder home, searching drawers and peering underneath beds and carpets, Mary demanded to see a warrant, which was read to her. She told newsmen she and her mother and sister had moved only the day before because their old home had grown "too hot."

"Every flatfooted copper and detective in Indianapolis knew where we lived and took it as a personal social duty to call on us every day," said Mistress Mary, quite contrary.

Such constantly growing pressure from the Federal men was nothing Dillinger could escape, as he had been able to escape when his only real opponents were the state or local police. He could no longer take the "heat" off by leaving town. There were G-men everywhere, and only the faces changed if he moved from state to state.

For example, on Monday, April 9, the day after the family reunion, Dillinger had an appointment in a tavern at 416 North State Street, Chicago—and the G-men were waiting. Only the fact that Evelyn Frechette had a sudden premonition prevented his arrest and saved him for a harsher fate. No government agent had been killed by a Dillinger associate yet, and the chances are he would have been taken alive.

But as the two pulled up near the rendezvous, Evelyn grew suddenly wary. "I'll go in," she said, remembering Tucson. "The last time you went in somewhere you were arrested."

As she entered, she was seized by Federal agents. Dillinger, who had driven around the block to permit her to check the place out, quickly realized something was wrong and simply kept on going. He did, however, telephone Piquett at the Willard Hotel in Washington that night and asked him to represent Miss Frechette.

Evelyn, a couple of days later, infuriated G-man Purvis by blandly (and untruthfully) assuring newspapermen that the evening she was picked up Dillinger had been in the same bar "when the agents walked in and told me to put up my hands. Dillinger was standing in a crowd near the door. He walked right through them as quiet as you please. He strolled down the street and got into a car not fifty feet away. Then he waited until the agents brought me out of the place, and I saw him drive away."

Said the frustrated Purvis, "I have no comment to make on such a ridiculous statement."

Miss Frechette's cunning mixture of truth and fancy seems to have been her way of getting back at the agents, who, she maintained, questioned her for more than twenty-four hours without permitting her to sleep, a charge the government men denied.

What with one thing and another—the raid in St. Paul, the wrecked car in Indiana—Dillinger and his mob were running low on weapons and especially bulletproof vests. The answer to this minor problem was found in Warsaw, Indiana, early on the morning of April 13 by Dillinger, who was accompanied by Homer Van Meter.

Judd Pittenger, night patrolman of the Warsaw force, told a graphic and somewhat unbelievable tale of his encounter with the two gangsters.

He was walking down Buffalo Street, Pittenger said, when two men approached. One, whom he recognized at once as Dillinger, shoved the muzzle of a machine gun into Pittenger's stomach and Pittenger as promptly shoved it into the air, only to be menaced from behind by Van Meter. Dillinger, Pittenger reported, swore and snarled, "Don't try to get funny, copper, we don't want to kill you!"

"I asked Dillinger if his gun would shoot," Pittenger's account goes on, "and he asked me what the hell I thought he was carrying it for. Just then the clip fell out, but Van Meter had a gun on me and I hesitated to draw my own revolver—a .38-caliber special. Dillinger stooped and picked up the clip and put it back in the machine gun.

"The odds were against me, so I gave up and said I would go along with them. We started down an alley and then turned east a block and a half to the city hall. While we were walking Dillinger said I was the biggest damn fool he ever saw, and Van Meter suddenly snatched my gun from my holster and cracked me over the head with it.

"They asked me how many officers were on duty at night and I told them four, although there really were only two of us. I tried to scare them by saying I expected the other three along soon."

At the city hall, Pittenger went on, they demanded the keys to the room where the guns were kept, and he tried to stall, but finally opened it. Dillinger then said, "Let's take the old boy along with us so he won't squawk too soon."

At this, according to one statement credited to Pittenger, he backed out unobserved, slammed the door, and fled when he discovered the key was no longer in the lock. At the top of the stairs he slipped and hurt his knee, but managed to hobble down the stairs and dart into an alley behind the Continental Theater. When he reached the intersection of the alley and Buffalo Street, he saw a car drive away from the city hall with Dillinger and Van Meter in it. They had taken two revolvers and some steel vests.

(In a gaudier version of the Pittenger account, the policeman trips Dillinger who falls downstairs, then flees without reprisal.)

By this time the Mooresville *Times* was out with a story bearing the headline DILLINGER ATTENDS FAMILY REUNION IN MIDST OF MAN-HUNT, and reporters began arriving to interview the elder Dillinger. He made no attempt to hide the fact that his son had been there, and is quoted as saying, "Oh, yes, John came down here to look in on me. He was hurt in the leg a little, but not much. I don't aim to tell no lies, even to keep things like that quiet. I didn't tell the police because they didn't ask me. John's not in Indiana now."

This enraged Al Feeney, Indiana State Police head, who said, "It is unusual for a community to withhold such information for days and then let it reach the newspapers in such a way that it disparages the police. I simply can't understand it."

Matt Leach took the matter philosophically and said he had no intention of questioning the elder Dillinger. "What good would it do?" Leach asked. "Dillinger's been and gone, and under the law the old man has the right to protect his son."

Kyle Crichton, in his book *Total Recoil*, describes a visit to the Dillinger farm and his talk with the father, who kept insisting that "Johnny is a good boy. You can ask anybody in town and they'll tell you the same thing."

Crichton decided to test this out in Mooresville and asked a young gas station attendant if he knew John Dillinger.

"Sure" was the cheerful reply.

"What do you think of him?"

"I like him fine."

Crichton said he was a reporter for *Collier's* magazine and wanted to know something of Dillinger's background.

"You could have talked to him yourself right here about ten days ago. He came in to get gas and have his oil changed."

"After he broke out of Crown Point?" asked the amazed Crichton.

"Sure," said the other. "He stayed with his old man two days."

Crichton then checked further and discovered that the local

banker had seen Dillinger on the street "visiting around with his old friends."

"You mean to say that the most-wanted criminal in America could stroll around here in his home town, eighteen miles from Indianapolis, without anybody turning him in?" asked Crichton.

The banker had a perfect answer.

"Nobody ever did," he said.

FOURTEEN

● ● ● ● ● ● ● ● ● ● ● ● ● ● **"SO FAR AS THE GUN USED IN THE ESCAPE IS CONCERNED, THE GRAND JURY BELIEVES THAT, FROM ALL THE EVIDENCE GIVEN, IT WAS A WOODEN ONE."**
—GRAND JURY REPORT

In the meantime, eighteen days after the special grand jury began its investigation, it turned in its report to Judge Murray. Although the jurors seemed to have followed his instructions to the letter, the jurist was not amused.

Based on a tour of the jail, and testimony from more than fifty witnesses (Mrs. Holley was questioned three times), the jurors' report of April 3 called Judge Murray's failure to permit the transfer of Dillinger to Michigan City the prime cause for the escape!

The jurors, given *carte blanche* by Judge Murray, had fallen to with enthusiasm. In addition to their swipe at Judge Murray, they traced the success of the escape to: (1) the coolness, alertness and reputation of Dillinger himself; (2) the help of Herbert Youngblood; (3) laxity of jail officials; (4) collusion of Cahoon and Blunk (both of whom were indicted); (5) an indifferent and unreliable trusty working as a turnkey.

The report added that Dillinger could have been sent to Michigan

City as a parole violator, thus saving about $150 a day in special guards who were without experience at such work, "and unfit to guard a hardened criminal of the Dillinger type."

Sheriff Holley was *not* relieved of the responsibility of getting efficient guards by Judge Murray's refusal to transfer Dillinger, the report declared, and the Crown Point jail, properly manned, "could hold any hardened prisoner."

The jurors also decided that Dillinger's only gun, at least when the break started, was a wooden one, and explained the fact that everyone who saw it said it seemed larger than the one he displayed when about to leave "possibly is ascribable to the fright felt by those who saw it."

The investigation found no link between crime and politics, but did cite eleven jail employees, including Baker and Bailiff Ralph Pierce of the Lake County Criminal Court, as "sharing blame" for the escape because of their negligence, poor judgment and failure to obey jail rules. The report also recommended changes in jail procedure.

Judge Murray, obviously piqued, said he would put Dillinger back in the Crown Point jail if he were recaptured, and demanded to know why he should have paid any heed to a "prosecutor who had just finished hugging Dillinger." (The report held Estill blameless for the notorious photograph, saying it was taken when Estill "had been without sleep for 48 hours and had been under a nervous strain.")

Judge Murray also pointed out that he had no power to transfer Dillinger unless the prisoner's life were endangered by mob violence. He added, "The report is worded in language not contemplated in law. It is lacking in the respect due courts of justice and judicial officers, and is particularly disrespectful to this particular court and its judge. It is in defamation of the judge, and contains language which scandalizes the court."

The judge was also upset over criticism of his bailiff, Ralph Pierce, for not making a proper search of Dillinger and his jail quarters, and over the suggestion that it was "important that citizens hereafter look into the qualifications of all candidates for office," a suggestion Judge Murray characterized as "contemptuous."

Judge Murray started contempt proceedings against the entire six-man jury April 6, and ordered them to appear in court on Monday, April 9, to show cause why they should not be held in direct contempt.

Both Estill and Smith, the special prosecutor, had commended the jury for a job well done, and promised to defend it if the report were criticized. After the contempt order was issued, Smith announced that he would appear in court as attorney for the jury. The contempt hearing, however, was continued until Friday, April 13, when Smith requested a postponement. Smith said he, as prosecutor, had made some changes from the stenographer's notes before the report was written.

Judge Murray objected to Smith's serving as attorney for the jurors, saying, "You may be a witness in this case, and have you thought you might be a principal? You are still an officer of this court and if there is an appeal it may be your duty to represent this court. You certainly can't represent both sides."

Smith replied that he understood his work as special prosecutor was finished and that he was now acting in his private capacity as a lawyer. Judge Murray did not rule that Smith, his predecessor on the bench, could not serve.

The judge then took the offensive, criticizing Assistant Attorney General Barce for trying to act for the jurors. "He is, I understand, the personal attorney for the governor. This jury spread criticism of the governor throughout the state, notwithstanding the fact that the governor sent Matt Leach of the state police to Arizona to bring Dillinger back. State's Attorney Estill took a plane there and beat Leach to the prisoner. If he had let Leach alone Dillinger would have been safe in the state prison. So I don't see how in common decency Mr. Barce can represent this jury."

When the jurors returned April 13, Murray listened to an answer in which they declared they had tried to carry out the court's orders and had no intention of casting personal aspersions on Murray. He then directed that the grand jury's report be expunged from the record and the jury itself discharged.

"I am sorry that this has come up, gentlemen," Murray said. "It is not pleasant for the court. I accept the answer. It was unfortunate that you were not better advised. The indictments against Blunk and Cahoon will stand."

Blunk, however, was freed in May when Special Judge Maurice E. Crites of East Chicago refused to hear closing arguments and ruled that there had been insufficient evidence given to convict. During the trial Blunk repeated that Dillinger had been armed with a "fully loaded .45 automatic." Cahoon also was freed.

With the added publicity impetus given by the grand jury report, the St. Paul gun battle, the wrecked car, the raids, and the arrest of Miss Frechette, the rumor crop was ready for harvesting again. Dillinger and Hamilton were reported seen in Pittsburgh on April 10. Dillinger was said to have had a haircut in Brownsburg, Indiana, on the thirteenth, presumably after the Warsaw holdup, and to have passed through Elkhart the following day. And on the fifteenth he was "seen" in South Bend and Niles, Michigan, with Homer Van Meter. On April 10, too, a guard was posted at Yuma, Arizona, at the Colorado River bridge in case he came that way.

The deluge of stories about Dillinger and his exploits also revived the letter-writing members of the Dillinger fan club, an unorganized but nonetheless existent body. There were poems composed to celebrate his deeds, and several persons wrote to urge that he run for governor of Indiana.

In addition there were the wags. Indianapolis police discovered a lottery with the prize depending upon the date of Dillinger's capture. A story out of Duluth maintained that a street peddler, with larcenous leanings, was selling envelopes supposedly containing photographs of Dillinger for fifty cents. When the gullible buyer found the envelope empty, the salesman reportedly chuckled and said, "He got away from you, too!"

Nor were the legitimate commercial tie-ins overlooked. A Pennsylvania restaurant owner erected a billboard which read: HELLO, DILLINGER—YOU'LL LIKE LEE HOFFMAN'S FOOD! LEE HOFFMAN'S TAVERN, LORETTO, PA."

The elder Dillinger also began to get offers, one from a vaudeville circuit for $500 a week and the other from a Coney Island sideshow for $100, if he would appear to discuss his son for the cultural enrichment of the curious. He refused. The Universal Newsreel Company announced a reward of $5,000 for Dillinger's capture (presumably so they would be notified in advance and could get some exclusive footage), and a gossip columnist announced that a movie actor (famous but unnamed) was planning to hire private detectives to track down the outlaw so that the actor could make the actual capture and enhance his already shining image.

There was, however, a growing tide of feeling that the Dillinger problem was overemphasized, badly handled, and in need of reappraisal. One letter in a Voice of the Reader column urged police not to make a martyr of Dillinger by shooting him without a chance, and Clarence Darrow, the nation's most famous lawyer since the Loeb and Leopold and the "monkey" trials, said in an interview that Dillinger's first sentence had embittered the outlaw. Darrow also said that he did not believe Dillinger should be sentenced to life if caught, and attacked the government's "shoot to kill" attitude.

One Middle Westerner wrote to suggest that Dillinger news be removed from the front pages and put inside, and added, "The attempt of the newspaper to manufacture news by ascribing to him every holdup and bank robbery in the country is an absurdity which the public should not be expected to swallow."

Point was given this complaint a short while later when a gang of five men and a woman held up a bank in Flint, Michigan, and all but one of the men were identified as Dillinger.

Newspaper editorials were beginning to regard the Dillinger hunt in the light of its implications rather than treat it as an isolated phenomenon. One said, in part:

> Dillinger is not just one bad man against the United States. He is, unfortunately, a symbol of crime in its latter day aspects in America. His is crime on rubber tires, crime armed with the finest killing devices known to science. Unlike Billie-the-Kid, Charles Quantrell, the Jameses, Fords, Youngers and other famous outlaws of the past, this bandit killer is at large over five states. The laws and police of Indiana and neighboring states seem helpless to catch and punish him.

(The *Christian Century*, in an editorial printed after the Dillinger hunt was over, seems to have wrapped the whole thing up in faultless fashion:

> But it is hard to escape from the feeling that in the latter stages of his career, Dillinger became the perverted and lethal social menace that he was because of the incapacity of local police forces and because of his desire to measure up to a fictitious role that a sensation-seeking public had been assured fitted him.)

The hunt, of course, went on. On April 16 Federal authorities announced that a cottage near Alma, Wisconsin, had been raided and the cottage owner, a former bootlegger, arrested, because Tommy Carroll, Van Meter, Baby Face Nelson and Opal Long apparently had been using it as a retreat. The government agents were tipped off by a farm youth who had pulled a new Ford, with three men and a woman in it, out of a ditch near Alma three days earlier. The Ford was believed to be one bought by Tommy Carroll in Mankato after leaving the Hudson to be repainted.

Opinion in Mooresville at this time was divided. A clerk in the town's only bank told newsmen, "I wouldn't be afraid if John walked in here right now. He's a town boy and I don't think he would hurt any of us. We don't even take any precautions against him!"

Further, two residents of the Mooresville area, neither of whom knew Dillinger personally, got up a petition to Governor McNutt urging that Dillinger be given a pardon if he surrendered and pledged to remain within the law.

The petition cited a precedent (the pardon of Frank James in Missouri), declared that Dillinger "has never manifested a vicious, revengeful or bloodthirsty disposition, there being considerable doubt as to whether he ever committed a murder," and said that such action would prevent probable bloodshed "and salvage a being who, no doubt, has considerable worth if his energy were properly directed." The authors of the petition, who later denied having written it, also stated their opinion "that many of the financial institutions of the State have just as criminally robbed our citizens without any effort being made to punish the perpetrators."

Amazingly enough, this document was signed by many Morgan County residents and delivered to Governor McNutt. When it became public, however, a number of the signers disowned their signatures and interest in the petition dwindled away. Dillinger's father, asked about the suggested pardon, said he thought his son "would make a good policeman."

The Mooresville *Times* commented editorially on the move in this fashion:

> The unfortunate fact that a notorious outlaw, John Dillinger, happened to begin his career in Mooresville, an orderly, law-abiding

and respected community, is something that could not have been prevented, perhaps, but can certainly be judged with intelligence and reason. The probability that the pursued bandit has on occasion found refuge there among members of his family, or even that in fear of him some who should have spoken remained silent, is in no way a reflection on the people as a whole. The reported circulation of a petition asking that he be pardoned has been regarded as fantastic or of no authority in speaking the sentiments of the people.

The editorial then praised the Mooresville Town Board, which had asked higher authorities for protection against Mooresville's most famous son, and declared that "the Citizens of Mooresville are ready and willing and anxious that John Dillinger be placed in the custody of the law." It then continued:

The failure is not at Mooresville nor among the people as a whole. It is with public officials or with the system of nominating and electing public officials who cannot match the ingenuity and recklessness of desperate criminals. Dillinger is at large because officials were less faithful to their duties than citizens seeking public office should be. In some degree it is probable this laxity in law enforcement and indifference toward public safety emboldened the young desperado to believe that he could escape punishment for his early misdeeds.

So confused was the Mooresville civic attitude by now that when a petition was circulated demanding that a company of Indiana National Guard troops be stationed in town as a protection, some of those who signed the pardon petition also signed this one.

By this time Dillinger was heading north once more. On April 17 he and Hamilton and a woman were visiting Hamilton's sister, Mrs. Isaac Steve, in Sault Ste. Marie, Michigan. The Federal agents learned of the visit two days later, and called on Mrs. Steve on the nineteenth. The trio had departed for an unannounced destination, leaving a Ford sedan behind.

Despite extensive questioning of Mrs. Steve and her son, Charles Campbell, the agents learned nothing to indicate which way the fugitives had gone. Once again Dillinger had disappeared without a trace.

FIFTEEN

●●●●●●●●●●●●●●●● "IT WAS THE WORST THING
THAT HAD HAPPENED TO ME
SINCE I HAD A BRAND NEW
PAIR OF BOOTS BURNED OFF
IN A FOREST FIRE."
—CONSTABLE CARL
CHRISTENSEN

Little Bohemia Lodge, thirteen miles south of Mercer in northern
Wisconsin, was the only resort in that lake country open the year
around, a financial measure dictated by the fact that its owner, Emil
Wanatka, was trying to pay off a sizable mortgage.

Wanatka, a former circus roustabout, was born in Bohemia in
1888 and came to the United States as a steerage passenger when he
was eighteen. After a varied career as a boxer, bellboy and café
proprietor, during which he ran the old Little Bohemia in Chicago
(visited by Gene Tunney after the famed "long count" victory),
Wanatka came to Wisconsin and opened Little Bohemia Lodge in
1930. It seems worthy of note that while a resident of Chicago,
Wanatka had occasion to retain Attorney Louis Piquett, a fact which
may explain the visit to Little Bohemia which now concerns us.

The lodge itself, on the shore of Star Lake, was about 650 feet off
Route 51, the highway running to Mercer, Hurley, and Ironwood,
Michigan, and completely hidden by a thick growth of trees and

dense underbrush. It was a two-story timber structure facing the tree-shielded highway, with a concealed beach below and behind it. Some cabins were clustered nearby to handle any overflow of guests from the main lodge.

About one o'clock Friday afternoon, April 20, a car came up the winding driveway and two men and a woman got out, leaving a Boston bull terrier pup in the car.

Although they were strangers to Wanatka, who came out to greet them, one of the men said, "Hello, Emil, how are you?"

Wanatka said he was fine, and the three (Homer Van Meter, Pat Riley and Marie Conforti) asked if they could get lunch. After eating, one of the men explained that they were on their way to Duluth and would be joined by friends later in the afternoon. He asked if there was room to put up ten or twelve people for two or three days. Emil said there was, and eagerly showed them the rooms and the heated garage they asked about.

The strangers said everything looked fine and that the rest of the party would be along soon. No one left the lodge, and no one asked for liquor. They played the slot machines (five, ten and twenty-five cents) and fed the dog.

About 5:30 two other cars pulled in, and Wanatka met—though not by name—four more men and three women (Dillinger, Hamilton, and Pat Cherrington, from Sault Ste. Marie, and Tommy Carroll, Jean Delaney, and Baby Face Nelson and his wife Helen, who had come from Chicago).

Two young employees, George Baszo and Frank Traube, carried the bags into the lodge and one of the cottages, and found them heavy. The sixteen-year-old Baszo grumbled to Wanatka, "There must be lead in this one. What are these guys, hardware salesmen?"

Wanatka, delighted with the unexpected windfall during the slack season, told his aides to mind their own business. But he, too, was a little curious. Mrs. Wanatka, who had started upstairs to get the rooms ready, was stopped by Nelson, who explained that the girls would take care of such chores.

Dinner was ready about 6:30, and Mrs. Wanatka served steak. One of the women guests peeled the garlic which went on it. After dinner one of the men asked Wanatka if he played cards.

"Yes," Wanatka said, "my favorite is pinochle."

"We can't play that," was the reply. "How about poker?"

Wanatka demurred, saying he was too tired and that the proposed dollar limit was too steep. But he finally got into the game with four of the guests. He was sitting across the table from a sandy-haired man about thirty, who had been introduced as Johnnie, and the third or fourth hand was a spirited one. Finally everyone dropped out but Emil and Johnnie, who was content to call Emil's last bet. Wanatka reached for the pot, saying, "Too bad, Johnnie."

"What have you got?" asked the other.

"A little more than you," Wanatka said confidently. "Kings and sixes."

"Too bad," his opponent replied. "I've got kings and eights."

As Johnnie leaned forward to rake in the money, his coat opened and Wanatka saw two guns in shoulder holsters. He immediately began wondering who his guests might be, and thought at once of Dillinger.

"There had been several poses of Dillinger in the papers, showing him in profile, giving his weight and height, mentioning a scar here and there," Wanatka said later. "But I couldn't think that with all that, Dillinger would show up. As we continued to play I was looking over the others, and as two of them reached for their cards I saw guns in shoulder straps.

"In half an hour or so Johnnie went to the men's room. As he got up, I went into the kitchen. There were some pictures on the front page of the *Tribune,* and I looked them over. I thought he weighed about a hundred and fifty. The paper said a hundred and sixty. I compared sizes and pictures, then I went back and played until it got to be about ten o'clock. I started to yawn. I had a little winnings —maybe twenty-five or thirty dollars—and was very anxious to break up the game.

"Their good night wasn't very friendly. Two of them went to the cottage next door. I went upstairs with my dogs—two collies, Shadow and Prince. One of the men didn't even say good night when I left. They'd made me think there were two factions. The one who didn't say good night was stone-faced, a mean guy.

"I went up with the dogs. I was tired, and I went to sleep after Mrs. Wanatka asked me half a dozen times who they were. I told her I thought, after I got back from the kitchen, that one of them was Dillinger. In the morning she told me she heard somebody walking up and down the hallway all night."

(Mrs. Wanatka agreed that they didn't know for certain who their visitors were until Friday night, but said she knew they were hoodlums even before that "because nobody comes north at that time of year. We figured somebody had held up a bank and was staying off the highway.... You can bet there wasn't much sleep that night. In the night, when the dogs bark and you hear door keys and walking in the hall, you lay on your back with donkey's ears sticking way out.")

Wanatka got up about six o'clock to let the dogs out, and found Carroll, who was staying in the cottage next door with Pat Delaney and the Nelsons, already up. Carroll stretched and said, "Good morning, Emil. Boy, did I sleep. How about breakfast?"

"I told him, 'You come in and get the gang up, and we'll eat.' "

Carroll came in and went upstairs, where Dillinger and Riley had rooms to themselves, Hamilton shared a room with Pat Cherrington, and Van Meter was with Marie Conforti.

"In a little while the whole gang was together in the family kitchen," Wanatka went on. "The girls came down also, in their dressing gowns. Pat Cherrington asked if we had an ironing board she could use to iron her dress, and everyone helped set the table.

"We had breakfast—a long-winded breakfast—and during it I said, 'Johnnie, could I talk to you?'

" 'Absolutely,' he said. 'Is something wrong, Emil?'

"I said, 'No, I just want to talk to you.'

"I took him into my little office and slammed the door. I made up my mind to face it. He said, 'Emil, what's wrong? What do you want?' I looked him right in the eye and said, 'You're John Dillinger.'

"He looked at me, very calmly, and said, 'You're not afraid, are you?'

"I said, 'No. But everything I have to my name, including my family, is right here, and every policeman in America is looking for you. If I can help it, there isn't going to be any shooting match.'

"He patted me on the shoulder.

" 'Emil, all we want is to eat and rest for a few days. We'll pay you well and get out. There won't be any trouble.'

"From then on we got very friendly. He even tried to satisfy me by playing pinochle with me, and I cheated him every hand. It was very friendly."

After breakfast the visitors wanted to have a little target practice and asked Wanatka if he had a gun. He brought out a .22, and they shot that until it jammed. Dillinger then said, 'Go on, Van, get one of our rifles.' Van Meter came out with a rifle and the whole bunch shot at a can placed against a snowbank about three hundred feet away."

Wanatka remembers that only he and Van Meter hit the target.

"The boys wasn't very good marksmen," Wanatka said, "but I guess they were good with the sprayer [*machine gun*]."

The girls wanted some laundry done, and the men wouldn't let Mrs. Wanatka do it. So Van Meter and Wanatka took it to a woman living nearby who did such work. The woman, obviously surprised at the amount of dirty clothing, jestingly said to Wanatka, "You haven't got Dillinger over there, have you?"

This remark so upset Van Meter, Wanatka says, that he threatened to go back and shoot her. Wanatka, however, persuaded the jittery gunman that the woman was joking, and reminded him that stories about the gang were in every paper.

"This is how I know there were two factions," Wanatka went on. "The day after we came back from taking the laundry, Homer Van Meter said to me, 'I want to talk to you. There are too many of us here. You know some place I could go away to?' I could see Nelson watching us. Later Nelson asked me, 'What were you fellows talking about?' When I told him, he said, 'Listen, Emil, when he wants any cottages you tell him to see me!'"

Although his guests seemingly trusted Wanatka, they remained watchful. When the milkman, an electrician, or anyone else drove into the yard, one of the men was always at the window to ask Emil, "You know who this is?" When the telephone rang, one or another of the gang, apparently by chance, was always within earshot.

The visitors were astute enough not to attempt to interfere with the regular customers who dropped in while they were there. Mrs. Ruth Voss (Mrs. Wanatka's sister) and her daughter Audrey came in Friday night and saw Wanatka playing cards with the four strangers. Dillinger asked who the two women were, and when Wanatka told him, he bought drinks for them. Audrey wondered why the stranger's hair was so much lighter than his eyebrows.

Dillinger himself seemed completely at ease on Saturday and

spent some time playing catch with Emil, Jr., Wanatka's eight-year-old son. During the morning Riley and Miss Cherrington left in one of the cars.

Saturday evening young Emil was sent to his cousin's birthday party at the home of Mrs. Wanatka's brother, George Laporte, in the village of Spider Lake (now Manitowish Waters) two miles away. Mrs. Wanatka soon said she wished she had gone along, and the girls urged her to go, saying they would do the cooking. Mrs. Wanatka then went into the lounge and asked if it were all right to leave. The men, by now filled with an incredible and foolhardy self-confidence, told her it was.

"I got into the car and started it, then stalled it," Mrs. Wanatka said, "to give them a chance to change their minds. Then I went to the party, but I wouldn't stop. I had used the party as an excuse to get out and mail a letter to George Fisher [a friend who was an assistant district attorney in Chicago]."

Mrs. Wanatka was sure she was being followed as she drove to Manitowish and picked up another brother, Lloyd Laporte, then continued to Mercer, where Laporte mailed the letter. On the way she told him that Dillinger was at Little Bohemia. The "following" car, if there was one, disappeared, and Mrs. Wanatka and her brother returned to the birthday party at Spider Lake. There a conference was held with her brother-in-law Henry Voss, owner of Birchwood Lodge, two miles south of Little Bohemia.

After a conference with Voss and her two brothers, Mrs. Wanatka said she would tell Emil their plan—to have Voss telephone a friend in the Milwaukee police department Sunday. If Emil approved, a message to this effect was to be slipped to Lloyd Laporte in a cigarette package Sunday morning. This was done.

Voss then drove 60 miles to Rhinelander (to avoid having his call overheard) and telephoned Milwaukee. On advice from the police there, he also called the FBI in Chicago. Finally he talked with Melvin Purvis, who told him that a group of G-men would fly into the Rhinelander airport that very afternoon, and asked Voss to meet them, wearing a white handkerchief around his neck so Purvis would know him. Voss agreed and Purvis at once arranged for government agents from Chicago, Duluth, Milwaukee and the Twin Cities to rush to Rhinelander by plane and car.

Purvis and his men—equipped with steel vests, machine guns,

tear gas and revolvers—flew by chartered plane to Rhinelander. Rough weather delayed them, and by the time they arrived, the agents from St. Paul already were on hand and trying to rent enough cars to carry the raiders to Little Bohemia. Purvis conferred with Voss, who told him the gang planned to leave Monday morning. This, although Voss did not know it, was no longer true.

"Everything went smooth until Sunday," Wanatka said. "Then about ten o'clock in the morning Dillinger called me on the side. He paid me five hundred dollars and said, 'We'll be leaving in the morning.' He told me how nice everything was, and that was it. From then on the boys packed the cars and the girls were in the lounge.

"We had customers there Sunday afternoon, including one fellow from Winchester. While he was in the barroom John Hamilton came in. This was about four or five o'clock. This fellow from Winchester said, 'Hey, you, have a drink!' Hamilton said, 'Thank you. I don't drink.' And the man said, 'God damn you, you'll drink this or I'll pour it down your throat!' So Hamilton said, 'This man is pretty tough. You'd better give me a small beer.' "

By this time Dillinger had told the Wanatkas that plans were changed, and he and the others would leave that evening as soon as Riley returned from St. Paul. Providentially, Mrs. Voss dropped in a little later, and Mrs. Wanatka casually suggested that there was extra meat in the big icebox if Mrs. Voss cared to pick some out to take home. Once inside the storage room, Mrs. Wanatka whispered the news, and Mrs. Voss quickly excused herself. Moments later Mrs. Voss, her mother and her daughter Audrey were speeding over the blacktop toward Rhinelander, where they met Voss and the Federal agents as they were leaving for Little Bohemia in a five-car caravan, with Voss and Lloyd Laporte as guides.

Told of the gang's imminent departure, Purvis had no choice except to rush to the lodge and attack virtually without preparation, a circumstance which goes far toward explaining the debacle that followed.

A dollar dinner was served at Little Bohemia on Sunday nights, a bargain which on this evening had attracted around seventy-five patrons. The gang mixed with the customers generally, but avoided those Emil signaled he didn't know. Among the patrons that evening were John Hoffman, twenty-eight-year-old oil station operator from Mercer, and two men from the nearby Civilian Conservation Corps camp: John Morris, fifty-nine, a cook, and Eugene Boiseneau, thirty-five, a specialist.

Wanatka showed Boiseneau around after the other customers had gone, and finally the three from the CCC camp decided to leave. Baszo and Traube walked onto the porch with them and stood watching as the 1933 Chevrolet coupé, with Hoffman driving, started away. The dogs were barking furiously, but no one paid any attention.

The radio was playing as the car backed out, turned toward the right and headed for the road. Boiseneau was sitting in the middle and Morris on the outside. The government agents, some of whom had ridden on running boards after two of their cars broke down, had just arrived and were not yet in position. When they saw the trio leaving, someone shouted to Hoffman to halt. Morris heard the warning, but Hoffman did not. There was a fusillade of shots, and the side window vanished.

"I just got turned and started," Hoffman said, "and it was just like a big windstorm—whiffff! I stopped the car and left the motor running and jumped out."

Hoffman's right arm was bleeding as he headed for the lake, sprinting hard, with the guns still chattering and Baszo and Traube shouting from the porch, "Don't shoot! Those are customers of ours!"

Morris, meanwhile, came out of the car, at so slow a pace that no one thought to fire again at him. He had two bullets in his hip and two in the shoulder, and the agents watched as he walked painfully into the lodge, where he took all the money from the cash register, to save it—he thought—for Wanatka, since he, like Hoffman, believed he had been shot during an attempted holdup.

Boiseneau lay dead in the car, whose headlights were shining into the trees. The motor still ran and the radio was blaring. No one approached the car until dawn.

Wanatka was in the bar when the shooting began, and he ran into the basement with the three girls, where he later was joined by Baszo and Traube. All the outlaws but Nelson and Carroll (who were in the cottage next door and presumably slipped into the woods at once) were upstairs. Purvis's account of the raid tells of heavy fire from within the lodge—fire that continued for some time

—although Wanatka says he believes the gang fled without wasting time shooting back. Some went out the upstairs window and over the roof. One or two, including Dillinger, ran downstairs and out the back door, which was not yet covered by the Federal men.

"After Hoffman was shot and Boiseneau dead," Wanatka said, "I was in the basement under the telephone when Morris called Alvin Koerner [in whose place the switchboard was located] and said, 'Alvin, I'm at Emil's. Somebody held up the place. Boiseneau's dead and we're shot.' Then he fell.

"When I heard him fall, I went upstairs. I could hear machine guns spraying, so I went back and asked the girls to lend me a hand so we could drag him to the basement. But the girls said, 'If you want to give him help, you help him. We're staying here.' Which I don't blame 'em for."

In the meantime Pat Riley was nearing Little Bohemia with Pat Cherrington—who had gone along for the ride—after an overnight trip to St. Paul, where he had been sent to collect some money a night-club owner had been holding for Van Meter.

Shortly after the shooting of the three unsuspecting customers, his car whirled into the driveway at Little Bohemia and was challenged by agents hiding beside the road. Instead of halting, Riley flicked off the lights, jammed the gears into reverse, and backed out to the highway at amazing speed. Although the following shots were accurate enough to hit the car, there seems to have been no attempt to pursue.

Riley and his companion—the latter very much upset by this explosive welcome home—went as swiftly as one flat tire would permit in the direction of Mercer. The sound of their coming was unmistakable in the crisp night air, and Mrs. Lillian Collins, whose husband Richard was about to lock up their gas station at the main intersection in Mercer, told him to wait.

"You're either going to sell a tire or fix one," she told him.

"I ain't going to fix it," Collins retorted. "He's coming in on the rim."

Collins was shortly changing the tire. While doing so, he had trouble with his jack, and asked Riley if he had one. Riley said the car wasn't his and he didn't know. Collins offered to take a flashlight and look, but Riley said he would do it—probably because a bag with $2,500 of Van Meter's was in the trunk.

As Collins worked, Pat Cherrington kept peering down the road, in the direction from which they had come, and Riley asked, a shade too casually, whether they had a telephone. Collins said there was none, that the wires went only to the ranger's station.

When the spare was on at last, a car with a couple of CCC boys in it approached, and Riley spun the gravel in his haste to leave. He had already asked the best route to St. Paul, but said he did not want to return the way he had come. So he headed toward Ironwood, disregarding warnings that the road was washed out in spots.

"I wanted to get out of there," Riley said, "but I couldn't show it. It took fifteen or twenty minutes to change because he had no spare wheel to fit it. It was a Ford, and he didn't have the size. Then we went towards Ironwood and got stuck in the mud. We were stuck for an hour or better, and I had to go and wait for a farmer to get up and pull us out. Pat was hollering, scared. She wanted to get out and walk."

Hoffman, who had caromed off one agent and kept running after bailing out of his car, jumped down the bank to the lake shore behind Little Bohemia and lay there. Someone came and peered down through the darkness, asking, 'Is that you, Red?' but went on when Hoffman failed to answer. Finally, Hoffman went out the driveway of the next resort to the main road.

"There was someone walking on the highway," Hoffman said. "I hollered to the guy [*quite possibly Tommy Carroll*] but he didn't answer. He was walking towards Mitchells'. I was scared and sat in the swamp again. It was April and the ice was on the lake. I could hear shooting and hollering. Then Ray Jorgenson [*owner of the resort*] came in [*to the drive*], and I told him what had happened.

"He said, 'It's probably a holdup. Take my car and drive over.'

"I went back because I wanted to see what the hell was going on."

Hoffman drove into the yard at Little Bohemia and asked if it was all over. The government agents asked why he had run, and he said, quite sensibly, because they had been shooting at him. The agents began searching the wounded Hoffman, but a doctor from the CCC camp identified him and he was taken to the hospital.

"There were twenty-eight holes in my car," Hoffman said, "one right behind where my head had been. I was hit just above the right elbow and bruised on the right leg by a bullet that came through the door. They said, 'We got information that Dillinger was in there and we weren't taking any chances.' They were scared, that's what was the matter with 'em."

Later Hoffman was paid for his ruined car.

The doctor had been brought by George Laporte, who had been sitting on a hill near Little Bohemia when the shooting began about 8:30. Laporte drove in to find that Wanatka, Baszo and Traube had come out of the lodge with their hands in the air, in response to orders given by a listening G-man when Wanatka had telephoned Koerner's to ask that a doctor be sent for the wounded Morris. The three were not permitted to return to the lodge.

Purvis and Wanatka, who apparently took a quick dislike to each other, got into a violent argument after Wanatka asked permission to drive to Koerner's for some winter jackets to shield them from the cold. Permission was granted at last, and he left with Laporte and his two helpers, and Carl Christianson, the stationmaster, who was riding with Laporte.

As they walked into Koerner's, the group found itself facing a snarling Baby Face Nelson, who was behind the door with a .45 in his hand. Mr. and Mrs. Koerner and Mr. and Mrs. Paul Lange already were in the room.

Wanatka said, "What are you doing with these people? They're friends of mine."

Nelson ignored the question and asked whose car they had come in. Laporte said his, and Nelson ordered Koerner and Emil Wanatka to accompany him outside.

As this was happening, word had reached the agents' headquarters at Birchwood Lodge that a car without lights was parked in front of Koerner's place. Agents J. C. Newman and W. Carter Baum were at Birchwood with Carl C. Christensen, thirty-two-year-old constable from Spider Lake. Christensen, who had been elected constable only two weeks earlier, had just been recruited to help the agents set up roadblocks in case anyone escaped from Little Bohemia.

Baum and Christensen were outside when Newman came out of Birchwood and relayed the message. He then jumped behind the wheel of their 1932 Ford coupé, one of the cars rented in Rhinelander. Baum sat in the middle and Christensen on the outside. They left for Koerner's place.

"We started out hell-a-whooping," Christensen recalled. "I said, 'Go easy now, we're coming to the bridge and might meet somebody.' Then we saw a car at the side of the road. I checked the license and knew it was Lange's [which Nelson had commandeered and abandoned because it was running poorly]. We got to Koerner's and there was an auto there. There was nobody around. We couldn't see a soul. I thought it was damned funny, with the house lighted up like a church. . . ."

Wanatka, Baby Face Nelson and Koerner were in Laporte's car, and Emil had just told Nelson he didn't know where the switch was.

"I told him I was excited," Wanatka said later. "He said, 'Put that switch on!' which I did. As we talked I could see a couple of lights in my looking glass. We just got moving when a car drove up right next to us and someone yelled, 'Halt! We're Federal officers.' Nelson jumped out from the right side of the front seat. . . ."

"I saw that it was George Laporte's car," Christensen said, "a neighbor's car, and I know it. We didn't get abreast of it when this little jackrabbit flew right out of nowhere. Our car wasn't even stopped when his gun came through the window.

"I know he swore at us, but I can't remember what he said. I tried to duck behind Baum, and he tried to duck behind Newman. I had a Smith and Wesson thirty-eight in a holster on my left side and couldn't get to it. Baum had a machine gun on his lap. Nelson opened the door and fired into the car. He shot right away, with a forty-five Colt converted into a machine gun with a long clip and a pistol grip. Newman was hit over the eye by a bullet, and rolled out.

"I got out and our machine gun came out on top of me. Baum fell out, then got up and tried to run. He was hit in the throat above his steel vest. I started to run for a woodpile, but I was in the headlights. I was turning back when he caught me. The bullets knocked me down. Newman fired at Baby Face and I tried to wriggle out of the headlights' glare. I rolled on the ground to Baum's gun. Nelson got into our car and started out the driveway. I didn't know how to operate the machine gun and had dropped my revolver.

"I tried to crawl to Baum, who had fallen across the fence. I could still hear him breathing, but he died before anyone got there. They let us lie there about an hour before anyone dared to come."

While this was happening, Wanatka, who had dived into a snowbank as the shooting began, was missed by one shot Nelson threw at him. When the outlaw left, spinning the wheels so hard that Baszo, still in the house, heard gravel shower against the siding, Wanatka took off on a run for Little Bohemia. As he came panting into the yard, all the agents shouted to him to put his hands up, but a Dr. Roberts recognized him and yelled, "Don't shoot! It's Emil Wanatka!"

"Then Purvis and I got into a big argument," Wanatka said, still disgusted at the thought. "He asked me how I spelled my name, and how to spell Manitowish. I said, 'All your men are dead. Did you come here to get Dillinger or me?' All because I couldn't spell Manitowish. I never could."

Purvis then asked where the shooting had taken place, and Wanatka told him. The innkeeper tossed some hay and blankets into his pickup truck, had another argument with Purvis about putting the truck lights on, and left, after calling Purvis a number of names.

At Koerner's Baum was gently placed on the hay and covered up, but Christensen was left behind, simply because he still could talk and no one realized how seriously hurt he was. Newman, although creased by a bullet, was not badly injured. Wanatka says he was told to drive Baum to Ironwood, 35 jolting miles away, but went instead to the CCC camp, where a doctor removed the useless bulletproof vest and pronounced the agent dead.

Sheriff Thomas McGregor of Eagle River, who had been called by the government forces after the trap failed, and brought a small posse with him, took Christensen and Newman to Ironwood, where it was found that the constable had wounds in the lungs, liver, chest, hip, arm and ankle. He fooled everyone by recovering.

Long before this, and about the same time Nelson was terrorizing the people at Koerner's, Dillinger, Hamilton, and Van Meter had walked through the woods, circling the attacking forces, and crossed the road to a resort run by E. J. Mitchell, a mile from Little Bohemia. There they knocked on the door and gained admittance. After jerking the telephone connection loose, they demanded a car.

The seventy-year-old Mitchell, whose wife was ill with influenza and was lying on a couch in the kitchen, told them his only car was a Model-T, which had been standing outside all winter. They asked who owned the Model-A parked nearby, and were told it belonged to Robert Johnson, a carpenter, who occupied a cottage a hundred feet away.

While Dillinger stayed with the Mitchells, the other two knocked at Johnson's door and told him that Mrs. Mitchell was ill and needed to be taken to the hospital. After Johnson had dressed and come outside in his carpet slippers, he was told at gunpoint that he must chauffeur the three gangsters. Before they drove away, however, Dillinger ordered everyone at Mitchells' to stand on the porch where they could be seen as the auto left. Mitchell said everyone but his wife would go outside, but that she was too ill. Dillinger thereupon wrapped a blanket around her and said, "She'll have to come out, too. Just stand there until we get away."

"For an outlaw," Mitchell said later, "that Dillinger was a gentleman. He made the others behave. No foul language, and cool as a cucumber."

Johnson was forced to drive the trio over back roads to Park Falls, about 25 miles from Manitowish Waters. Dillinger and Van Meter rode inside in the 1930 Ford coupé, and Hamilton huddled in the rumble seat despite the cold. Johnson was warned to mind his own business, and drive as he was told. Near Springstead, with the gas supply low, one of the bandits roused a filling station attendant and bought ten gallons of gasoline. About midnight they ordered Johnson out three miles from the Pixley power station, gave him seven dollars, and promised to leave his car where it would be found. He reached a telephone an hour later.

The sixth male member of the mob, Tommy Carroll, effected the cleanest escape of all. He simply walked the two miles from Little Bohemia to Kuhnert's Northern Lights resort in Manitowish Waters and stole a Packard from the front yard.

When daylight came at last, the government agents moved cautiously against the silent lodge, tossed some tear gas into the building, and had no difficulty in capturing the three women, who walked out with their hands in the air.

It was not a glorious moment.

SIXTEEN

●●●●●●●●●●●●●●● "EVEN SOME RED INDIANS
JOINED THE HUNT TODAY,
WITH BOWS AND ARROWS."
—LONDON (ENGLAND)
NEWSPAPER

The word out of Little Bohemia was confusing, to put it politely, in the hours between the opening volley and daylight, when the Federal agents moved in and captured six machine guns, twelve shotguns, five bulletproof vests and three young women.

J. Edgar Hoover announced at 2 A.M. in Washington that Dillinger was surrounded. At 3:30 came a flash from Mercer that posses would join battle with Dillinger and his gang within a matter of hours. Shortly thereafter a third report said Dillinger had been seen at Antigo, heading toward Chicago. Not until 6 A.M. was it admitted officially that four of the gang "may" have broken through the cordon.

If the main highway had been guarded properly, none of the gang could have escaped, except afoot. As it was, Riley and Pat Cherrington not only managed to turn around and come back through Mercer after daylight (Mrs. Collins, the wife of the gas station operator, saw them as they sped by) but continued on

Route 51 past Little Bohemia. Collins, meanwhile, who had finally learned of the shooting at Wanatka's place, was trying in vain to get through to the authorities by telephone to warn them that Riley was on the road.

Riley and his companion abandoned the Ford at Owen, Wisconsin, and hired a car to drive them to the suburbs of St. Paul. There they took a taxi downtown in an effort to throw dust across their trail.

Dillinger and his companions also had luck breaking their way until they ran into a roadblock near Hastings, Minnesota, where three deputies had set up an ambuscade at a bridge. When the bandit car refused to halt, the lawmen gave chase.

During the ensuing gun battle, a bullet fired by one of the deputies, who was aiming at the tires, split when it hit a fender brace and a piece of lead ricocheted through the back of the car and struck Hamilton in the back; it proved to be a mortal wound. The fugitives finally pulled away after riddling the windshield of the police car.

Fearing that their license number and the make of car were now known, the fleeing trio curbed a new Ford V-8 driven by Roy F. Francis, a young St. Paul businessman, who was taking his wife and infant son for a noontime ride. The mobsters stopped Francis near a newly built cutoff, and Dillinger, .45 in hand, opened the driver's door and ordered Francis and his family into the rear seat.

The wounded Hamilton climbed into the front seat and Van Meter got in back with the machine gun. They started away, with Dillinger driving, but returned while Van Meter parked Johnson's car just off the road where it was less visible. Then, finding Francis' car low on gas, they pulled into a station, warning Francis and his wife to say the three men were friends if anyone asked questions.

Hamilton said he needed a drink, and they bought some pop, including a bottle for the youngster, paid for the gas and left.

During the ride Van Meter asked Francis where he worked and was told the Northern State Power Company. He asked if Francis had seen the noon papers. Francis said he had not.

"You don't know how lucky you are," Van Meter said suddenly. "You've got a good job and a nice family."

"He sounded like a kid in a trap," Francis recalls.

Dillinger halted the car between roads, half an hour or so after the kidnaping, and let the passengers out, half a mile from a farmhouse.

Riley, who reached St. Paul about noon, was joined by Dillinger, Van Meter and Tommy Carroll a short time later.

"They laughed about my arrival at Little Bohemia," Riley said. "They had heard the shooting and knew I was driving in. I gave Van Meter the money. They went back to Chicago and I stayed in St. Paul."

(Hamilton was not with the others, and Riley believes he already had died and his body had been hidden in the country near St. Paul, where it later was picked up and driven to Chicago for burial. Another version of Hamilton's end is that he survived for a few days, and finally died in a Chicago suburb after having hidden out in the apartment of a woman acquaintance of the gang.)

By this time Michigan, Minnesota and northern Wisconsin were crawling with police and unofficial or volunteer searchers. All roads along the Wisconsin-Michigan border were guarded, from Ironwood to Iron Mountain, and Chief of Police Matt H. Mitchell of Sault Ste. Marie announced that a crack shot had been posted in each of that town's three banks in case the gang was heading that way.

Federal agents swarmed into the Mercer area all day Monday, and local law officials, belatedly apprised of the presence of the nation's top gun in their area, also were patrolling the roads. The Federal Bureau of Investigation asked Chicago police to broadcast a request to northern Illinois and Wisconsin authorities to watch all highways and be on the alert for two Fords and a Packard. Dillinger, it was said, was "positively" riding in one of these.

The Packard, however, was found in a ditch near Marenisco, Michigan, later that day, where it had been abandoned by Carroll, who then managed to make his way to St. Paul.

It was "admitted" in Washington April 23 that Federal agents would probably kill Dillinger on sight rather than risk a gun battle by trying to take him alive. There was talk of demoting J. Edgar Hoover because of the Little Bohemia affair, and President Roosevelt was urging speedy passage of new Federal crime laws recommended by Attorney General Cummings, which would permit Federal agents to pursue fleeing criminals across state lines.

Interest in the hunt for Dillinger and his men remained high

223

overseas. Chief of Police Thomas Dahillat of St. Paul Park received long-distance telephone calls from both *The Times* and the *Evening News* in London, and one caller told him, "It's quite an interesting story over here, you know."

By this time, it had become obvious that Dillinger and the men with him had gone to earth in St. Paul or Chicago. But the whereabouts of Baby Face Nelson remained a mystery to all but the members of an Indian family living at Stearns Lake, not far from Lac du Flambeau, Wisconsin.

The diminutive Nelson had driven the car stolen after the deadly battle at Koerner's until it became mired in the mud about 20 miles from Mercer, near the Michigan line. He then had taken to the woods.

Mary Schroeder, a Chippewa Indian woman, was staying with her uncle and aunt, Mr. and Mrs. Ollie Catfish, in their cabin near Stearns Lake. The Catfishes were visiting in Lac du Flambeau on Sunday, and Mrs. Schroeder was alone in the cabin with two daughters, Gertrude, two, and Dorothy, fifteen. She was awakened early Monday morning by what she thought was a gunshot.

"I lay there for a while," she said, "then got up. I had a big washing to do and wanted to get done early. So I carried water from the lake and did the wash that morning. I had an old female dog named Geegans, and she had five puppies. She wasn't around and the puppies were hungry. I whistled and looked—she'd never left them before—and every once in a while I'd go and look around in the woods for her.

"The kids were up by this time and tried to feed the pups some canned milk. Dorothy went looking for the mother dog, and I gave up. I started working and got all the clothes hung up, eight or ten sheets on the line. Towards evening Dorothy said, 'Ma, I'll hang those colored clothes up.' I was baking bread at the time. When she came in she said, 'Ma, there's a man coming.' She had dropped her socks and run in.

"I looked out and could see a man's legs under the sheets. Then he came around to the front door and I said, 'Tell him to come around to the back.' Through the window, Dorothy told him to go to the back, and he came in. He was very friendly, said, 'Hello, Mother, could I buy lunch from you? Your baking smells good.'

"I looked at him, and I looked at Dorothy, and I gave him some bacon and fried eggs, gave him some fresh bread and made coffee. He gave me two dollars—put it down on the table—and gave Dorothy a dollar. After he finished eating—there was a cot along the wall—he asked, 'Would you mind if I lay down for a while? I've been walking a long ways.' But he wasn't muddy and he was well dressed.

"I kept the kids out of the room, but he didn't really sleep, I don't think. He asked me if we had any neighbors or a radio or a telephone. I said no. He said, 'Don't you get the papers either?' And I said, 'No, we're in the sticks. We could be killed, and no one would know anything about it.'

"I kept looking at him. His head was towards the front door. There were two windows facing out on the lake.

"He asked me where my husband was, and I said he was out trapping. He'd gone to his folks, been gone three or four days. He trapped beaver, muskrat, and got some deer.

"He was very friendly with the kids, playing with them and joking with Dorothy. He was about five-six and slim. He kept the guns hid all the time. Soon after he got done eating he asked me, 'Does your husband have any kind of old clothes?' I said, 'All we have is old clothes.' So I went and got George's khaki-colored pants and jacket—a plaid jacket with the sleeves cut off—and a stocking cap. He took them and put them on over his good clothes. He hung his hat up on the door and said, 'Your husband can have that.'

"I was afraid, but I didn't let on. I saw to it that the kids stayed in sight. I told him I expected my uncle and aunt home at any time: 'They went into town, said they'd be back today.' Then we saw 'em coming across the lake on the ice. We'd been making maple sugar out there and that's why they wanted to get back.

"They came in through the door—we were only using one—and my uncle said in Indian, 'An awful thing happened in town.' Then he saw the man lying there. I kind of motioned for him not to talk too much. Just about that time the man got up, and Ollie said, 'When did he come home?' Ollie thought it was George [*Mary Schroeder's husband*]. I told him the man walked in on us.

"He got up and shook hands with Ollie and Maggie. 'Hello, Uncle and Auntie!' She just laughed at him and looked at me and said in Indian, 'Who is that to come and be so friendly?' He kept on talking and after they were done I gave them something to eat.

About that time Dorothy said, 'Mommy, you should see the guns he has under his pillow!' He was wearing a light jacket, and I guess he had a gun in every pocket.

"When they were done eating we went to the woodpile and Ollie and the man sat down. They talked part in English and with writing on the ground. He asked me where Eagle River was, how far it was to the highway and to Rhinelander. I told him I didn't know much about this country, that I had just come over from Flambeau.

"We had one car sitting in the yard, an old Dodge that wasn't running, but he thought it was a running car. I think one or two of the pups died before the day was over. I told Ollie and Maggie, 'I don't know what's become of that dog.'

"I got supper for them, and he ate. It was getting kind of dusk, and he asked Ollie, 'Would you mind if I stayed overnight? It's getting dark and I wouldn't be able to find my way.' He had asked me and I told him to ask them because I was just staying here while we were boiling the sap.

"There was a mirror hanging on the wall, and I could tell by his face that he wasn't a 'right' man. Every now and then he'd look in the mirror, and I could tell by his eyes he wasn't honest. He wasn't acting right, though he was nice and polite.

"He stayed there that night, and the next morning early—four or five o'clock—we got up to go to the sugar camp. The sap was running real good. We took all day boiling sap. The fire was just going good when he thought it was too windy to make a fire. He spilled all their sap—two or three barrels full—to put out the fire. They were mad. They knowed something was wrong somewheres and said in Indian, 'I'll bet he's one of those men in that place there.' (We were just as deceitful as he was, laughing and making a joke of it.) I think he gave them seventy-five dollars when he spilled all that sap.

"Wednesday morning I had a hatchet and he must have seen it. He took the stocking cap and a mackinaw and said, 'We don't have no wood. I'd better go out and cut some.' I said I'd go and help. I told Maggie, 'You stay in here with the kids.' Maggie offered to go too, but he said, 'No, we're younger than you.'

"He sawed stove lengths and split it. I showed him how to split that wood. At the same time an airplane was going by. It seemed to be following the railroad tracks and the roads. I said, 'That plane is flying low.' I'd look up at it, but he wouldn't. He kept on sawing wood and said, 'Oh, they're just looking for somebody.' Then he said, "That's enough. That will last you until tomorrow morning.'

"He told me about himself and asked me where I went to school and what religion we had. I said, 'We're Catholics.' 'Oh,' he said, 'I was raised in a convent.' He said he was from Chicago. Said he walked in from the road, was lost. He didn't say where he was going, but said he wanted to get to Eagle River. Said something about 'I got to get to Eagle River and see whether my friends got there or not.' After a while he said, 'You're not as dumb as you let on you are. You know a lot, but you won't let on.'

"I think Ollie kind of spilled the beans. He watched them more than he did the two kids. They knew who he was.

"It was getting late on Thursday. He was getting kind of mad, asked if I would put up a lunch. I made some meat sandwiches and some strawberry jam ones and put them in a big sack. I think I took a couple of maple sugar cakes and threw them in.

"He kept asking Ollie if he'd go with him, been after him since Wednesday noon. There still was no dog. Maggie said, 'What's become of that dog?' Him and Ollie walked up the road. I told her, 'I think I heard that dog barking and I thought I heard a shot.' Maggie said, 'I bet you he killed that dog.' The puppies all died.

"He gave me twenty dollars for putting up the lunch and making the meals. He said, 'You're the one that got the meals. Was it their groceries or yours?' I said they were mine. Then he gave me fifty dollars more for his board.

"Ollie came in and said, 'He wants me to go as far as the highway.' This was about three miles. Ollie went as far as the road, then came back. 'I can't walk fast,' he said.

"Maggie said to me, 'If anything happens to your uncle you'll be to blame for it.' What money I got I gave to Dorothy. 'You keep it in case I don't come back.' 'All right,' she said. She was in tears then. 'Never mind, Dorothy,' I said. 'Things will come out all right—or let's hope they do.'

"I took a sweater and scarf and started walking. He was waiting in the road. I started walking down the road. It was quite a ways to the curve. I walked toward where he was. He saw me. I pretty near got to him and he said, 'Well, Mother, you going with me?' I said, 'I'll take you as far as the highway.' 'All right,' he said. So we started out.

"A little while after that Ollie hollered at us and said in Indian, 'I'll go and show him the road.' I didn't say nothing. I looked at Ollie and the other guy. Ollie started up the road and the guy said, 'You going to show me or is she?' 'I'll go,' Ollie said. We hadn't any more than gotten around the curve. He stood behind Ollie. 'Walk fast, it's getting late,' he said. He had a gun on him. Every now and then he'd look back to see if one of us was following.

"In an hour or so, Maggie left for town. Said she was going to follow them. I told her in Indian to be careful, to watch out. She grabbed a shawl and left. She knew the shortcuts, and I wouldn't have. She took a trail that came out by a place on the highway, walked a little way on the highway, and then cut across again and came into the town the back way. But they done the same thing, and then went along Fence Lake and took a different trail.

"It was getting dark by the time they got to the highway, walked, then cut across again. There were some people fishing, catching suckers. They seen a lot of cars. He asked, 'What are those cars doing there?' Ollie told him they were fishing. He said, 'Let's go fishing too.'"

Shortly after Nelson and his unwilling companion reached Fence Lake and joined the fishermen, Adolph Goetz—a mailman and deputy sheriff from Merrill—arrived with a friend, Al Snow, a policeman from the nearby reservation.

"They were just chasing the kids off the street," Goetz remembers. "It was dark when we got to the lake. I parked the car so I could scoot out if I had to. Nelson already was with the others, and he said, 'I want the keys to that car.'

"I thought, 'Who's this son of a gun?' But I figured that he might be a warden or something, so I said, 'Who are you? What's your authority for this?' He said, 'Never mind, I want the keys to the car.' Then he showed me a gun. He had been sitting with his hands crossed, holding a gun under his coat.

"Herman Weber, who'd been bringing wood to the fire, was sad about this later. He said, 'If I'd known, I could have hit him on the head with one of them clubs.'

"Nelson lined up the whole bunch: Catfish, Herb Ackley, Al

Snow, Bill Grunewald, Herman Weber. He kept away from us after his gun was out. I had to fumble for the keys, and when I handed them to him the gun was ready. Then he went to Ackley's car and yanked the wires out. He started questioning us about the affair before he pulled the distributor wires. He wanted to know about the roads. We told him the roads were all right, none were blockaded. He asked Snow who I was. Snow told him a friend from Merrill, up to get some fish. I told him one agent had been killed at Little Bohemia and the next question his voice kind of quivered, so I figured, 'Aha, you're the son of a gun that did it!' He had a police positive thirty-eight.

"Nelson told me, 'I'll give you twenty dollars to take you home.' I said all right. He peeled off a couple of tens and let them fall to the ground. I asked, 'You want me to start it for you?' He said, 'No. I know all about these cars.' I had the door locked and he couldn't open it. I reached in through the window and opened it.

"He was a nice guy to talk with, real polite. He asked me for the title to the car, wanted to buy it and pay cash, but I said I didn't have the title with me. Before he got in with Catfish he said, 'I know you guys are gonna report this, but gimme a little time.'

"Al Snow and I walked to town, and when we got there we saw Catfish. It was a cold day."

Nelson had stopped in town for gasoline, giving the attendant ten dollars and telling him to keep the change, then driven on, letting Catfish out of the car about half a mile from the main highway, after giving him seventy-five dollars.

Said Catfish, "He left me there. Said goodbye. He went west."

The next day, near Greenwood, Wisconsin, about a hundred miles southwest of Fence Lake, Nelson ran the stolen car into a farmer's shed (seemingly to keep it out of sight) and told the farmer that he had burned out a connecting rod and that a friend would be out from St. Paul to pick it up. He told the farmer he was a CCC worker and hired him to take him into Marshfield, where he bought a secondhand car. Goetz later recovered his car and found nothing missing but the keys and a road map.

Nelson reached St. Paul Friday without attracting any notice on the way.

By Friday the hunt had widened to the extent that official and civilian groups in every state between Minnesota and New York were guarding crossroads and keeping watch for the fugitives. In northern Wisconsin Indian guides and lumberjacks were hunting two men, one believed (erroneously) to be Nelson. In Ohio, authorities were in an uneasy state of alertness because of another tip that members of the mob were in Columbus and planned to kidnap Governor White and his daughter, presumably as the prelude to arranging a swap for Pierpont, Makley and Clark.

It was the second such report in two weeks, and two National Guardsmen were stationed day and night at the Governor's mansion. The number of guards near Death Row in the Ohio State Penitentiary was also increased on orders of Warden Preston E. Thomas.

Extra guards were assigned to the St. Paul jail in which Miss Frechette was awaiting trial for harboring Dillinger, and there were rumors that she had been moved secretly to a different place to prevent Dillinger's finding her in case he was looking.

Dillinger himself was reported seen in Pennsylvania, New York and New Jersey, and twice was said to have driven up to a building on East Oak Street, in Chicago, in a new sedan. Although the source of this information was a Hindu crystal gazer (feminine), police laid on a guard just for luck.

The repercussions in Wisconsin were heavy after the Little Bohemia raid. Purvis was the target of harsh criticism, and a petition circulated in Mercer County asked for his dismissal "at least until Dillinger was caught or killed." This petition, which was sent to the Justice Department, protested the "irresponsible conduct of federal operatives" for having raided Little Bohemia "in such a stupid manner as to bring about the deaths of two men and injury to four others." None of the dead or injured, the petition pointed out, was a gangster.

The Federal agents also were blamed for their early failure to seek aid from the local sheriff's police familiar with the Mercer area, who—conceivably—could have sealed off the key escape routes simply by barricading three bridges, and the petition stressed "the criminal stupidity of two United States agents, evidently either with insufficient instructions or in disregard of orders for caution, in approaching a suspicious parked car near the Koerner home with no attempt at concealment and with weapons held so they could not be drawn for defense."

Actually, the agents—one killed and one wounded—had taken the word of Constable Christensen that the car was Laporte's (which it was), and Nelson, acting with tigerish speed and ruthlessness, had simply caught them unawares. The worst that could be said for the unfortunate trio was that it was taken off guard.

The FBI came in for attack on several fronts. The papers in the Mercer area carried highly critical articles, and in Michigan Commissioner Oscar Olander of the Department of Public Safety charged that failure of the Federal men to cooperate with the Michigan State Police probably permitted the escape of Dillinger and Hamilton when they visited Mrs. Steve.

Olander said the Chippewa County authorities were told that the state police "were not needed," and added that the government agents refused to permit Sergeant Fred Kune of the state police to attend a conference at which the Dillinger hunt was planned. Olander inferred that the Federal men were motivated by a desire not to share the credit for Dillinger's capture, and pointed out that the state police—who had been very successful in tracking down fugitives with the aid of radio—were forced to pick up what news they could of Dillinger and his men from the newspapers and press associations.

In Germany, where Adolf Hitler was Chancellor, the Little Bohemia story rated front-page space in the Berlin newspaper *Zwoelf Uhr Blatt*, which said that with Dillinger loose there should no longer be criticism in the United States of Hitlerism (a non sequitur which defies explanation) and advised the United States to sterilize its gangsters.

In London, the *Express* explained that the Dillinger mob's methods could be attributed to changes in gang procedure brought about by the Roosevelt administration: "The Roosevelt revolution, shaking up the whole structure of the American government, has upset organized crime which fattened on corrupt officialdom. Capone had got that business down to a fine art. Nobody has followed him because conditions have been changed. In the present confusion of the economic crisis it is the lone raider type you would expect to flourish. Hence, Dillinger."

By Thursday the search for Dillinger was pretty much concentrated in the Chicago area, even though Francis' bloodstained car was not found there until May second. The Town Hall police were searching their North Side district after a waiter told them that Dillinger and two women had been in a restaurant at 3203 Broadway at 5 A.M. on April 26 and left in a cab.

At 2 A.M. on Friday, April 27, Sergeant John Cunningham and twenty-five policemen from the Sheffield Avenue station raided an apartment at 2822 Cambridge Avenue, rousing an indignant young lady from her blameless sleep, after receiving a false tip. The police apologized and the young woman went back to bed.

Later that day Edward J. O'Hare, a Cicero publisher and president of Sportsman's Park racetrack, was in a sedan chased by State Policeman William Gallagher from Barrington into Des Plaines. Gallagher, who thought Dillinger might be in the car, managed to get the license number before being outdistanced, and O'Hare, found later in his South Side home, said he had been coming back from his summer cottage in Wisconsin and had outrun the police accidentally, since he didn't know he was being chased.

(O'Hare, incidentally, was killed some years later in a gang-style shooting which still is unsolved.)

Attorney General Cummings summed up the general feeling about Little Bohemia and allied matters very well, after attending the funeral for Baum at Rock Creek Cemetery in Washington.

"It has been a rather depressing episode," he said. "In any event, it will serve to accentuate the seriousness of the problem which confronts the people of this nation. As I have said before, those who had expected that the campaign against organized crime would be easily won were those who did not realize the situation. As things move along there inevitably will be disappointments, setbacks and sorrows. We have had a setback, we have been touched by sorrow. That is the part which makes all of us the more determined to go on. We will go on, and this campaign against predatory crime will be finished."

Cummings denied that the hunt for Dillinger had been hampered by any friction between Federal and state authorities, or between himself and J. Edgar Hoover.

Dillinger now had less than two months to live.

SEVENTEEN

●●●●●●●●●●●●●●●● "WE HAD A LOT OF FUN.
IT'S SURPRISING HOW
MUCH FUN WE HAD."
—POLLY HAMILTON

Whether it was because Baby Face Nelson had killed a Federal
agent at Little Bohemia, bringing greatly increased pressure to the
chase, or simply because after a year of playing cops and robbers
even the most elusive robber grows weary at not being able to call
off the game and go home to supper, it seems evident that by this
time Dillinger was anxious to step out of his starring role and leave
the limelight to someone else.

Probably he would have preferred dropping out of sight completely and permanently, although there were indications during
the last ten weeks of his life that thoughts of surrender were much
in his mind. As early as March, according to testimony by Arthur
O'Leary, Piquett's talkative messenger and handyman, Dillinger
had begun to discuss a face-lifting operation and asked O'Leary to
check with Piquett on such matters as price and a safe hideout.

Shortly after that, again according to O'Leary, Piquett introduced
his assistant to James Probasco, a longtime friend of the attorney's.
Probasco, sixty-seven years old, and reputedly in need of money

to finance a tavern, lived at 2509 North Crawford Avenue, well out of the area in which Dillinger had been known to hide. Probasco had been arrested a number of times during the previous thirteen years on suspicion of receiving stolen property, but never convicted. Negotiations began, and Probasco said he would rent a room to Dillinger for thirty-five dollars a day.

The hunt for Dillinger and Van Meter was centered firmly on Chicago with the discovery, the afternoon of May 2, of an abandoned car in front of 3333 North Leavitt and its identification as the one stolen from Francis near St. Paul. Neighbors said it had been there since two o'clock the previous morning. There were bloodstains and an emergency surgical kit on the seat and several packets of matches with Emil Wanatka's name on them, as well as a copy of the Dubuque *Telegraph-Herald* for April 23 with a headline reading DILLINGER ON RAMPAGE.

It was obvious that the car had come down Route 20 from Dubuque, since it bore license plates stolen from Dr. E. E. Shelly of Freeport, Illinois, between seven and eight o'clock the evening of April 23, with his physician's insignia still attached. But the drive from Minnesota must have been made at dangerous speed, since it is more than 300 miles from South St. Paul to Freeport. Heading south was a smart maneuver, however, because at that time the police search still was confined mostly to the St. Paul area.

The car gave mute evidence that its occupants had been ready for battle. The rear window was knocked out so that a machine gun could be fired through it, the taillight was disconnected, and two empty .45-caliber shells were found on the front seat. Because there were only three gallons of gasoline in the tank, the police theorized that the car had been abandoned for fear of running out of fuel.

In St. Paul the next day, Evelyn Frechette pleaded not guilty to a charge of having harbored Dillinger and was held in bond of $60,000. In Chicago at the same time, the forty-man Dillinger squad was reactivated with Sergeant Reynolds in charge and with an arsenal consisting of submachine guns, bombs, riot guns and other weapons. No new clues were found that day, although thirty-five apartments were searched in a building on Washington Boulevard near Central, and that evening several squads went to Niles Center, in the western suburbs, after a report that the gang leader had been seen there. Another house in the suburbs was searched simply because a car with Missouri license plates had been parked in front of it for several days, and two policemen were sent to Midway Airport in response to a rumor that Dillinger was about to board a plane.

There was some belief in police circles that Dillinger might be wounded and in hiding, and a detail went through the Northwest Side searching barns and vacant buildings and questioning the occupants of apartments and houses. By this time, too, the three women arrested at Little Bohemia had implicated Pat Riley, and he was being sought in St. Paul.

The lack of cooperation between the government agents and Chicago police (so obvious a couple of months later at the Biograph Theater) was evident at this point also. Reporters were barred from the office of Melvin Purvis, and one Federal man told newsmen there was nothing to say because the police were telling the FBI men nothing. The police, in turn, explained that in their view the Federal men would simply be in the way if Dillinger were located.

When Dillinger had not been found by Saturday, May 4, the Chicago police cabled Scotland Yard to ask that all ships arriving from the United States or Canada be watched, and that special attention be paid the *Duchess of York* and the *Pulaski*, both out of Halifax. The *Duchess* was scheduled to reach Glasgow May 5 and the *Pulaski* was due in Copenhagen May 8. Canadian Pacific Line officials at Montreal admitted that a "guarded" message had been sent the master of the *Duchess of York* but said that no reply had been received.

"We wouldn't mind if he were heading for England," said Sergeant Reynolds, but he added that a local search was being pressed. Most Chicago police thought Dillinger was "too smart" to flee to so small a place as England.

The *Duchess* docked in Glasgow on Saturday, and although Dillinger was not found, Scotland Yard officials said the ship would be searched again in Liverpool. The same day Ohio authorities were hunting for Dillinger after a holdup of a bank in Fostoria, in which Van Meter was identified as one of the gang which took $17,200 and wounded five persons with machine-gun fire. Toledo police said Dillinger may have been standing by to help if needed, an unlikely theory.

On May 8 Chicago police posted a guard on a car parked on South Ashland Avenue because (1) it was souped up and (2) it was only half a block from the home of Nelson's sister. The next day in St. Paul, Ralph Alsman of Brookville, Indiana, Dillinger's double, was arrested while on his way to the police station to tell the police he wasn't The Man. This made the sixth time he had been picked up since December. Suspicious St. Paul police took his fingerprints before being convinced of their error.

In St. Paul the action continued. Mrs. Beth Green pleaded guilty to a charge of harboring Dillinger in the apartment raided March 31, and shortly thereafter was sentenced to fifteen months' imprisonment. She had cooperated with authorities by letting them inspect a safe-deposit box rented three days after the Mason City robbery. They found $4,500.

The trial of Evelyn Frechette, Dr. May, and Nurse Salt opened in St. Paul on Tuesday, May 15. Attorney Piquett declared his belief that Dillinger was by this time in Mexico or South America, but extra guards accompanied Miss Frechette from jail to court, and police squads armed with tommy guns patrolled the streets. Although, as one news story pointed out, "John Dillinger, who boasted no friend of his would stay behind bars, failed to keep an appointment in St. Paul today," Miss Frechette almost succeeded in escaping without him. During the noontime recess, she joined a crowd of spectators heading for the stairs and was almost out of the courtroom when a bailiff stopped her.

On May 23, after the jury had deliberated for seven hours, Miss Frechette and Dr. May were found guilty of charges of having conspired to harbor Dillinger, and each was sentenced to two years in prison and fined $1,000. Mrs. Salt, whose thirteen-year-old son Wallace testified to having bought magazines and newspapers for Dillinger during the latter's stay in Mrs. Salt's apartment, was acquitted.

The thirty-nine government witnesses included Thomas J. Dodd (now senator from Connecticut), a government operative who also had been at Little Bohemia. He said that when he and some fellow agents introduced themselves to Dr. May, the physician turned to Mrs. Salt and said, "They've got us!"

The finding of guilty against Miss Frechette and Dr. May was made despite Piquett's impassioned plea that she was bemused by love and that Dr. May and Mrs. Salt were fearful of death if they turned Dillinger in.

"Evelyn Frechette loved Johnnie Dillinger," Piquett said in his closing address, "and although she knew he was a desperado, she was willing to take a chance with him. We all know where Dillinger belongs, but are we going to punish three people because they were brought innocently into this net? Miss Frechette was willing to go to the end with this Public Enemy Number One because she loved him. She did not harbor him under the statute. Give her back her freedom."

The jury, however, paid more attention to the wry reminder by Judge Gunnar H. Nordbye that Miss Frechette was aware that Dillinger was an escaped convict and had stolen an automobile and brought it across a state line (thus making a Federal case out of it).

The day after the St. Paul trial ended, two East Chicago policemen, Lloyd Mulvihill and Martin O'Brien, were ambushed and slain in their police car on a desolate road on the outskirts of East Chicago. Mulvihill was one of the policemen who had been at the East Chicago bank the day it was robbed.

There were no witnesses to the murder, although a night watchman said he had passed the spot earlier and noticed a large sedan with four men in it parked beside the macadam road. Twenty-five minutes later, he said, the strange car was gone, but the riddled squad car with its two dead occupants was standing in the middle of the road in a lonely industrial area, only fifteen minutes after the two officers had left the station at 11:10.

Dillinger or his men were blamed, although why he should have wanted to kill these two policemen was never established. There were whispers, however, that the real reason the policemen were killed was that they had learned too much of how Dillinger's escape from Crown Point was effected. It is doubtful that this double murder ever will be solved or the reason for it known. Although the men were experienced officers, their holstered guns lay on the seat beside them and each man had been shot eight or nine times in the head and neck.

The next day a reward proclamation was signed by Governors Henry Horner of Illinois, Paul McNutt of Indiana, George White of Ohio, William A. Comstock of Michigan, and Floyd B. Olson of Minnesota, for payments totaling $5,000. The same day Marie

Conforti, alias Rose Ancker; Helen Gillis, alias Marian Marr; and Pat Delaney were found guilty of harboring Dillinger and Tommy Carroll at Little Bohemia. Federal Judge Patrick T. Stone sentenced them to a year and a day, then suspended sentence and granted eighteen months' probation. Judge Stone, perhaps cooperating with the FBI which may have wanted the women at liberty in hopes they could be followed to the gang, urged the three to return home and avoid bad company. All said they would go back to Chicago.

Whether this official willingness to part with a sizable chunk of cash in return for Dillinger was the final straw, or merely coincidental, the fact remains that on May 27 Dillinger, O'Leary, and Piquett (the story is O'Leary's) sat around the kitchen table in Probasco's house discussing a face-lifting operation for Dillinger, which could be performed "by a very reliable surgeon, Dr. William Loeser."

O'Leary had first met Dr. Loeser (alias Ralph Roebind) about May 1, at which time the surgeon told him it would be easy to alter Dillinger's appearance. Some time later O'Leary had recommended Loeser to Dillinger and said he could be trusted. Dillinger's reply was "I'll let you know shortly."

Dr. Loeser, fifty-eight, was a native of Germany and had been educated there and at Northwestern. With Piquett's help he had been paroled from Leavenworth two years before after serving time for violation of the narcotics laws, and three months after leaving prison had broken his parole by fleeing to Mexico under an assumed name. After locating Anna Patzke, his "secretary," with whom he had lived for fifteen years, he returned to Chicago in 1934 and got in touch with Piquett because he needed money to get his furniture out of storage. Piquett, Loeser said, told him he had no money but did have a plastic surgery job on "Public Enemy Number One."

"I told him I had done some plastic work on myself," Loeser said afterwards. "While I was in Mexico I removed my fingerprints because I was a parole violator. He told me it was not against the law."

O'Leary said he and Piquett went to Probasco's home the night of May 27 and found Dillinger walking up and down on the sidewalk waiting for them. The three went in together, and Dillinger, after some discussion, agreed to the operation. Piquett, according to O'Leary, telephoned Dr. Harold Cassidy and asked him to help in an operation to be performed by an unlicensed doctor on a man who was "hot."

Dillinger, according to O'Leary, turned over $3,000 of the promised $5,000 fee—of which Piquett later paid O'Leary $1,400 with instructions to give $600 of it to Dr. Cassidy. (According to later statements by Dr. Loeser, Dr. Cassidy was to get $600 and the rest of the $5,000 was to be split among Piquett, O'Leary and himself.)

When the two doctors arrived, Dr. Loeser examined Dillinger, tested his heart, and asked what the gang leader wanted done. Dillinger said he wished two moles removed from between the eyes, a depression erased from the bridge of the nose, a lip scar removed, a dimple taken from the chin, and his cheek pulled higher.

Loeser retired to the bathroom to wash his hands and soon heard a commotion from the bedroom, where Dillinger was lying on a cot while Cassidy administered the ether, using a towel as a make-do mask. Loeser found that Dillinger had swallowed his tongue and was choking to death. He grabbed the forceps, pulled the tongue up, banged the unconscious Dillinger in the ribs with an elbow, and got him breathing normally again.

The two doctors began work at once. The moles were removed, the cheek cut along the ear and jaw and tightened with kangaroo tendons, and some flesh moved to fill in the dimple. Dillinger remained at Probasco's for five days after the operation, with Cassidy in attendance. Then, on June 2, he sent word to Loeser that he wanted more work done and that a friend was also in the market for a face-changing job.

Loeser and O'Leary returned to Probasco's house by streetcar June 3 and met Homer Van Meter. Probasco, Piquett and Dr. Cassidy also were there. Dillinger said he didn't like his new face. Piquett had to calm him down by telling him it looked "wonderful" before he would pay the balance of the fee.

Dillinger produced a package wrapped in newspaper and counted out two thousand dollars. Handing it to Piquett, he said, "That makes five thousand for the doctors." Van Meter, having taken five thousand from a similar package, gave it to Piquett and said, "Remember, I want a good job."

According to Loeser, "Piquett came to pay me the next day, but he only gave me seventeen hundred. He said he had been borrowing, stealing, anything, to get money to cover a bond in Wisconsin where he was indicted for selling securities without a license."

Work included blurring Dillinger's finger tips with acid and giving further treatment to his face, since the kangaroo tendons were not holding properly. A wedge of skin was taken from near one ear, and the dimple was touched up. An operation also was performed on Van Meter's nose and lip, and the removal of a blue-and-red tattoo (an anchor with the words "Good Hope") was started on Van Meter's right arm. His finger tips were also burned with acid.

The next day Piquett gave Cassidy $600, Loeser $1,700 and O'Leary $2,100, and the fifth of June when the group returned to Probasco's, they found Van Meter "a very disgruntled and greatly excited man" who threatened to shoot Loeser if the job didn't come out to his satisfaction. One of the patients—the remark has been ascribed to both Dillinger and Van Meter—complained of "looking like I'd been in a dogfight." Baby Face Nelson was also present on that occasion.

Dillinger left Probasco's place in early June—a departure that was a relief to his temporary landlord, who had complained of Dillinger's insistence in going out and walking around the neighborhood. About that time—and perhaps the same day he left Probasco's —Dillinger, looking for some feminine companionship, was steered by a cab driver to the home of Mrs. Anna Sage, who had formerly run a disorderly house in Gary, Indiana.

Mrs. Sage, rather than phone a call girl, invited Polly Hamilton Keele, twenty-six, a 5-foot 3-inch, 120-pound redhead, to come over to meet Dillinger, and the three sat around and talked for a while. Dillinger later told Mrs. Sage he wanted a "date" with Polly, and he and Polly, who was divorced from a Gary policeman, saw each other virtually every day from then until he was killed, except for two or three times when he was out of town for periods ranging from two to five days.

Polly, a blue-eyed girl with an off-and-on smile, eventually moved into the Sage apartment (where Dillinger also stayed the last two days of his life) after telling the owner of the restaurant where she worked that she was ill.

"I was crazy about him," she later said. "He had a marvelous personality. He really *couldn't* have been kind and good and do the things he did, but he was kind and good to me. He had very good innate intelligence, and was interested in what was going on, and I don't just mean cops and robbers, but daily events.

"We went out a lot. He was crazy about movies, and we went to nightclubs. He looked like an average businessman type, and always had plenty of money."

Although Dillinger himself drank little, she said, "That's when I first started to drink. Probably the first drink or two I ever had were with him. I used to order Alexanders—anything fancy. Anna used to make us Romanian coffee, and later told me, 'I knew who he was right away.' I don't think he was careless, he just made one mistake. He trusted her.

"We were at the Grand Terrace one night and some people kept looking and looking at him. You never saw anyone call for a bill as fast as he did. I don't think he even waited for his change. We took a cab to the Loop, then got another cab and went to the Chez Paree.

"He had a low voice, rather pleasing, and was a terrific card player. He was crazy about cards. We played pinochle [*Wanatka would have been pleased*] and regular rummy. Penny-ante stuff, a nickel limit. One time I wouldn't pay my card bill, and he started twisting my arm. I don't know if he was serious or not, but I paid.

"Dillinger was short and stocky and *very* solid. He was broad-shouldered and had a fascinating smile, especially when he was playing a joke. It was a very tricky smile. He was a good dresser, clean and neat. I didn't particularly care for his taste in suits, but he was always immaculate.

"There was one song Dillinger was crazy about, from a picture we saw with Joan Crawford at the Marbro: 'All I do is dream of you the whole night through . . .' He used to sing it and sing it to me. Did he have a good voice? At least he could carry a tune.

"It was the Depression and I was broke. I got a thrill out of going around in cabs. We cabbed everywhere. Twice he gave me money so my girl friend and I could go to the World's Fair. He was very good-hearted but he was no sucker. He was very conservative for the kind of money he had. I remember I said I couldn't go to the beach because I didn't have a decent bathing suit. He wasn't about to go out and buy you any fur coats, but he handed me forty dollars and said I should go and buy something with it.

"One time he said he had to go to Ohio. He was gone four or five days once, another three or four. I think the longest was five days. Once he said he was going to be gone five days and came back in three. He was rather jealous, and I wondered if he thought he was going to catch me.

"We had a lot of fun. It's surprising how much fun we had."

Dillinger also gave Polly money to get her teeth filled, and bought her one dress or gave her the money for it. They exchanged presents, Polly giving him an inexpensive ring and Dillinger presenting her with a garnet one.

He was very fond of his father, Polly said. After one trip, he brought back a watch of his father's to have it repaired and said he had left his own in Indiana.

Polly later told government agents that she hadn't the slightest idea of Dillinger's identity until he was slain—a statement they were polite enough to accept. It seems certain, however, that Mrs. Sage's son, Steve Chiolak, was completely ignorant of Dillinger's identity.

Mrs. Sage introduced Dillinger to Steve and his girl as "Jimmy Lawrence." Chiolak said this meeting took place late in June, and that he went on one drinking party and to a couple of movies with Dillinger, Polly and his own girl friend. He said he also saw Dillinger three times at his mother's apartment.

They saw *Viva Villa* with Wallace Beery at the Granada, and W. C. Fields in *You're Telling Me* at the Marbro, both times attending the 8 P.M. show, in Chiolak's words, "just like regular people." Dillinger paid, since Chiolak was not working.

Chiolak said Dillinger always picked up the check, and seemed unworried and unconcerned. He said they went to the Stables, a nightclub on Broadway, one evening, where Dillinger commented on the floor show, chatted easily, and drank nothing but mild gin fizzes.

"He never flashed a roll on me, though," Chiolak later commented. "I never saw any great amount of money on him. If he was the man they said he was, he was an all-around fellow. He didn't act tough and he didn't talk rough.

"I didn't even ask him where he worked. My girl friend asked him if he lived in the city and he said, 'Yes, up north.' She said, 'Working?' and he said, 'Yes, at the Board of Trade.' It was just like talking about the weather."

Chiolak said he often noticed the scars on Dillinger's face (the ones left by the plastic surgery), "but I didn't like to ask a guy about his face. I'd get mad if anyone asked me about mine."

June was a busy month for those searching for Dillinger, and if the outlaw read the papers regularly he must have felt that the trap was closing.

On June 1 Virginia Hughes and Opal Long (alias Bernice Clark) were arrested in the Chateau Hotel, 3838 Broadway, on the North Side of Chicago. Miss Hughes was identified at a court hearing as Patricia Young, but said her name really was Pat Cherrington. Both women were accused of harboring Dillinger in St. Paul, and Miss Cherrington, pleading guilty a few weeks later in Madison, Wisconsin, was sentenced to two years in the Federal Reformatory for Women at Alderson, West Virginia. She told the court her own husband was in prison, and that she had taken up with the gang five months before.

Mrs. Clark, who will be remembered as having slammed the door that broke a policeman's finger during the Tucson affair, was sentenced to six months in the Minneapolis city jail when convicted in St. Paul late in June.

On June 4 Joseph Fox, one of the Michigan City escapees, was caught in Chicago and returned to Indiana to finish his sentence. Three days later Tommy Carroll and Jean Delaney Crompton, who had returned to him shortly after being put on parole, were surprised in Waterloo, Iowa, and Carroll was killed. The two had spent the night of June 6 in a tourist cabin near Cedar Rapids, and the next day Carroll's car had developed engine trouble. He had driven it to a garage, where a mechanic spotted some guns and an extra set of license plates, and called police.

Detectives Emil Steffen and P. E. Walker found the car parked near the garage and hid nearby. When Carroll and the girl appeared, they were challenged, and Carroll reached for a gun. He was still reaching for it when he fell with five bullets in him.

The dying man admitted his identity on the way to the hospital, and added, "Take care of the little girl. She doesn't know what it's all about. I've got seven hundred dollars on me. Be sure she gets it."

Mrs. Crompton, who visited the morgue for a brief and tearful farewell to Carroll, said they had been married a week or ten days, but later admitted this was untrue. Actually she was the estranged wife of a Chicago entertainer whom she had wed in May of 1932 at the café where they both worked.

Carroll had been sought for questioning in the murder of H. C. Perron, a San Antonio detective who had been killed in December, 1933, and for questioning in the $32,000 holdup of a Brainerd, Minnesota, bank—and banks at Sioux Falls and Mason City. The license plates on the car he was driving had been stolen in St. Louis on May 8.

The day after the shooting Mrs. Crompton's parole was revoked by Judge Stone, and she was ordered to start serving her year-long sentence.

On June 16, taking cognizance of rumors, the elder Dillinger had a letter printed in an Indianapolis newspaper in which he denied that his son had visited Mooresville on April 22 and April 28, but some time in mid-June the outlaw did indeed visit Indianapolis. He parked his new Essex Terraplane in front of the home of Tubby Toms, the reporter to whom he had given the rabbit's foot in Tucson, and waited until Toms came out to ask what he was doing there.

"Get in," said Dillinger. "I want to talk with you a minute."

Toms reluctantly did so, and the two chatted briefly about Tucson, several jobs of which Dillinger had been erroneously accused, and the numerous reports of his whereabouts. Toms, however, felt that Dillinger was trying to work around to something—which he never did—and later decided that the outlaw had been trying to ask him to arrange a "truce" and possible pardon from the Governor.

Dillinger never did state the reason for his visit, perhaps realizing the futility of such a suggestion, and when it came time to leave, raised no objection when Toms said he would have to report the incident. He did, however, ask for half an hour's start, which Toms let tick by before calling Captain Matt Leach.

On June 19 Fred Weber, a thirty-seven-year-old Chicagoan, was swept up in the net while attending the Uptown Theater, 4814 Broadway (not far from the Biograph), after a fellow patron called police to say that Dillinger was there. Weber, who bore a startling resemblance to the bandit, "surrendered" to six squads armed with riot and tear-gas guns, after they surrounded the theater. He was so indignant at the the mistake that he refused to identify himself at first. Later he did so and was freed with apologies.

On June 20 Dillinger, angered by word that Piquett had not paid the persons to whom he owed money, wrote the lawyer as follows:

> No doubt you know by this time how I feel toward you. You know I sent you the money to pay everyone that I owe. Now I find out you have never paid any one of them a cent. I'm telling them I have sent you the money. And when they come to you you can tell them why you did not pay them. So far as I'm concerned, you and I are through. Johnnie.

Captain Stege, who released the letter, quoted Piquett as having said of it, "Well, he is right. I did not do the right thing. I was busted and I owed office rent and office help."

On June 22 the personal columns of an Indianapolis paper carried this message: "Birthday greeting to my darling brother, John Dillinger, on his 31st birthday. Wherever he may be, I hope he will read this message. Audrey Hancock."

Mrs. Hancock, queried by reporters after her message appeared, said she had not heard from her brother in some time. "John has sent no message home," she said. "He's smarter than that."

The following day Attorney General Cummings announced that the Federal government was posting a reward of $10,000 for Dillinger's capture or $5,000 for information leading to it, and one-half of those amounts for the capture or a tip-off on Baby Face Nelson. This information must have ended any lingering hopes Dillinger may have had of an amnesty.

On June 24 the quest for Dillinger himself veered suddenly to Branson, Missouri, where sixty state and Federal officers with the usual machine guns raided an Ozark ranch after a tip that both Dillinger and Charles "Pretty Boy" Floyd had been brought there by ambulance the night of June 22, one of them badly hurt. The raiders searched, found nothing and left.

On June 27 Harry Copeland was finally sentenced to twenty-five years for helping rob the Greencastle bank. The same day, in St. Paul, Pat Riley was arrested while he slept, by three carloads of

Federal agents with machine guns ready. There was no shooting. Riley, who had been implicated by statements from the three women seized at Little Bohemia, pleaded guilty and was given two consecutive sentences of one year and nine months, and fourteen months. He also told authorities that Carroll had told him, during a conversation in Minneapolis, that Dillinger was dead.

While the law was catching up with other gang members, Dillinger, perhaps emboldened by the at least partial success of the plastic surgery, was living virtually under the noses of the police. On one occasion, so a well-authenticated story still current in Chicago police circles goes, a barber telephoned to report that he had cut Dillinger's hair, and was told by a bored desk sergeant that he had called the wrong precinct, to try another number. Either the barber did not do this, or he was brushed off once more and quit. Dillinger also bought a shirt from Jerry Ward, of the Ward Mitchell Company clothing store, near Mrs. Sage's apartment, a few days before he was killed. He wore it to the Biograph the evening of July 2 and later to the morgue.

And there seems no doubt that Dillinger indulged his love of baseball by visiting Wrigley Field more than once that summer.

Both Mrs. Patzke, whom he had kidnaped during the Racine bank holdup, and Volk, the mailman who had seen him when he escaped from Crown Point, said they saw and recognized Dillinger (despite surgery) in Wrigley Field on June 26, when the Cubs were playing the Dodgers. Volk said he exchanged a few words with Dillinger before the latter disappeared, and both Volk and a companion identified photos of Dillinger as the man they had seen.

Chicago detectives also visited the ball park one day and, spotting Piquett, asked when he planned to surrender Dillinger. The lawyer said he hadn't seen the outlaw for weeks. Later, according to one of the detectives, Piquett admitted that Dillinger had been sitting within twenty feet of them during this conversation.

Whether this day or another, Piquett told his wife on one occasion that he had bumped into Dillinger at Wrigley Field.

"Who do you think I saw at the game today?" he said, on reaching home. "Dillinger. My heart was in my mouth. He was practically brushing against policemen."

Mrs. Piquett asked if Dillinger had given any sign that he knew

Piquett, and her husband reported, rather desperately, that Dillinger had given him a mock salute and said, "Hi, counselor!"

On June 28 the state of Indiana—through the medium of a speech by Wayne Coy at the Central States Parole Conference in Chicago —took public blame for the phenomenon that was Dillinger.

Said Coy, "There does not seem to be any escape from the fact that the state of Indiana made John Dillinger the Public Enemy Number One he is today. There is no doubt in my mind that Johnnie Dillinger's life would have been entirely different had the administration of justice in his case and in the case of his partner, Edward [Edgar] Singleton, been comparable considering their previous records."

In July the hunt seemed to be drifting away from Chicago again. On July 3 a man who stopped for gasoline at Whitinsville, Massachusetts, was "positively" identified as Dillinger, and on July 7 Dillinger was reported seen near Palmer, Massachusetts, with three other men. On the same day a filling station owner in Iola, Kansas, said Dillinger and a companion had stopped there the night before, asking where a physician might be found.

On July 9 Pierpont and Makley, still waiting for death in Columbus, Ohio, talked briefly to newsmen.

Makley said, "We have heard nothing from Dillinger since they kidnaped him out of the Tucson jail and took him to Indiana."

Both men scoffed at rumors that Dillinger was robbing Middle Western banks in an effort to finance an appeal for them. Said Makley, "They say Dillinger is sending me fifteen thousand dollars. I wish he'd send me a few fins right now so I could buy cigarettes."

After a rambling statement in which both said they had not killed Sheriff Sarber, that the Indiana authorities knew who had, and that Dillinger had not sent the guns with which the Michigan City break was made, Pierpont concluded, "They [the authorities] know, too, why Dillinger got loose from the escape-proof Crown Point jail with a wooden gun, just fifteen minutes before he was to make a deposition in our case. He was to tell who delivered him. I can tell you it was not us.

"I wish Dillinger all the luck in the world. We don't expect any help out of him."

Makley added, "Why should we? I wish they never catch him."

While their declarations of innocence cannot be believed, it is probable that both were sincere in their expression of goodwill toward the elusive Dillinger. He seems to have had a capacity for inspiring loyalty among his comrades in crime.

On July 19 twenty policemen raided the Lawson YMCA on Chicago Avenue at LaSalle Street in response to a report that Dillinger, Nelson and Hamilton (or perhaps the latter's ghost) had just gone to a nearby parking lot, changed their California license plates to Alabama plates, and driven off with two women. This was only three days before Dillinger was trapped and killed.

At approximately this time, according to Piquett's later statements, the lawyer was attempting to arrange to surrender Dillinger to the authorities through Nate Gross, a reporter for the Chicago *American*. The reward money was to have gone to Dillinger's father. There seems to have been some validity to this tale, since Gross was called as a defense witness when Piquett later was put on trial for having harbored Dillinger.

Another story is that Dillinger, rather than surrender, was planning to escape to Mexico: a Chicagoan was to have driven him there for $3,500 in advance and $6,500 on crossing the border, with Dillinger posing as a member of the tourist's family. This trip was to have started July 23.

Whatever plans Dillinger had—surrender or flight—they were destined to be changed by a circumstance beyond his control: the desire of Anna Sage to escape deportation.

Some time prior to July 22, and probably about the nineteenth or twentieth, a member of the East Chicago police force (never identified by Purvis in later accounts) came to the FBI office with word that he knew someone who could turn up Dillinger. (It is known that Martin Zarkovich had come from East Chicago to work on the case, and that he and Anna Sage had been good friends in Indiana.)

The "someone" was Mrs. Sage, and Purvis met her at a rendezvous some distance from her apartment, then rode in a car with her for some time while she talked. She and Purvis made a deal—at least in so far as Purvis had the authority to do so. In return for a share of the reward and Purvis's promise to do what he could to halt the deportation proceedings then pending against her, she would deliver Dillinger to the Federal men.

On the evening of the twenty-second Steve Chiolak came to his mother's apartment. Whether his mother talked him out of going to the movies or not is unknown. At any rate, he and his girl friend left. Mrs. Sage, meanwhile, had managed to telephone Purvis about 5:30 to say she was going to the movies with Polly and Dillinger, and they were going to one of two shows. When evening and show-time came, she excused herself, went into the bedroom and put on a bright orange skirt—a flag of betrayal, a sign to the government agents that Dillinger had decided to attend the Biograph rather than the Marbro. Then they set out.

The three went around the corner and into the theater, and the men with the guns waited for them to come out. Two hours later John Dillinger lay dead in the alley a few steps away.

EIGHTEEN

●●●●●●●●●●●●●●●●●● "HE WAS THE KIND OF
GUY ANYONE WOULD
HAVE BEEN GLAD TO
HAVE FOR A BROTHER."
—CHARLEY MAKLEY

After the shooting on that hot Chicago night, word spread as if by
jungle drum that the dead man was John Dillinger. Purvis refused
to confirm it, perhaps because he still had no proof of identity. But
it was obvious to anyone that the aura surrounding the shooting
could be associated only with the hunting down of Public Enemy
Number 1; for a month past he had led Attorney General Homer
Cummings's roster of men least likely to succeed, and there was a
Federal reward of $10,000 on his head.

Anna Sage and Polly Hamilton had done their best to remain un-
connected with the affair. Polly had stepped back into the entryway
of the National store when the shooting began, bumping into a revolver held by one of the posse who didn't even give her a second
look, he was watching Dillinger so intently.

Polly moved quickly to the sidewalk again and found Anna, who
asked, in apparent puzzlement, "What happened? What happened?"

"He's been shot," said Polly in a low voice.

Anna wanted to run, but Polly warned her not to. Both began walking north and the Federal agents made no effort to stop them. They met two men, obviously policemen in plain clothes, who asked where they were going.

"Someone's been shot," one of the women answered, and the police officers hurried by.

At the corner north of the Biograph the two frightened women tucked up their skirts and ran, panting, to Altgeld Street. Polly, to whom the deadly ambush had come as a total surprise, caught the elevated train at a station nearby, while Anna continued on toward her apartment. Polly got off at Wilson Avenue, the first stop north, for fear someone might have seen her board the train, and then went to the restaurant at 1209½ Wilson, where she worked as a waitress. She said she was ill and would not be in the next day. She also told Maxine Dunn, a fellow waitress, that Dillinger had been shot.

"How do you know?" Maxine asked.

"Wait till the papers come out," Polly replied. "You'll see."

By this time Anna Sage had reached home and changed her signal-flag skirt. She was to become an integral part of the Dillinger legend as the Lady in Red. (The lights of Lincoln Avenue or some phrase-making reporter transmuted the orange of her skirt into scarlet.)

Having changed, Anna returned to the Biograph for a discreet look around. Spectators were pouring into the area. Some were innocently curious, others morbidly so. A few fashioned macabre souvenirs by dipping handkerchiefs into the blood which stained the alley bricks. Others, more experienced in the routines of violence, went winging toward the Morgue with the unerring instinct of carrion birds.

Dillinger's body was there ahead of them, already stripped and checked in. A tag on each big toe bore his name and the information that his was the 116th corpse to reach that cheerless storehouse during July. Only $7.70, two keys tied with string, a magazine clipping, a fancy kerchief, and a watch were found on his person. A photograph of Polly Hamilton was in the back of the watch. The $7.70 later aroused some curiosity among those who had known the slain man well and maintained that he would as soon have ventured forth barefoot as without his money belt with at least two or three thousand dollars in it.

Anna Sage returned home once more, forced open the linen closet (the key was in the dead man's pocket), took from the shelves a machine gun, pistol and bulletproof vest, and persuaded a woman friend to accompany her to the beach. The two women, carrying blankets which covered the guns and vest, hailed a taxicab. During the short ride to the edge of Lake Michigan they talked loudly of how hot it was and what a comfort it would be to sleep on the sand.

While the guns were being disposed of, an autopsy was performed on their late owner. One of the attending physicians had refused to leave his home until assured that the Indiana badman was indeed quite dead. Doctors, internes and nurses from nearby hospitals crowded the postmortem room, and their number was increased by newsmen and by some of the avidly curious who had talked, bluffed, or bought their way in.

"Dillinger," said one of the newspaper stories, "lay in a basement room. None of the dignity of death was his. A winding sheet draped his bullet-torn body like a travesty of a Roman toga. The whole place was soaked in a penetrating, persistent odor of formaldehyde."

Hundreds of sensation seekers waited outside the dingy stone building. Many pressed their faces against the protective wire mesh of the windows, peering eagerly in hopes of glimpsing the corpse of the man who had commanded the headlines so many times. Some of them lingered hopefully until the small hours. Others left and returned long before the inquest, which was scheduled to begin at 11:30 Monday morning.

The Federal agents were a little late arriving for the inquest, which gave the press photographers time to persuade Coroner Frank J. Walsh to pose with the body. He was pictured examining the wounds, or pointing out the plastic surgery scars.

Coroner Walsh, red-faced and sweating, presided in his shirt-sleeves at the inquest. Earle L. Richmond, one of the Federal agents, testified that fingerprints (the acid had failed to blur the lines completely) corresponded to those taken when Dillinger was serving time in Indiana. Samuel Cowley, Hoover's special assistant, told the jurors that information had been received that Dillinger would attend the Biograph or Marbro Sunday night and the trap was set.

"As he came out," Cowley went on, "he turned to his left. He was approached by one of the agents. He drew a gun and was killed."

"Shot by a government agent?" Walsh asked.

"Yes, sir."

"Did he have a gun?" Deputy Coroner Jacob M. Schewel inquired.

"Yes, sir, and he drew it."

"And was shot before he could fire?"

"Yes, before he could get the gun in firing position."

The gun taken from Dillinger was not introduced into evidence, however, and Purvis was not on hand. Nor was Anna Sage's name mentioned. Finally the jury retired, taking with it the autopsy report prepared by Dr. J. J. Kearns, which described the deceased as "a medium developed white male, 32 years of age [*he was thirty-one*], 5 feet 7 inches tall, weighing 160 pounds; scalp hair brown–dyed black–mustache same, eyes brown." The report added that the deceased had been shot four times, but that only one of the bullets caused his death.

Two shots had grazed him; one cut a superficial hole in his right side, and the other–the payoff shot–struck the back of his neck, smashed a vertebra, ripped through the spinal cord and lower portion of the brain and came out the right eye, severing two sets of veins and arteries.

The jury returned in short order with a verdict of justifiable homicide on the part of the Federal agents, and a postscript saying they were to be "highly commended for their efficient participation in the occurrence as shown by the fact that there was no further loss of life in the capture of a man of this type."

The whole thing, however, struck the Associated Press correspondent as lacking a few parts. The wire service story, after telling the verdict, added, "The man who ran him down was not present; the man whose bullet killed him was not named, and the informant who led him to his death was not mentioned."

The reaction to the news that Dillinger had been killed was not, oddly enough, unanimously approving. Many persons, understandably including Dillinger's father, felt that it should have been possible for so large a force, having the advantage of surprise, to take the hunted man alive.

Also, there were the rumors usual in a case of this kind that certain persons in Indiana much preferred Dillinger dead than alive and perhaps talking. The East Chicago police, it was said, regarded the tracking down of Dillinger in the light of a crusade, since many witnesses had identified him as the bandit whose machine-gun bullets cut down and killed Patrolman O'Malley during the holdup of the East Chicago bank on January 15.

The government men, too, had no reason to hold Dillinger in anything but low esteem, perhaps mingled with a touch of grudging admiration for his ability to scramble out of tight places. Whatever the reason for failing to take him alive, eyewitnesses felt that no effort had been made to do so.

Edgar l'Allemand, a mechanic, who was standing outside Barth's garage at 2424 Lincoln Avenue, said, "I glanced across the street as I stood there. Everything seemed calm and peaceful. There were not many people around and very little traffic. I had a clear unobstructed view of the sidewalk in front of the theater on the opposite side.

"Suddenly I saw a tall man fire two shots in quick succession. He seemed to be standing almost beside the man who was shot. The wounded man fell to the alley without uttering a sound."

Mrs. Esther Gousinow, who had been sitting in her second-floor parlor at 2427 Lincoln, and looking down at the street, told a similar tale. She had, she said, been viewing the front of the Biograph for some time and noticed some young men waiting, as though for girl friends.

"Then I saw a young man walk out of the theater, accompanied by two girls. They were only about ten feet from the alley and I was looking right down at them when I saw three men walk up behind them. I heard two shots—there may have been more—and the man with the two girls fell to the sidewalk. I thought at first that it was a holdup and that the victim was killed. Then I thought of Dillinger, and because it appeared to me that the three men shot without giving a warning, I thought immediately that the victim was Dillinger.

"I sent my brother-in-law running downstairs and he called to me in a few minutes that the man who had been shot had been carrying a gun."

Also indicative of the suddenness with which the shooting began is the statement attributed to one of the plainclothesmen from Sheffield after things quieted down. This man, Frank Slattery, reportedly told friends that a government man had congratulated him after Dillinger's death, saying he was "lucky to be alive."

"When we got the signal" the agent was quoted as saying, "you were close to Dillinger. You looked like Dillinger, and I was about to shoot you when the other fellows let loose and killed the right man."

After the inquest on "the right man" adjourned, undertaker Ray G. McCready, who had been hired by the elder Dillinger, asked Coroner Walsh if he could now embalm the body. The coroner refused, saying, "The government may want the body or something. I'll tell you—we'll let you have the body in the morning. Come around any time after nine and you can get it. You can't get near it now."

The reason McCready couldn't get near the body was that Walsh had ordered the Morgue doors opened so that the curious could file past the little room where Dillinger lay, propped up at an angle for better viewing, and stare their fill through the plate glass at the man they would have scrambled to stay clear of twenty-four hours before.

Men, women and even children lined up for so rare a treat, and a bulging blonde, carefully applying lipstick after emerging from the basement, with its reek of disinfectant, expressed disappointment.

"He looks like any other dead man," this connoisseur of corpses said fretfully. "But I guess I'll go through again."

Morgue attendants estimated that fifteen thousand persons made their shuffling pilgrimage past the body before it was removed to the McCready Funeral Home at 4506 Sheridan Road the following morning. Both at the Morgue and at McCready's it was a come-as-you-are party; costumes included beach attire for women and pants and undershirts for men. The funeral home was almost inundated Monday afternoon and evening by a jostling army of five thousand, loud in their belief that the body had already been brought from the Morgue. Police were needed to clear Sheridan Road for traffic.

That afternoon, too, a gray eight-year-old hearse ended its dusty 225-mile trip from Mooresville, and was taken immediately to a garage to be put in shape for the return journey. The hearse was driven by E. F. Harvey, Mooresville undertaker, who was accompanied by the elder Dillinger, somber and dry-eyed, his son Hubert and Everett Moore, editor of the Mooresville *Times*, who had an inside track on the biggest news story of the year and intended to use it.

The two undertakers—McCready and Harvey—finally were given permission to embalm the body, and this work went on at the Morgue while crowds of chattering spectators continued to file past. Both government men and newsmen questioned the elder Dillinger and Hubert. The Federal agents were anxious to learn anything at all about other members of the gang or the whereabouts of whatever loot Dillinger might have squirreled away. But they learned nothing of value. (Hubert charged that he was pushed around during this interrogation.)

The elder Dillinger answered the newspapermen's questions politely, saying, among other things, that it was his first trip to Chicago since the Columbian Exposition of 1893, and stressing his belief that his son was slain needlessly.

"They shot him down in cold blood," said the sixty-nine-year-old farmer, wiping his face with a handkerchief. "I don't approve of shooting a fellow down in cold blood. He was surrounded by fifteen men, and that ain't fair. I'd rather have had him shot than captured, though, and John would rather have had it that way."

Hubert, who bore a strong resemblance to his dead half-brother, greeted questions from the press in surly silence, but finally shouted, "You God-damned newspaper reporters get out of here!"

Numerous interested persons were quickly notified that Dillinger was no more.

Attorney General Cummings, being told the news in Washington just before boarding a train for the first leg of a trip to Hawaii, smiled and said, "Gratifying as well as reassuring."

At the Ohio State Penitentiary in Columbus, Harry Pierpont and Charles Makley, still occupants of Death Row, greeted the news with regret. Pierpont, at first cautious in accepting it, finally said, "If it's true, I'm sorry. John was a good friend of mine. He didn't owe me anything, though, for I wasn't in Lima and didn't spring Dillinger."

Makley, always the comedian, also expressed sorrow, and told the interviewer, "Why, I would even be sorry if they bumped *you* off."

Asked what kind of man Dillinger had been, Pierpont inquired if the questioner had a brother. Told he did, Pierpont continued, "Then just write a description of your own brother and you will have the right dope on Johnnie Dillinger."

Makley agreed, adding, "Yes, he was the kind of guy anyone would have been glad to have for a brother."

Captain Jess McMurtry of the Indianapolis Police Department was unsurprised. "That's the way I thought Dillinger would go," he said. "No man can ride high all the time."

A reporter spoke to Mary Kinder as she sat behind the wheel of a small car outside the Green Lantern Resort near Indianapolis. She was visibly upset and refused to say when she had last seen the slain man.

"Every girl who has been associated with him is 'in,'" she said. "I'm the only one who's out." She then admitted having talked with Dillinger shortly before his death, but would not disclose their conversation. "You can't expect a girl to say much," Miss Kinder demurred, "when you've just told her that one of her best friends has been killed. There never was a finer fellow." She paused, then turned to the reporter. "Is it true?" she asked doubtfully. "Is he dead?"

There was no doubt in the minds of the waiting throngs of Chicagoans that Dillinger was dead when shortly before 11:45 Tuesday morning the body, covered with black oilcloth, was carried in a wicker basket from the undertaking home. Six men, who had to force their way through the crowd, carried it to the waiting hearse. It was loaded in back and the homeward journey began.

The elder Dillinger—haggard and drawn—shared the front seat with Harvey and Moore. The two brothers occupied the van, Hubert on a chair and the dead outlaw on a cot.

Newsmen followed the hearse, and crowds gathered from place to place along the route, as they would have done if some national hero were being taken home for the last time. The temperature reached 105 during the afternoon.

Chicago police, with screaming sirens, served as an escort down Route 41 to the Indiana border. Only two stops were made during the journey. The first was at Kentland, Indiana, where it was discovered that despite repairs to the hearse the oil was dangerously low. The other was at Lebanon, where the elder Dillinger climbed wearily into the back of the vehicle to finish the trip with his dead son.

Finally, after more than six hours on the road, the hearse, its brakes smoking, pulled into Mooresville, and the body was carried into the Harvey Funeral Home. There most of the waiting crowd were quieter and more solemn than the mobs in Chicago had been. Men stood with their heads bared, and women spoke in whispers. This was a tribute to the elder Dillinger and reflected the high regard in which his neighbors held him, despite his son's misdeeds.

Yet, as out-of-town reporters noticed, Mooresville (population 1,000) had thoughtless and callous ones who could compare with their big-city counterparts.

"Sockless flappers," said one story, "chattering like gay magpies, and shouting, 'Should I go in?' 'Is it bad to look at?' 'What did he look like?' were among the curious visitors to the town morgue. They came in rumble-seated Fords, on bicycles and hand in hand with boy friends."

The dead man's sister was not convinced that the body was that of her brother (despite the mute evidence of a bullet scar attributed to the shooting in St. Paul) until Harvey urged her to look for a scar on the back of the thigh, souvenir of a barbed-wire fence encountered during a watermelon raid many years before. Mrs. Hancock did so, then said, "It's all right. Go ahead, Mr. Harvey. That's Johnnie!"

A mortician skilled in facial repairs was summoned from Indianapolis to work on the terrible wound under the right eye, and not until his task was finished did the Hancocks permit the curious to enter. Before Harvey called a halt, a line of approximately five thousand persons filed past the body as it lay on a cot in an amber-lit room. Among the "mourners" was Mary Kinder.

Early stories out of Mooresville said the family had chosen a "$7,000 lavender casket" for the slain outlaw. This was either deliberate falsehood or a careless disregard for facts. The body was placed in a $165 coffin, covered with rose-colored cloth. ("The same little casket as we buried his stepmother in—a little octagonal plush casket," said Harvey. "This was no gangster funeral.") The undertaker had suggested that Dillinger be buried in black, but the father sent a Mooresville clothier to Indianapolis for a new suit of gray herringbone. One sharp-eyed newsman recorded that the sleeves came well down beyond the wrists; Dillinger alive would not have tolerated so poor a fit.

About 10:15 that Tuesday evening the body was removed to the Hancock cottage in Maywood, with an escort of two Indiana State Police cars. The casket was carried into the living room, from which photographs of Dillinger and Evelyn Frechette, his French-Indian sweetheart, had been removed. The casket was opened and Mrs. Hancock wept.

"The last time I saw Johnnie," she said, "he had a big smile on his face and said, 'Don't worry.'"

Outside the crowds had begun gathering again, and extra squads of state police were sent under the direction of Captain Lewis Johnson. Before their arrival, however, members of the throng, frantic for something to remember this golden moment by, stripped leaves from the trees and shrubs around the house. And rumors began flying: There would be an attempt to steal his body (the elder Dillinger had revealed an offer of $10,000 if he would "lend" his son's corpse to a Wisconsin showman for a brief period). John Hamilton (already dead but the crowd didn't know it) and Baby Face Nelson, another whisper went, were planning to drop by to pay their last respects.

So patrol cars cruised the quiet Maywood streets, and two police wagons stood nearby, ready for anything. The policemen guarding the house were invited in for coffee, an invitation they accepted in relays, and the uniformed officers moved past the casket, caps in hand, gazing into the face of the man who would run no more.

The following morning the Hancocks agreed to let the public at large walk through the front parlor and view the body, in order to relieve some of the pressure from the still-swelling crowd. Among those who came were a couple of youngsters from St. Louis whom Mary Kinder personally guided, after checking to see that they had no camera, because she was touched at the thought of the long trip they had made for the purpose of seeing Dillinger.

This public viewing came to a halt within an hour, however, when one of the visitors, making drunken progress past the coffin, lost his balance and almost fell after extending a bottle toward the corpse with a muttered invitation to have a drink.

Soon thereafter Mrs. Hancock yielded to the urging of the harassed police and agreed to hold the funeral that day, instead of waiting until Thursday, as originally planned. Burial was to be in the family plot at Crown Hill Cemetery, on the outskirts of Indianapolis, in spite of protests from other lot owners.

A quartet sang "God Will Take Care of You." The Reverend Charles Fillmore, who had married Dillinger's father and stepmother in 1912, conducted the service. The Reverend Mr. Fillmore, author of the hymn "Tell Mother I'll Be There," began praying: "We believe in a God of forgiveness, a God of mercy, a God of grace...."

After he finished, the quartet sang a second hymn, "We Say Good Night Down Here and Good Morning Up There," and the Reverend William J. Evans of the Mars Hill Christian Church gave the closing prayer.

Outside, the crowd shifted restlessly, waiting for the service to end and the show to go on. A photographic plane droned overhead. Some newspaper cameramen were attacked by self-appointed guards, who were quickly warned by Captain Johnson that they were not to interfere with the press. Among the outside watchers were Al Feeney, the Indiana State Police head; Attorney General Phillip Lutz, Jr., of Indiana, and Ralph Alsman, Dillinger's "double."

At last the coffin was carried out, but here the dignity the family was trying so hard to preserve took another blow. The pallbearers were preceded by a flying wedge of seven men, who waved their arms and warned against picture taking. One cameraman was knocked down and his equipment broken during this charge to the hearse.

A further contribution to the confusion came when Mrs. Hancock collapsed and Mary Kinder quickly followed suit. Both were revived and helped to waiting cars. Only five vehicles followed the hearse. Others—whose drivers had asked for funeral flags, which would have permitted them to enter Crown Hill, where the gates had been guarded all day by uniformed policemen—were beguiled by Harvey's vague promises that the flags would be forthcoming "later." They never were.

The hearse took an unannounced route to Indianapolis, throwing many newsmen off the trail, and when it reached the cemetery went in through a supposedly locked gate, while decoy policemen guarded an entrance which was not opened. Rain began to fall as the procession neared Crown Hill, and a severe thunderstorm forced the tiny cortege to halt near the open, unlined grave for about fifteen minutes until the downpour ceased.

Then the mourners gathered beside the grave, over which a canvas canopy had been placed. The two ministers intoned a brief service and Mrs. Hancock sagged against her husband Emmett. Miss Kinder wept, as though on camera, and the dead man's two young half sisters, Doris and Frances, sobbed less noisily. The elder Dillinger brushed at his tears with a finger.

It was 3:15 when the body of the man the entire law enforcement organization of the country had sought was at last lowered into the wet earth. Three cemetery employees began at once to shovel dirt on top of the coffin. A few of the mourners and a handful of bystanders who somehow had managed to gain entrance tore flowers from the funeral wreaths as souvenirs. Some of the policemen did the same.

When mourners left, a police guard was posted, as precaution against ghouls, and a day or so later cemetery officials persuaded the elder Dillinger to have the grave reopened so that concrete slabs could be placed above the vault. Two Indianapolis policemen were left on guard, however, until July 30, although there seemed little reason for their presence after the concrete was laid down.

As someone said, "If they get him out of there now, the whole world will know it, because they'll have to blast him out."

Crown Hill was not the sort of resting-place anyone would have been likely to blast with impunity. Among the dignitaries sleeping within hailing distance of John Herbert Dillinger were Benjamin Harrison, James Whitcomb Riley, three United States Vice-Presidents and Abraham Lincoln's Secretary of the Interior.

Shortly after the shooting of Dillinger outside the Biograph, some anonymous scribbler, touched by the drama of it all, chalked on a building in the alley, near where Dillinger had fallen:

> Stranger, stop and wish me well,
> Just say a prayer for my soul in Hell.
> I was a good fellow, most people said,
> Betrayed by a woman all dressed in red.

NINETEEN

●●●●●●●●●●●●●●●●●●● "I HAD A GOOD EX-
PERIENCE. I DON'T
REGRET A BIT OF IT."
—MARY KINDER

John Dillinger was dead, but the trouble he stirred up during his short but lively life continued to affect those with whom he had associated. Sometimes the effect was a deadly one.

James Probasco was arrested for questioning on July 25, three days after Dillinger was shot down. The following morning Probasco was killed in a plunge from the nineteenth-floor office in the Bankers' Building, where the FBI had its Chicago headquarters.

Curiously, there had been charges earlier in the year that John J. "Boss" McLaughlin, a former Illinois state legislator, was held out of the window of that same room in an effort to make him confess complicity in the Charles Bremer kidnaping.

Government agents said they were not in the room when Probasco went out of the window, and after Cowley had testified that Probasco was neither intimidated nor given any rough treatment, and that a chair was found near the window indicating that Probasco had climbed on it to jump out, the jury returned a verdict of "suicide while despondent."

Anna Sage was taken to California for safekeeping shortly after Dillinger was killed, and there she was given the $5,000 reward, then deported. She died in 1947 in her native Romania.

Homer Van Meter managed to last one month and a day longer than Dillinger. On August 23, as dozens of bystanders watched, Van Meter was chased up an alley by four members of the St. Paul police force—after ignoring a surrender demand—and was killed by machine-gun fire and blasts from a shotgun. He managed to get off two shots from his pistol before dying.

At the close of a criminal career which had begun in Aurora, Illinois, with the theft of a motorcar in 1924, Van Meter had $923 in his pocket, an extra clip of bullets, and an Illinois motor registration slip in the name of Henry Adams. He had been on his way to keep a date with a waitress when he walked into the police trap. Word in the St. Paul underworld was that the finger had been put on Van Meter by his "banker," who had a dual purpose: to keep some of the money he was holding for the hunted man, and to take the heat off himself.

The next to go was Fat Charley Makley, and it is probable that he counted on dying as he did in preference to the chair. Makley and Pierpont had managed to fashion two highly realistic-looking guns out of a potpourri of soap, bits of jigsaw puzzle, wire, fountain pens, cardboard, thread from their blankets, shoe blacking and tin foil.

On September 23 they tried to bluff their way out of Death Row at the prison in Columbus, and managed to slug one guard and get through two doors and free several other prisoners, including Russell Clark, before running into a guard who turned in an alarm when faced by their "weapons." Clark promptly returned to the safety of his cell, but Makley and Pierpont were battering at a steel door with wooden table legs when an eight-man security squad arrived.

Both prisoners were shot, and Makley died a few moments later. Pierpont was saved for the electric chair, in which he was electrocuted on October 17 while his parents and Mary Kinder waited at a shabby hotel nearby to claim the body.

By this time Drs. Cassidy and Loeser, O'Leary and Piquett had been picked up, and all but the attorney had admitted their parts in the hiding of Dillinger and Van Meter and the facial operations. Piquett steadfastly insisted that he had done nothing for Van Meter and only as much for Dillinger as he was entitled to do for a client.

On November 27, Baby Face Nelson and his wife, accompanied by John Paul Chase, a bank robber, were speeding from Wisconsin to some undisclosed point in Illinois when they were intercepted by two government agents, Samuel Cowley and H. E. Hollis. In the chase which followed, the bandit car slid into a ditch on the Northwest Highway near Barrington, Illinois, and a pitched battle ensued.

Both agents were killed, and Nelson's nude body was discovered the next day in a field near Niles Center. Two days later Mrs. Nelson was caught; she was sent to the Federal Correctional Institution at Milan, Michigan. Chase was picked up in California in December.

The hunt for Hamilton went on, despite the fact that there had been no confirmed sight of him for months. But in November he was promoted to the rank of Public Enemy Number 1 anyway. Later in the year he was "identified" in Kansas as having taken part in a five-dollar holdup—a report which probably would have annoyed him.

On December 16, 1934, Joseph Burns was seized in a flat on Chicago's South Side without the firing of a shot, although there were machine guns, rifles and revolvers in the apartment. He had been hunted since a jewelry salesman was held up a few days before.

The trial of Piquett opened in January, 1935, and he testified that the money paid him by Dillinger was for legal services, not for the face operation. He also denied that he had paid $500 to Mrs. Patzke, Dr. Loeser's "secretary," with the understanding that she would try to persuade Dr. Loeser to back up his story. He was acquitted on January 14, to the great surprise of everyone including U.S. Attorney Dwight H. Green, who told him, "You are a very lucky man, Mr. Piquett."

But in June, 1935, a second jury came in with another surprise, at least for Piquett. He was found guilty of having harbored Van Meter, a man he claimed to have seen only once, and who was not his client. In the pressroom after the verdict Piquett said, "I had three witnesses: Dillinger, Van Meter and Probasco, and the government killed all three of them."

After fruitless appeals, Piquett went to Leavenworth on May 9, 1936, and served twenty months before being released January 11,

1938. Piquett was forced to return to his former trade as bartender, was given a pardon in January, 1951, by President Truman, and died the following December while proceedings were under way to have him reinstated to the bar.

All speculating about Hamilton ended on August 29, 1935, when government men uncovered a shallow grave near a gravel pit outside Oswego, Illinois. Hamilton apparently had been there more than a year. His right hand (with the telltale missing fingers) had been removed, and lye had been used in a further attempt to prevent identification. A horseshoe was lying on the body, apparently a sentimental gesture from Dillinger or Van Meter.

Various minor figures also were rounded up and sent to prison for their parts in having helped Dillinger escape the law for so long. In Indiana, too, Warden Baker and Blunk and some others were arrested and questioned, then released once more.

Melvin Purvis quit the FBI in July of 1935, and after practicing law in San Francisco, writing a book, working briefly as a screen writer, and organizing the Junior G-Men for Post Toasties, he went to Florence, South Carolina, where he published a newspaper. He served as a colonel in World War II, then bought a radio station in Florence. In February, 1960, he shot and killed himself in his home. He was fifty-six and had been in poor health, but his widow said the shooting was an accident.

Singleton, Dillinger's first partner in crime, was sitting on a railroad track in Mooresville late one night after the taverns had closed and was killed by a fast freight.

The elder Dillinger joined a carnival sideshow, lecturing on "Crime Does Not Pay," and also served in 1935 and 1936 as caretaker, during the season, for the Dillinger museum that Wanatka established at Little Bohemia. Dillinger replied to criticism of this method of earning money by stating the simple truth: he needed money to support his family. He died about 20 years ago.

Leach was killed in a turnpike crash in Pennsylvania while returning from New York, where he had appeared in a television program built around the Dillinger story.

Evelyn Frechette, after her release from prison, traveled with side shows, billed as Dillinger's girl friend. Then she dropped out of sight.

The strange delight some men take in tormenting their fellows was demonstrated in 1955 when Mrs. Hancock received a letter with a New York postmark in handwriting which resembled Dillinger's. It warned her not to let the police know she had heard from him and was signed "Johnnie."

Mrs. Hancock was quite upset for a day or so, but she soon calmed down, observing, "He wouldn't have stayed away from me that long, I know that."

In Mooresville Dillinger is still a favorite topic of conversation and, inevitably, the story has sprung up that someone else's body rests beneath the headstone marked John Herbert Dillinger in Crown Hill Cemetery.

"Just to be honest with you," one Mooresville resident said, "I think Dillinger is down in Mexico. That fellow they buried didn't have dyed hair, and he was too short."

This belief would have pleased the Indiana farm boy who became one of the most publicized "bad men" in the nation's history. It would have delighted him to know that he has become a legend at last.

ABOUT THE AUTHORS

Robert Cromie was a reporter, sports writer, and book editor for the *Chicago Tribune,* as well as the host of the TV show *Cromie's Circle* and the public radio program, *Book Beat.* He has written books about the Chicago Fire, poetry, golf, and Chicago history.

Joseph Pinkston, the curator of the John Dillinger Historical Museum in Nashville, Indiana, was a criminal investigator for the U.S. Air Force and an undercover investigator for the Pinkerton National Detective Agency.

OTHER BOOKS BY CHICAGO HISTORICAL BOOKWORKS

Resurrection Mary: A Ghost Story. By Kenan Heise
    Buddy Wojcik, an almost 100 year-old patient at Peoria State Hospital, had a secret and he was about to reveal it: he had danced with Resurrection Mary, a ghost.
Softcover $10.95

The Cliff Dwellers: The History of a Chicago Cultural Institution. By Henry Regnery.
    This book spans the history of the club from its auspicious beginnings to the present.
Hardcover $20.00

If Christ Came to Chicago. By William T. Stead. (1894) Reprint.
    One of the most soul-stirring, muck-raking books ever written about an American city.
Softcover $14.95

Catalogue of the WPA Writers' Program Publication:s September, 1941. By the WPA Writers' Program. (1941) Reprint.
    A catalogue listing more than 1,000 WPA books, plays, pamphlets, etc.
Softcover $ 7.50

A Bibliography of Illinois, Chicago, and Environs. By the WPA Writers' Program. (1937) Reprint.
    A guide to literature and materials prior to 1937 on the state of Illinois, the city of Chicago, and its suburbs.
Softcover $15.00

The Chicagoization of America: 1893-1917. By Kenan Heise.
    Fascinating evidence of Chicago's profound cultural and moral impact on the United States between the World's Columbian Exposition and World War I.
Softcover $12.95

Check List of Chicago Ante-Fire Imprints: 1851-1871. By the WPA Writers' Program. (1938) Reprint.
    Bibliography of 1,880 books and pamphlets printed in Chicago in the 20 years before the Chicago Fire.
Spiral-bound $35.00

Alphonse: A Play Based on the Words of Al Capone. By Kenan Heise.
    Contemporary newspapers and the transcript of the trial of Al Capone contributed the material from which this play was written.
Softcover $ 6.95

The Cost of Something for Nothing. By John Peter Altgeld. (1903) Reprint.
    Strong words from the man whom Darrow called "one of the most sincere and devoted friends of humanity this country has ever produced."
Hardcover, D.J. $ 9.95